Sean Gilsdorf (ed.)

The Bishop: Power and Piety at the First Millennium

Neue Aspekte der europäischen Mittelalterforschung

herausgegeben von

Prof. Dr. Natalie Fryde (TU Darmstadt)
Prof. Dr. Michael Gelting (Universität Kopenhagen)
und Prof. Dr. Hanna Vollrath (Universität Bochum)

Band 4

LIT

Sean Gilsdorf (ed.)

The Bishop: Power and Piety at the First Millennium

LIT

Bibliographic information published by Die Deutsche Bibliothek
Die Deutsche Bibliothek lists this publication in the Deutsche
Nationalbibliografie; detailed bibliographic data are available in the
Internet at http://dnb.ddb.de.

ISBN 3-8258-7488-5

© LIT VERLAG Münster   2004
Grevener Str./Fresnostr. 2   48159 Münster
Tel. 0251-23 50 91   Fax 0251-23 19 72
e-Mail: lit@lit-verlag.de   http://www.lit-verlag.de

Distributed in North America by:

Transaction Publishers
New Brunswick (U.S.A.) and London (U.K.)

Transaction Publishers   Tel.: (732) 445 - 2280
Rutgers University   Fax: (732) 445 - 3138
35 Berrue Circle   for orders (U. S. only):
Piscataway, NJ 08854   toll free (888) 999 - 6778

In memoriam
Timothy Reuter
Comitis, magistris, amici

Contents

List of Illustrations ... ix
Contributors ... xi
Preface ... xiii
Acknowledgments ... xix
Abbreviations ... xxi
Editor's Note ... xxii

1 The Bishop: Prince and Prelate
Michel Parisse ... 1

2 Bishops, Rites of Passage, and the Symbolism of State in Pre-Gregorian Europe
Timothy Reuter ... 23

3 The Bishop as Aristocrat: The Case of Hugh of Chalon
Constance Brittain Bouchard ... 37

4 Bishops in the Middle: Mediatory Politics and the Episcopacy
Sean Gilsdorf ... 51

5 The Bishop as Cultural Medium: Berthold of Toul, Byzantium, and Episcopal Self-Consciousness
Anthony Cutler and William North ... 75

6 Modelling the Bishop: Egbert of Trier, Gregory the Great, and the Episcopal Image
Hiltrud Westermann-Angerhausen ... 113

7 The Bishop Makes An Impression: Seals, Authority and Episcopal Identity
Brigitte Miriam Bedo Rezak 137

8 The Bishop as Artist? The Eucharist and Image Theory Around the Millennium
Pierre-Alain Mariaux 155

9 Elusive Bishops: Remembering, Forgetting, and Remaking the History of the Early Danish Church
Michael Gelting 169

Bibliography 201

Index 231

Illustrations

Tables

1) The Counts of Chalon
2) Kings of Denmark, c. 948-1134
3) Bishops of Ribe (Jutland), 948-1134
4) Bishops of Schleswig, 948-1134
5) Bishops of Odense (Funen), c. 988 - c. 1134/39
6) Bishops of Lund (Scania), c. 1000-1137 (or 1020/22-1137)
7) Bishops of Roskilde (Sealand), 1020/22-1134

Figures

1) Hodegetria, second half of tenth century. Berlin, Museum für Spätantike und Byzantinische Kunst.
2) Hodegetria (detail), second half of tenth century. Utrecht, Rijksmuseum Het Catharijneconvent.
3) Crucifixion ivory (c. 870) on the cover of the Pericope Book of Henry II (before 1014). Munich, Bayerische Staatsbibliothek, MS Clm. 4452.
4) Hodegetria ivory (second half of tenth century), on the cover of the Aachen Gospels. Aachen, Domschatz.
5) Ivory of Bishop Adalbero of Metz, 984-1005. Metz, Musée d'art et d'histoire.
6) Ivory with Crucifixion and Women at the Tomb, c. 1010 (?). Nancy, Cathedral treasury.
7) Front cover of Bernward of Hildesheim's "Precious Gospels" (c. 1000-1010), with Deesis ivory (late tenth century). Hildesheim, Domschatz.
8) Rear cover of Berward of Hildesheim's "Precious Gospels". Hildesheim, Domschatz.
9) Front cover of the "Codex Aureus" of Echternach (c. 989). Nürnberg, Germanisches Nationalmuseum.
10) Portrait of Otto II, originally from the frontispiece to the *Registrum Gregorii* (c. 983/4). Chantilly, Musée Condée, MS 14b.
11) Portrait of Pope Gregory the Great, frontispiece to the *Registrum Gregorii* (c. 983/4). Trier, Stadtbibliothek, MS 171/1626.

12) Egbert of Trier, dedication portrait from the *Egbert Psalter* (977-80). Cividale del Friuli, Archivi e Biblioteca di Palazzo dei Provveditori Veneti, MS 136, f. 17r.
13) Egbert of Trier, dedication portrait from the *Egbert Codex* (*ante* 985). Trier, Stadtbibliothek, MS 24, f. 2r.
14) Egbert Shrine (c. 980). Trier, Domschatz.
15) Egbert Shrine (front view).
16) Incipit page to Gospel of St. Matthew, from the *Codex Aureus* of St. Emmeram (c. 870). Munich, Bayerische Staatsbibliothek, MS Clm. 14000, f. 16v.
17) Egbert Shrine (rear view).
18) Staff reliquary of St. Peter (c. 980). Limburg, Domschatz.
19) Seal of Bishop Peter Lombard of Paris, 1159.
20) Seal of Henry I of France, c. 1031.
21) Seal of Bishop Notker of Liège, 980.
22) Choir capital with Adoration of the Magi. Church of St.-Pierre, Chauvigny.

Contributors

Brigitte Miriam Bedos-Rezak, Department of History, New York University.

Constance Brittain Bouchard, Department of History, University of Akron.

Anthony Cutler, Department of Art History, Pennsylvania State University.

Michael Gelting, Danish National Archives, Copenhagen.

Sean Gilsdorf, Department of History, University of Chicago.

Pierre-Alain Mariaux, Institute d'Histoire de l'Art, Université de Neuchâtel.

William North, Department of History, Carleton College.

Michel Parisse, UFR 09 (Histoire), Université de Paris I-Sorbonne.

Timothy Reuter (†), Department of History, Southampton University.

Hiltrud Westermann-Angerhausen, Schnütgen-Museum, Cologne.

Preface

Ruotger, the biographer of the archbishop of Cologne (and Otto the Great's brother) Brun, offers us an ideal image of the tenth-century bishop. As a *dux* and prelate, as a kinsman to emperors and a teacher of bishops, Brun seemed constantly to be pulled this way and that by the demands of his position. Yet as Ruotger tells us, this external behavior was only the visible indication of Brun's deeper, "interior" purpose—the conversion and correction of his flock, and the establishment of the blessings of peace.[1] Ruotger's description, part of a tradition extending back to Gregory the Great, might be read in two ways. One is to see Brun, and by extension the bishops of his time, as betwixt and between, as "liminal individuals", structurally situated in a kind of nether land between the more definite social positions, values, and expectations represented by monasticism on the one hand and the warrior aristocracy on the other. The other, and more productive, way to read this description, however, places the bishop not "between two worlds", but at the very center of a complex social whole. In such a reading, the episcopacy is in the middle of things, not as a permeable membrane or medium of interaction, but as a node, a nexus, a mediator in the fullest sense of the term.

Indeed, while monasticism is often seen as the definitive expression of early medieval Christendom, it was in fact the episcopacy that served as the cultic and political backbone of society in the first millennium. As Timothy Reuter has pointed out, before the rise of the reform papacy in the eleventh century and of centralized monarchies in the twelfth, episcopal traditions, institutions, and territories were the most homogeneous, transregional entities in Europe.[2] Despite its central role, however, the early medieval episcopacy has received far less attention from modern scholars than other contemporary social and religious phenomena, such as monarchy, lay lordship, or reformed monasticism. While studies of individual bishops and bishoprics have a long history, far fewer works have attempted to examine bishops as a whole, or in comparative perspective, in

---

[1] Ruotger, *Vita sancti Brunonis*, in *Lebensbeschreibungen einiger Bischöfe des 10.-12. Jahrhunderts*, ed. Hatto Kallfelz [*AQDGM* 22] (Darmstadt: Wissenschaftliche Buchgesellschaft, 1973), especially chapter 23 (212-14).

[2] See Timothy Reuter, "Property transactions and social relations between rulers, bishops and nobles in early eleventh-century Saxony: The evidence of the *Vita Meinwerci*," in *Property and Power in the Early Middle Ages*, ed. Wendy Davies and Paul Fouracre (Cambridge: Cambridge University Press, 1995), 193-94.

the pre-Gregorian period—a striking contrast to the episcopacy of the later Middle Ages, which has been the focus of careful and comparative studies by Robert Benson, Robert Brentano, Bernard Guenée and others[3] This situation has only recently begun to change with the publication of compelling, albeit regionally-focused, studies of Italian episcopal architecture by Maureen Miller, the Bavarian and Swabian episcopacy by Geneviève Bührer-Thierry, and Ottonian and Salian episcopal biography by Stephanie Haarländer.[4]

This book, therefore, is intended as an open invitation to a more comparative, synthetic history of early medieval bishops and the early medieval episcopacy. Written by scholars from a variety of regional, theoretical, and disciplinary perspectives, it provides a rich portrait of the political, religious, intellectual, and artistic dimensions of the episcopacy around the year 1000, revealing the many ways in which all roads led through the bishops, their churches, and their institutions. This central role is made clear by Michel Parisse, who in his introduction surveys the political and social function of bishops as both "princes and prelates." As Parisse points out, bishops were crucial players not only in high politics, but in the daily life of early medieval societies. At the same time, their importance across Europe has not been adequately reflected in modern historiography—a result, he suggests, not simply of inattention or misappraisal, but

---

[3] Robert Benson, *The Bishop-Elect: A Study in Medieval Ecclesiastical Office* (Princeton: Princeton University Press, 1968), Robert Brentano, *Two Churches: England and Italy in the Thirteenth Century* (Berkeley: University of California Press, 1988), and Bernard Guenée, *Between Church and State: The Lives of Four French Prelates in the Late Middle Ages*, trans. Arthur Goldhammer (Chicago: The University of Chicago Press, 1996). An outstanding example of this kind of approach in the context of the early Middle Ages is Heinrich Fichtenau's chapter on the bishop in his *Lebensordnungen des 10. Jahrhunderts: Studien über Denkart und Existenz im einstigen Karolingerreich* [Monographien zur Geschichte des Mittelalters 30] (Stuttgart: Anton Hiersemann, 1984), 248-92; cf. the less fully annotated English version, *Living in the Tenth Century: Mentalities and Social Orders*, trans. Patrick Geary (Chicago: The University of Chicago Press, 1991), 181-216.

[4] Maureen Miller, *The Bishop's Palace: Architecture and Authority in Medieval Italy* (Ithaca: Cornell University Press, 2000); Geneviève Bührer-Thierry, *Evêques et pouvoir dans le royaume de Germanie. Les Eglises de Bavière et de Souabe, 876-973* (Paris: Picard, 1997); and Stephanie Haarländer, *Vitae Episcoporum. Eine Quellengattung zwischen Hagiographie und Historiographie, untersucht an Lebensbeschreibungen von Bischöfen des Regnum Teutonicum im Zeitalter der Ottonen und Salier* [Monographien zur Geschichte des Mittelalters 47] (Stuttgart: Anton Hiersemann, 2000). Cf. also Haarländer's earlier study (as Stephanie Coué), *Hagiographie im Kontext: Schreibanlass und Funktion von Bischofsviten aus dem 11. und vom Anfang des 12. Jahrhunderts* [Arbeiten zur Frühmittelalterforschung 24] (Berlin: Walter de Gruyter, 1997).

also of largely local and national historiographical traditions, as well as insufficient exploration of the extant sources, most notably the episcopal charters of which Parisse himself has been so assiduous an editor and commentator.

The following three chapters examine the role of early medieval bishops within contemporary aristocratic political life. Timothy Reuter focuses upon how the bishop's authority and presence were constructed not only by what he did during his reign, but by the way in which he began and ended it. As we discover, the ceremonies surrounding the bishop's installation in his see and his final departure from it were ideologically, symbolically, and performatively linked, forming a crucial frame for episcopal action; in turn, the content of these "sequences of symbolic action", as well as their transpersonal nature, highlights the degree to which bishops and kings were joined together within the common matrix of early medieval rulership. Constance Bouchard next uses the career of a tenth-century French prelate to demonstrate how traditional models of ecclesiastical reform, with their often stark distinctions between "lay" and "religious" interests, prevent us from adequately understanding the complex social, political, and spiritual position of the early medieval bishop. As she argues, the figure of Hugh of Chalon—bishop and count, cleric and soldier, reformer and conniver—epitomizes the close, and often productive, ties which existed between landed secular elites and ecclesiastical institutions and leaders, and reveals how the bishop could, and often did, reconcile seemingly distinct interests, ideologies, and traditions. Finally, in chapter four, I turn our attention to a less obvious, but equally important, form of episcopal politics—namely, the bishop's role as mediator and intercessor within aristocratic society. As I suggest, the "mediatory politics" of the episcopacy was an expression of the bishop's position in the middle (or alternatively, at the center) of a number of social and ideological networks, in which liturgical, political, and personal power were inextricably woven together.

Episcopal power, position, and prestige in the early Middle Ages were not, of course, expressed only through words and deeds, but through other forms of representation, in particular the medium of image production. The chapters that follow, therefore, turn our attention to the complex ways in which visual media were used to produce and disseminate an "image" of the bishop, literally as well as figuratively. Anthony Cutler and William North examine the role of the bishop as an arbiter of taste and supporter of artistic production and exchange, focusing upon a little-known German prelate, Berthold of Toul. Like many of his contemporaries in the Ottonian world, Berthold was a patron not only in a passive, but also an active sense, helping to introduce Byzantine objects and visual motifs into tenth- and eleventh-century Europe. As Cutler and North point out, without the willingness of episcopal patrons to accept these objects on their own terms and to reappropriate them for new purposes, Byzantine ivories in particular would never have enjoyed such a vogue in the Rhineland and elsewhere. Bishops thus served not only a conductive role within early medieval culture, but also a transformative one. Hiltrud Westermann-Angerhausen, on the other hand, demonstrates how visual resources were used to cast (and re-cast) the public image of a tenth-century bishop, Egbert of Trier. Egbert's patronage in a variety of media—architecture, manuscripts, and metalwork—thus is approached not simply as an expression of aesthetic interest, but as a key element in the bishop's ongoing attempt to define and strengthen his diocese's (as well as his own) ecclesiological, historical, and political position.

The interplay between social power, image production, and image theory is at the heart of the following chapter, in which Brigitte Bedos-Rezak demonstrates both the impact of sophisticated intellectual debate and reflection upon the episcopacy, as well as how bishops recast the terms and results of that debate in ways which would have a lasting impact in disparate areas of society. As she argues, northern French bishops were literally "in the middle" of the eucharistic debates of the early eleventh century. These debates, a continuation and elaboration of centuries-old conflicts over the nature and even reality of the central Christian sacrament, were conducted by an intellectual elite based in episcopal centers, employed by bishops, and responsible for the day-to-day business of the bishop and his diocese. In turn, the arguments of bishops like Gerard of Cambrai against Berengar of Tours and his supporters—generally summarized under the rubric of the "doctrine of the real presence"—were not confined to the realm of theology. Rather, as Bedos-Rezak suggests, the semiotic theory which they propounded had repercussions in the seemingly unrelated field of administrative, and particularly diplomatic, practice—a relationship mediated, quite literally, through the figure of the bishop, i.e., the bishop's seal.

In turn, Pierre-Alain Mariaux takes these same intellectual debates as the starting point for a quite different voyage, one in which he explores the relationship between the apparently disparate figures of bishop and artist. Mariaux is not interested, as one might expect, in bishops who were producers or designers of visual, musical, or literary artifacts. Instead, he traces the path leading from the bishop as confector of the body of Christ in the Eucharist to the artist as confector of the body of Christ in stone, glass, or ink. The crucial stage in this journey, Mariaux shows, was the assertion of the eucharist's physical identity with the body and blood of Christ. This assertion brought together—as the very term conficere suggests—the creative acts of the priest and the craftsman, both of them manipulating visible substances in order to produce something new linking the seen and the unseen. For Mariaux, then, the bishop as *sacerdos* served as the model and the inspiration for the image-maker's transformation into something altogether new: the artist.

As we have seen, bishops and bishoprics were crucial parts of the social and cultural fabric of early medieval society. The degree to which this was true is highlighted in unusual fashion by the final chapter, in which Michael Gelting explores the episcopal history—or rather histories—of a region on the margins of European Christendom, Denmark. In a masterful reevaluation of centuries of historiography, Gelting reveals how the often haphazard, even messy, development of the Danish church was "tidied up" by representatives of the German hierarchy, in particular Adam of Bremen, to match their own political as well as ideological models and aims. Notably, this process of "remembering, forgetting, and remaking" was one in which bishops, both real and imagined, played a central role. The invention of bishops and of an episcopal history for Denmark by the German ecclesiastical establishment thus demonstrates, if somewhat ironically, the degree to which bishops and their dioceses were a *sine qua non* for Christian corporate identity and history.

The picture of the episcopacy which emerges from these pages, while wide-ranging, is not of course comprehensive. It is our hope, therefore, that this book will encourage others not only to explore the territory which it has mapped and draw upon the suggestions which it offers, but also to expand and challenge its boundaries and horizons. In this way, the fascinating and complex figure of the medieval bishop will continue to attract the attention and insights he so richly deserves.

Acknowledgments

The Bishop had its beginnings at a conference on "The Image of the Bishop Around the Millennium," held at the University of Chicago in October 1999. The success of this event, which made it clear that a book on the early medieval episcopacy was not only feasible but also desirable, was due to many individuals and organizations—in particular, my colleagues on the conference organizing committee, Pierre-Alain Mariaux, Annika Fisher, Christina Nielsen, and Maureen Kupstas; the Divinity School, the Visiting Committee to the Division of the Humanities, and the Franke Institute for the Humanities; the Medieval Studies Workshop and its then-director, Christina von Nolcken; and many other departments and committees. Their involvement is emblematic of the spirit of interdisciplinary cooperation and exchange that defines not only medieval studies, but intellectual life in general, at the University of Chicago. The conference itself brought together an outstanding group of speakers from both sides of the Atlantic, whose energy and interests made for a truly memorable event. Each of these men and women both enabled and improved the book before you. Many thanks are due also to Barbara Rosenwein of Loyola University at Chicago, whose enthusiasm and interest have been invaluable; to my colleagues at the University of Richmond for their support during the final stages of manuscript preparation; to Dirk Reitz for his tireless work in preparing the book for publication; and to Natalie Fryde, Michael Gelting, and LIT-Verlag for bringing the book to press. Finally, I would like to acknowledge a personal debt of gratitude and love to my wife, Amanda, who has shared me with long-dead churchmen for far too long, and to my son Benjamin, who always brings me back to the present.

This book on the episcopacy is dedicated to the memory of our colleague and friend Timothy Reuter, whose own work on bishops and their worlds was cut short far too early, but whose accomplishments and kindnesses live on.

Abbreviations

AQDGM	Ausgewählte Quellen zur deutschen Geschichte des Mittelalters
CCCM	Corpus Christianorum, continuatio medievalis
CSEL	Corpus Scriptorum Ecclesiasticorum Latinorum
DA	*Deutsches Archiv für Erforschung des Mittelalters*
FmS	*Frühmittelalterliche Studien*
Jaffé-Loewenfeld	*Regesta Pontificum Romanorum ab condita Ecclesia ad annum post Christum natum MCXCVIII*, ed. Philip Jaffé, Samuel Loewenfeld, et al, 2 vols. (Leipzig: Veit, 1885).
MGH	Monumenta Germaniae Historica
AA	Auctores antiquissimi
Conc	Concilia
Const	Constitutiones et acta publica regum et imperatorum
DO I, II, etc.	Diplomata regum et imperatorum (Otto I, II, etc.)
Ep sel	Epistolae selectae
Fontes	Fontes iuris Germanici antiqui
SSRG	Scriptores rerum Germanicarum, separatim editi
SS	Scriptores
PL	*Patrologiae cursus completus . . . Series Latina*, ed. Jacques-Paul Migne, 221 vols. (Paris: J.P. Migne, 1844-64).
Settimane	Settimane di studio del Centro Italiano di studi sull'alto Medioevo
ZSfR	*Zeitschrift der Savigny-Stiftung für Rechtsgeschichte, kanonistische Abteilung*

Editor's Note

Although originally prepared for this volume, a slightly modified version of chapter five first appeared as "Ivories, Inscriptions, and Episcopal Self-Consciousness in the Ottonian Empire: Berthold of Toul and the Berlin Hodegetria," *Gesta* 42/1 (2003): 1-17. In turn, chapter six is a revised version of Dr. Westermann-Angerhausen's earlier article, "Egbert von Trier und Gregor der Große—Tradition und Repräsentation," published in *Sancta Treveris: Beiträge zu Kirchenbau und bildender Kunst im alten Erzbistum Trier. Festschrift für Franz J. Ronig zum 70. Geburtstag*, ed. Michael Embach *et al* (Trier: Paulinus, 1999), 709-31.

Chapter One
The Bishop: Prince and Prelate[†]
Michel Parisse

In Christian Europe, the bishop was everywhere. All Christianized territories were divided into dioceses, and at the head of each one was a bishop. It is impossible to know their precise number, but there certainly were hundreds. Of all the people who exercised power in the Middle Ages, the bishops were the ones whom people thought of right after kings and popes. We have mapped the dioceses they ruled, and we have drawn up systematic lists of prelates for each, with far greater ease than is the case for dukes and counts in their lay territories. Among the prelates, furthermore, we know the bishops much better than we know the abbots. Bishops played a major role in every aspect of life: political, religious, economic, social, and intellectual (as we will see, it is no accident that I mention the political before the religious). The bishop led the faithful, occupying the premier position that Peter had held in the first century of Christianity and which he had transmitted to his disciples and their disciples after them.

Throughout the Middle Ages, therefore, in no matter what region, the bishops held the most important position in daily life. Their presence and importance, however, leads us to wonder why they are so rarely studied by contemporary medieval historians. Certainly the sources privilege them over all other individuals, for the sources are mainly ecclesiastical and, for the period before the year 1000, are concerned above all with the activities of bishops and the goings-on of religious communities. Yet while Italian historians do concentrate on their bishops, there were so many, and the sources for them so abundant (far more so than elsewhere in Europe) that it is not possible to write their history in a satisfactory way.[1] Furthermore, among Italian historians, as elsewhere, the history of bishops is written from the point of view of their political activities but not their religious functions; the two are not treated together—and inseparably—as they had been in the Middle Ages. In turn, German historians have been attracted to

---

[†] Translated for this volume by Barbara Rosenwein, to whom the author expresses his warmest thanks.

[1] See e.g. the essays in *Vescovi e diocesi in italia nel medioevo (secoli IX-XIII)* (Padua: Antenore, 1964); *I poteri temporali dei vescovi in Italia e Germania nel Medioevo*, ed. Carlo Guido Mor and Heinrich Schmidinger (Bologna: Il Mulino, 1979); and Paolo Delogu, "Vescovi, conti et sovrani nella crisi del regno italico," *Annali della scuola speciale per archivisti e bibliotecari dell'Università di Roma* 8 (1968): 3-72.

the so-called "imperial church", the formation of episcopal principalities, and episcopal wealth and power; they have drawn up monographs on the dioceses and compiled lists of prelates; and they have written numerous biographies of powerful bishops, above all by using episcopal *vitae*. But while it is in Germany that we find the most thought and writing on the bishops of the Middle Ages, no one there has attempted a work of synthesis.[2] In England the bishops of the tenth century have attracted interest because of their key role in ecclesiastical reform;[3] likewise, scholars have turned their attention to other bishops in the entourage or in the service of kings, notably the archbishops of Canterbury from William the Conqueror to Henry VIII. The case of Thomas Becket alone has done much to focus attention on English prelates, but here too with regard to their political relations and not the whole of their functions.[4] In comparison with these national historical traditions, that of France is far behind. While there have been a few studies of the bishops of Reims, Chartres, Poitiers and Périgueux in western France, as well as the whole province of Reims,[5] here too there are no syntheses, and a project that I launched to fill this gap has not yet been realized.[6] It is clear, however, that the need for it is there.

---

[2] There are, however, numerous synthetic articles for different periods. See Rudolf Schieffer, "Der ottonische Reichsepiskopat zwischen Königtum und Adel," *FmS* 23 (1989): 291-301, the contributions by Schieffer and Odilo Engels in *Der Bischof in seiner Zeit. Bischofstypus und Bischofsideal im Spiegel der Kölner Kirche*, ed. Peter Berglar and Odilo Engels (Cologne: J.P. Bachem, 1996), and, most recently, Rudolf Schieffer, "Karolingische und ottonische Kirchenpolitik," in *Mönchtum-Kirche-Herrschaft, 750-1000*, ed. Dieter Bauer and Josef Semmler (Sigmaringen: Jan Thorbecke Verlag, 1998), 311-24.

[3] See in particular *St. Dunstan: His Life, Time, and Cult*, ed. Nigel Ramsey *et al* (Woodbridge: Boydell and Brewer, 1992), and *Bishop Aethelwold: His Career and Influence*, ed. Barbara Yorke (Woodbridge: Boydell and Brewer, 1988).

[4] See Raymonde Foreville, *Thomas Becket dans la tradition historique et hagiographique* (London: Variorum, 1981), and Frank Barlow, *Thomas Becket* (Berkeley: University of California Press, 1986).

[5] Jacques Boussard, "Les évêques en Neustrie avant la Réforme grégorienne (950-1050 environ)," *Journal des Savants* 3 (1970): 161-96; Jacques Duguet, "La famille des Isembert, évêques de Poitiers et ses relations (Xe-XIe siècles)," *Bulletin de la Société des antiquaires de l'Ouest*, 4th ser., 11 (1971-72): 163-86; Muriel Laharie, "Evêques et société en Périgord du Xe au milieu du XIIe siècle," *Annales du Midi* 94 (1982): 343-68. For the province of Reims, see most recently Patrick Demouy's *Actes des archevêques de Reims d'Arnoul à Renaud II, 957-1139*, Thèse du doctorat, Université de Nancy II, 1982, which offers a number of observations on the archbishop's role in the eleventh and twelfth centuries.

[6] This is the goal of the "Groupe de recherche pour l'édition des actes des évêques de France des origines à 1200." Two studies have been completed—the *Actes des évêques de Limoges des origines à 1197*, edited by Jean Becquet (Paris: CNRS, 1999), and the *Actes des évêques*

The period that I will discuss in the following pages is right in the middle of the Middle Ages, around the year 1000, after the Carolingian era and at the dawn of the Gregorian Reform. Concentrating on this period—one which has been generally neglected with the exception of the empire and the Ottonian realm—gives us the opportunity to take stock of the special power and position enjoyed by bishops before the popes, on the initiative of Leo IX, embarked on a policy of intervention vis-à-vis the episcopacy.

The Sources

Historians do not have a uniform knowledge of the activities of bishops and their personnel; the sources get richer only gradually in the course of the Middle Ages. Here I will survey rapidly what they tell us about the situation in the tenth and eleventh centuries, focusing upon three types of sources: narrative, hagiographical, and diplomatic.

1. Narrative sources

Modern historians write first about the elections of bishops and then, in descending order, about their relations with lay and ecclesiastical authorities, their family origins, and their participation in the religious life and connections to religious communities. The evidence for all of this comes from narrative sources: annals, chronicles, and the *Gesta* [deeds] of bishops (Auxerre, Le Mans, Cambrai, Liège, Metz, Toul, and Verdun) and of abbots. The *gesta*, unfortunately too few and too limited geographically, are of course the richest sources, because they record the facts about and deeds of successive prelates with a degree of precision that allows them to be useful for city historians, as a sort of aide-mémoire.[7] A good example of this genre is the *Gesta* of the bishops of Auxerre, recently published in a translated edition.[8] Between 971 and 1039, the first bishop was Heribert, son of Duke Hugh the Great and thus the half-brother of

---

de Laon des origines a 1151, edited by Annie Dufour-Malbezin (Paris: CNRS editions, 2001). The acts of the archbishops of Reims also should appear in the near future.

[7] See in general Michel Sot, *Gesta episcoporum, gesta abbatum* [Typologie des sources du Moyen Age occidental 37] (Turnhout: Brepols, 1981).

[8] *Les Gestes des évêques d'Auxerre*, ed. Guy Lobrichon and Monique Goullet [Les classiques de l'histoire de France au moyen âge] (Paris: Les Belles Lettres, 2002); this edition comprises only the first (and oldest) section of the *Gesta*.

Hugh Capet. He was succeeded by John, a man of humble origins. Finally came Hugh of Chalon, the son of Duke Hugh.[9] Whenever possible, the *Gesta* provides three catagories of information: first, on the bishop's social origins, the conditions of his election, and the date of his death and burial; second, on his participation in religious life and above all his foundations or restorations of churches and ecclesiastical communities; third, on political matters, such as the construction of castles, military campaigns, and conflicts with vassals. If the bishop is of humble origin, the writer focuses upon his intellectual formation and on the excellence of his morals. Quite precise (if often skewed) information is given concerning the election. The space given over to political activities is large: we even find a long account of King Robert's military campaign in Burgundy because Bishop Hugh was involved in it. The *Gesta* of Auxerre needs to be used with some care, but it offers material that many a diocese would envy. The *Gesta* of Cambrai is similarly rich, much more interesting than that for the bishops of Lorraine, which is relatively less forthcoming about the activities of the bishops it discusses.

2. Hagiographical sources

Certain bishops—alas, a very small number of them—were lucky enough to find a biographer. The *vitae* of the bishops of the tenth to eleventh centuries were of course written with the intention of bolstering their canonization, but the conditions for sanctity changed at the end of the tenth century: spontaneous canonization no longer took place, and we thus have many lives of German bishops that were never placed on the altars.[10] These too are quarries for factual information, although they must be used with caution. While they provide data which may compliment that found in the *Gesta* or the chronicles, they place particular emphasis on the prelate's requisite qualities, a feature which find in all saint's lives. These qualities are best set forth in a letter which appears to date from the twelfth century, where we find the virtues of the prelate enumerated as follows: a sense of moderation [*circumspecta moderatio*] and a good intellectual foundation [*sublimis scientia*]; impressive social origins [*nobilitas generis*]; high moral

---

[9] For Hugh, see *ibid*. 244-60 and chapter three below.

[10] This is the case with the *vitae* of Dietrich I and Adalbero II of Metz, Heribert of Cologne, Meinwerk of Paderborn, Bernward of Hildesheim, Adalbero of Würzburg, Altmann of Passau, Notger of Liège, and Werner of Merseburg.

development and comportment [*elegantia morum, continentia laudabilis*]; and a total devotion to those to whom they minister [*amor civium, sollicitudo pastoralis*], including but not limited to the faithful.[11]

To put it bluntly, in all biographical literature of the time, family origins hold pride of place, in particular the noble, even illustrious, character of the family (e.g. its royal or ducal origin). It is common to define one's noble character by stressing the antiquity and renown of the family, its courage (or strength), the quality of its morals, and its material resources. As a nobleman, the bishop must show these noble virtues, but he has to add others to them, including intellectual achievement and the capacity to care for others. As far as morality is concerned, the emphasis is on continence; the question of celibacy never comes up, both because it is assumed and because it is not essential. The *Lives* of the German bishops of the tenth and eleventh centuries are veritable gifts to historians. Consider in particular the admirable text of the Life of Ulrich of Augsburg, recently re-edited by Walter Berschin.[12] To be sure, historians need to be wary of all the traps hidden within these carefully literary and sometimes academic accounts of the heroes of the church, for it is not always easy to distinguish what happened from what the biographer would have liked to have seen happen. Nevertheless, these texts are still historical sources of the first order.

3. Diplomatic sources

Finally, there is another important body of evidence for the history of bishops, albeit one which is insufficiently known and thus poorly utilized: episcopal charters. After the acts of kings and emperors, and even before the bulls of the popes, the charters of the bishops are unexpectedly rich sources. Of course, not all regions are equally well furnished in this respect. The Empire is far behind France, while in the latter the north is far richer than the south. The documentation is very abundant in Italy and Spain-- so abundant, in fact, that much of it remains unpublished. England must be considered as a separate case. If we confine ourselves to the area between Poitiers and Cologne, Utrecht and Lyon, we could have at our disposal enough texts to provide precise information about the

---

[11] "Epistola ad regem pro eligendo episcopo," *PL* 162: 807.

[12] Gerhard of Augsburg, *Vita Sancti Uodalrici. Die älteste Lebensbeschreibung des Heiligen Ulrich*, ed. and trans. Walter Berschin and Angelika Häse (Heidelberg: Universitätsverlag Carl Winter, 1993).

bishops and their diverse activities. Unfortunately, this is not the case, due to the gap between our knowledge of the sources and the far greater possibilities which these sources would provide if only historians could exploit them fully.

Indeed, while we have been content for a hundred years with, on the one hand, episcopal registers[13] and, on the other, the cartularies that our forebears published long ago, both are notoriously inadequate and can easily lead to error. How can we be satisfied with registers—that is, brief notices about the actions of a bishop—without having the full texts of his acts, foundations, donations, and negotiations, without a record of those people with whom he worked and to whom he referred, and without any sense of the very words used at the time? After reading Gautier, the historian of the bishops of Langres and author of the register of their acts, how could I know that three of the charters of Bishop Lambert from 1018 and 1019 presented long and rich *arengae* full of information about the culture and spirituality of the bishop and his entourage? At the same time, had I not been able to consult all of the charters of the bishops of Langres for this period, I would have imagined that every bishop prefaced his acts with equally beautiful flourishes, whereas it seems that the charters of Lambert were in fact exceptional.[14] Thus, the first task in studying the bishops of the tenth and eleventh centuries is to examine, publish, criticize, and analyze their charters. These are not that numerous, and many of the dioceses in France have very few such sources for this period of time. It is regrettable that we still do not have at our full disposal the research that was completed (but never published) on the bishops of Tournai, Liège, Cambrai, Reims, Châlons, Metz, Toul, Verdun, Paris, Laon, Langres, and Besançon.[15] The delay is due not only to the difficulties involved in diplomatic criticism, but to the level of erudition required for the publication of important acts. Still, to the extent that we do not publish these sources, we are handicapped. While a project in England to publish epis-

---

[13] Known in French as "catalogues d'actes" and in German as "Bischofsregesten". Numerous such episcopal and archepiscopal *Regesten* have come out of Germany, but German scholars have not followed up with the necessary next step, which would be to publish the complete acts. The latter are available in other source series, but often are very dispersed (e.g. in regional cartularies, episcopal cartularies, or monastic cartularies).

[14] These acts have been placed at my disposal by Hubert Flammarion, who plans to produce a full edition. I thank him very warmly for his generosity.

[15] Complete dossiers for Tournai, Liège, and Cambrai have been compiled by Jacques Pycke, Jean-Louis Kupper, and Erik van Mingroot. Reims, Châlons, and Laon are the focus (respectively) of theses by Patrick Demouy, Marie-Josèph Gut-Bondil, and Annie Dufour-Malbezin, while I have gathered the acts for Paris, Metz, Toul, and Verdun.

copal acts is in progress and going well,[16] the one that I tried to initiate in France has not produced the results that we had anticipated. We have Limoges and Arras, and soon will have Laon and Poitiers.[17] That's not much.

In addition to registers, we also have recourse to cartularies, and we use them without hesitation. We now realize, however, all the surprises that cartularies can hide: incomplete acts, badly copied acts, even falsified acts whose originals have disappeared.[18] Of course, not everything in a cartulary is false or badly copied, but can we really run the risk of using charters whose validity is uncertain?

As an example of the kind of information that diplomatic texts give us about the activities of bishops, I did a survey of the extant original charters drawn up by bishops in what is present-day France during the thirty-year period from 985 to 1015. The research center at Nancy has found twenty acts dating from this period. They come from ten dioceses: Paris, Sens, and Strasbourg in the north; Anger, Le Mans, Tours, and Nevers in central France; and Chalon, Grenoble, and Marseille in the south. These acts primarily concern donations, either of churches and altars, of landed properties, or of rights. To these can be added a few foundations or refoundations and the procès-verbal of the election of an abbot.[19] Here we have precise evidence for subjects that never come up either in the narrative sources (with the exception of accounts of the conditions for monastic reform) nor in hagiographical sources in the same rich detail, unless the writer himself drew from archival sources. Moreover, the charters give lists of witnesses, both lay and ecclesiastical, who never show up elsewhere. It's only in this way that we can compile a list of members of a whole cathedral chapter or

---

[16] This project, begun at the initiative of Frank Barlow and supported by the British Academy, has resulted in the publication of numerous volumes of episcopal acts since 1980, including those of Lincoln, Canterbury, York, Norwich, Hereford, Winchester, Bath and Wells, Exeter, Worcester, Coventry and Lichfield, London, Salisbury, and Chichester.

[17] For Limoges, *Actes des évêques de Limoges*, ed. Jean Becquet; for Arras, *Les chartes des évêques d'Arras (1093-1203)*, ed. Benoît-Michel Tock (Paris: CTHS, 1991); for Laon, *Actes des évêques de Laon*, ed. Dufour-Malbezin. An edition of the acts of the bishops of Poitiers is in preparation by Georges Pon.

[18] For discussion and examples, see the papers in *Les cartulaires. Actes de la Table Ronde organisée par l'Ecole nationale des chartes et le G.D.R. 121 du C.N.R.S. (Paris, 5-7 décembre 1991)*, ed. Olivier Guyotjeannin, Laurent Morelle, and Michel Parisse (Paris: Ecole des chartes, 1993).

[19] During the same period, for the bishop of Langres alone, if we include copies along with the originals, we have an equivalent number of acts, including donations of churches, donations of land, and personal interventions by the bishop (a settlement and a judgment).

of a monastic community, and thus become aware of the immediate entourage of a bishop. As far as donations are concerned, the one example that we have brings us face to face with the serious problem of the sharing of churches between laymen and clerics, an issue that involved altars that were given by the bishop to the churches in his diocese. Thus, the three kinds of sources that I have just described are complementary. Each one tells us something lacking from the others, and on each we must cast a critical eye, keeping what is stated separate from what is implied, and what is authentic apart from what is wished for.

The Bishop over his Flock: Prelate and Prince

I will not repeat here everything that I have said on earlier occasions about episcopal recruitment, exercise of power, relations with the papacy, and so forth.[20] Rather, I would like to reflect upon the way in which bishops exercised power, both as heads of the church and the faithful, and as princes and thus associates of the sovereign. I've discovered with some astonishment that even in the many encyclopedias and dictionaries published over the last few years, no attempt has been made to broach the subject of the bishop's function in anything approaching completeness. Throughout this rapid review, therefore, please keep in mind the idea of the simultaneous presence of lay and ecclesiastical princes at the side of the sovereign, and of the clear superiority—at least in theory—of the clergy over the laity.

1. The choice of the bishop and his qualities

Medieval authors are often at pains to give a list of the qualities required of the bishop, something that they do not do for dukes and counts. The exception here are general requirements for nobles, such as we find in the *Vita Rictrudis*, where the author gives a definition of noble virtue that applies to lay princes, emphasizing brilliant ancestry [*genus*], courage, wealth, and morals.[21] These are characteristics that naturally accompany the high responsibility of exercising

---

[20] See in particular Michel Parisse, "Princes laïques et/ou moines: les évêques du Xe siècle," in *Il secolo di ferro: mito e realtà del secolo X* [Settimane 38] (Spoleto: Presso le Sede del Centro, 1991), 449-513.

[21] For women, these virtues and their classification were somewhat different; see Hucbald of St.-Amand, *Vita Sanctae Rictrudis*, c. 5 (PL 132: 834): "In uxore [i.e., Rictrude] autem pulchritudo, genus, divitiae, et mores, qui magis quam caetera quaerendi sunt, habebantur."

power in the name of the king. They apply just as naturally to the bishops, for it is out of the question for the prelate to have any but a noble origin. Only a nobleman has the right and the capacity to exercise power over others. This being established, the bishop may in fact come from a family more or less illustrious. But, as we saw before, these characteristics are not enough for the prelate; to them he must add intellectual credentials and the clear capacity to rule. If the second comes automatically, the first is specific to the clergy. In turn, even though the bishop is in principle a nobleman, a representative of the aristocracy, it is nevertheless important to realize that families who produce bishops become thereby even more illustrious. Thus there is a trade-off: the candidate for a bishopric is more likely to succeed the more illustrious his family, and a family is more illustrious if it has put its hands on an episcopal see.

There is a little treatise on the qualities of the bishop, the *Sermo de informatione episcoporum*, often attributed to Gerbert of Aurillac.[22] While this attribution is now known to be erroneous, there is no question that the text dates from around the year 1000.[23] It contains a list of about a dozen conditions that the bishop ought to fulfill, summed up in the form of adjectives that are then explained and glossed. He must be:

> without reproach . . . the husband of one wife . . . temperate . . . clear-headed . . . well-arranged . . . hospitable . . . willing to teach . . . a non-drinker . . . one who does not strike, but is instead gentle . . . not contentious . . . not greedy . . . in control over his own household . . . [and] not a novice . . .;

---

[22] Migne, *PL* 139: 169-78. The text is reprinted from that in Jean Mabillon, *Vetera Analecta, sive Collectio veterum aliquot Operum . . . nova editio* (Paris: Montalant, 1723), 103a-106b.

[23] It now is generally accepted that the pseudo-Gerbertian *Sermo* is an adapted and re-attributed version of the fifth-century pseudo-Ambrosian *Sermo pastoralis*, produced in the first quarter of the eleventh century by Ademar of Chabannes. See Flavio Nuvolone, "Il *Sermo pastoralis* pseudoambrosiano e il *Sermo Girberti philosophi papae urbis Romae qui cognominatus est Silvester de informatione Episcoporum*: Riflessioni," in *Gerberto: scienza, storia e mito* (Piacenza: Editrice degli Archivi Storici Bobiensi, 1985), 379-565, in particular 407-13 and 442-82, and Richard Landes, *Relics, Apocalypse, and the Deceits of History: Ademar of Chabannes, 989-1034* (Cambridge, MA: Harvard University Press, 1995), 110 and 362.

finally, "he must bear good witness from those who are without (that is, heretics and schismatics)."[24] Who could fulfill such requirements? At any rate, it's good that people had them in mind, although there must have been quite a distance between theory and practice.

In the same way, the procedure for episcopal election was continually recalled, but probably rarely observed! We have a whole series of form letters which serve as models for the correspondence called for in case of a vacant episcopal see: the announcement of the vacancy, authorization to hold the election, declaration of the result of the election, and so on, directed to the canons of the vacant city, the archbishop of the province, and the king.[25] All of this, although referring to the era of Archbishop Hincmar of Reims and Charles the Bald, is also applicable to the following century. The evidence available for the tenth century, however, shows that even if the authorities made an effort to follow legal procedures, they in fact chose the new bishop according to their own lights. Thus in the case of Hugh of Chalon, the bishop of Auxerre mentioned above, the *Gesta* noted the quasi-miraculous conditions under which he was elected, adding that his promotion took place with the approval of the duke of Burgundy (Hugh's brother) and King Robert of France. In fact, it is clearly stated that his election was decided—indeed, had even been prepared (*annuente*)—by these two interested parties themselves.[26]

2. Religious power

We know very little about how lay princes took power. Although the election of the king or his accession at the death of his father, the king's coronation, the rituals of homage, and the symbols of royal power are well-known and described, I have encountered only one *ordo* for the benediction of a duke (the duke of Aquitaine, as it so happens),[27] and we can only imagine the ceremony for the accession of a young count, presiding over the funeral rites of his father,

---

[24] ". . . irreprehensibilis . . . unius uxoris vir . . . sobrius . . . prudentus . . . ornatus . . . hospitalis . . . docibilis . . . non vinolentus . . . non percussor sed modestus . . . non litigiosus . . . non cupidus . . . suae domus bene propositus . . . non neophytus . . . Oportet illum et testimonium habere bonum ab his qui foris sunt, id est hereticis atque scismaticis."

[25] Migne, *PL* 129: 1382-1398.

[26] *Les gestes des évêques d'Auxerre*, ed. Lobrichon and Goullet, 246.

[27] "Ordo ad benedicendum ducem Aquitanie," in *Recueil des Historiens des Gaules et de la France*, new ed., vol. 23, ed. Léopold Delisle (Paris: V. Palmé, 1872), 451-53.

then greeting his important vassals and receiving their homage, and finally settling into a majestic seat in the grand hall of his castle. Yet while the sources are generally silent on this topic, this is not true in the case of the bishop.

The enthronement ceremony and the symbols of power

The advent of the bishop was a solemn affair.[28] After a *conventus* or meeting of a group of clerics and laity who proceed to acclaim the candidate, he was solemnly introduced into his cathedral by a colleague, seated on the throne, the symbol of majesty, and solemnly consecrated and blessed by three bishops of the province. One Sunday, in the presence of the people, he took up the insignia of power, which included the pastoral staff, the ring, and the pectoral cross. These, together with the miter and other episcopal accouterments, served as external signs of the bishop's power; in addition, he lived in a fixed central residence—the cathedral city.

Responsibility for faith and dogma

As soon as the bishop was enthroned, he became the man responsible for faith and dogma, and thus for the moral health and future salvation of his flock. He had to give evidence of his orthodoxy by reciting the *Credo*, and at the same time he became the touchstone for all problems regarding the faith. The bishop was still the sole master in his diocese. Everything that touched on heresy, whether from far or near, was his direct concern, as we see in the issues that bishops Gerard of Cambrai and Arnulf of Orléans had to deal with in the 1020s.[29]

If he delegated his right to baptize to the priests in the villages and the countryside, the bishop nevertheless remained the only one who could confirm the faithful. To do this, he had to traverse his whole diocese incessantly. He

---

[28] See below, chapter two.

[29] Guy Lobrichon, "Arras 1025, ou le vrai procès d'une fausse accusation," in *Inventer l'hérésie? Discours polémique et pouvoirs avant l'inquisition*, ed. Monique Zerner (Nice: Centre d'études médiévales, 1998), 67-85; Heinrich Fichtenau, "Die Ketzer von Orléans (1022)," in *Ex ipsis rerum documentis: Beiträge zur Mediävistik. Festschrift für Harald Zimmerman zum 65. Geburtstag*, ed. Klaus Herbers, Hans-Henning Kortüm, and Carlo Servatius (Sigmaringen: Thorbecke, 1991), 417-27, Malcolm Lambert, *Medieval Heresy: Popular Movements from the Gregorian Reform to the Reformation*, 2nd ed. (Cambridge, MA: Blackwell, 1992), 9-16; 22-25.

preached at the same time: numerous texts confirm this, with one of the most compelling descriptions coming from the *Vita* of Ulrich of Augsburg.[30] Of course we know that an annual visit to each place in the immense German dioceses was impossible, but the obligation remained.

The lone judge of the diocese: decision and punishment

The bishop, as the head of Christendom, was the sole judge for everything touching on religion and on membership in the Church. All extraordinary matters came under his competence, and the cases reserved for the bishop were numerous. The bishop judged behavior, determined the rules that had to be followed, intervened in social matters, and had a particular impact on the most wealthy and powerful members of the community. Because of his ecclesiastical function, he was more powerful than the powerful laymen with whom he interacted; it was he who could excommunicate an individual or a group and interdict the religious life of an institution or a territory. The anathema and interdiction that he imposed (and that he alone could lift) terrified the population, who quickly realized the danger they were courting if their children were not baptized, if their dead were banned from Christian soil, or if the Church condemned them. The threat was taken seriously. We should not underestimate the power of belief, the importance of fear, and the terrors of Hell. Christendom was thus hived off into dioceses and placed under the full authority of the bishops, and not an inch escaped them. Even sovereigns were subject to the will of the bishops; need we recall the firmness with which the bishop of Metz, Adalbero II, upbraided the king regarding the forbidden degrees of incest in marriage?[31] This case was hardly unique. Robert the Pious could not act without his bishops, and he knew that only the prelates could authorize a marriage that was normally impermissible. Nonetheless, he later was the victim of papal intervention, for the bishops of France, as powerful as they were, could not counter the will of Rome even if (as they sometimes said) it displeased them.

---

[30] Gerhard of Augsburg, *Vita Sancti Oudalrici*, c. 6.

[31] Robert Folz, "Adelbéron II, évêque de Metz 984-1005," in *Ex ipsis rerum documentis*, 399-415, especially 411-13.

A well-prepared function

Although the bishop bore a heavy burden, he was usually well prepared for it. On average, an episcopacy lasted fifteen years, about half as long as a powerful layman remained in authority. This was because the Church had fixed a minimum age for the office of bishop. The standard of thirty years established in the thirteenth century was not that followed in earlier times, for we know of prelates who held office in their early twenties. Normally, however, the prelate had already exercised some episcopal functions before his election. If he had been a canon in a cathedral chapter, he likely would have occupied some dignity or office such as archdeacon, schoolmaster, or provost. In other cases, the bishop was first an abbot or prior of a monastic community.

The definition of a bishop also included intellectual formation. Bishops were rarely uneducated. They had to know how to read and write, but they also received a scholarly education, knew the Old and New Testaments, and read the Church Fathers. Not all had attained a high level of cultural accomplishment, but in theory this ought to have been the case. Here too, we know that laymen were also prepared for their seigneurial function by their parents, for their inheritance was anticipated. Heredity thus played a role in benefiting the oldest son, although his degree of preparation was not as high as that of the bishops.

Should we say that, insofar as becoming bishop suppressed the privileges of heredity, there were no rights of succession for bishops, and only the best were elected? That would be going too far, since we would be ignoring the phenomenon of nepotism and its penetration into every region. Some cases are more striking than others, of course, such as at Poitiers where, over a long period of time, one family alone held the see.[32] Still, despite the role of nepotism, it was far from the equivalent of heredity pure and simple.

3. Economy and culture

The princes had to be masters of economic resources. Not only did they require abundant resources in the form of property, revenues, and rights, but they also needed to control the economy, which was the source of significant wealth. In this regard, the Church was far ahead of the laity. First of all, the bishops were either full or partial masters of the cities where they presided, and around

---

[32] On this see Duguet, "La famille des Isembert."

the year 1000 these were practically the only cities in the West.[33] Lay princes lived in the countryside, in castles from which they kept a close eye on transportation routes and points of weakness. The places in which they were ensconced, however, no longer were centers of production and exchange, as had been the villas of late antiquity.

Moreover, the sites of exchange—the markets and the fairs—were automatically placed under the authority and protection of the saints (and thus of those saints' churches) and were known only by their names. Monasteries and cathedral chapters therefore had at their disposal the very commercial exchanges that were important sources of money revenue, due to heavy taxes on the transport of merchandise (*tonlieux*) and its display and sale, and to their control over weights, measures, and coinage. The church was, after the king, the chief minter of coins, and each minting was a source of profit. We can well understand the interest that lay princes had in controlling the religious communities that were next to places of commerce, an interest made clear by the diplomas of the Ottonians, where we repeatedly find mention of three prerogatives: market, coinage, and tolls.

If the lay princes were not totally overwhelmed by the ecclesiastical princes in terms of economic resources, in matters of culture they were completely outclassed. The centers of education were entirely controlled by ecclesiastical communities, monasteries, and cathedral chapters. Of course, bishops did not have a monopoly over culture and education—they shared it with abbots. But the fact is that the great centers of instruction were episcopal cities—Chartres, Paris, Reims, Laon, Liège and many others of lesser importance—in the period around 1000.

This culture extended into episcopal government. At the bishop's permanent disposal were books containing the texts of councils, the canons, and the decretals, a whole set of materials that they could consult each time a delicate issue arose. Thus we find that in 991, when the time came to judge Archbishop Arnulf of Reims at the council of Saint-Basle de Verzy, the prelates had brought books with them in abundance, books that they read through tirelessly before and after

---

[33] Reinhold Kaiser, *Bischofsherrschaft zwischen Königtum und Fürstenmacht. Studien zur bischöflichen Stadtherrschaft im westfränkisch-französischen Reich im frühen und hohen Mittelalter* (Bonn: Röhrscheid, 1981), and *idem*, "Les évêques neustriens du Xe siècle dans l'exercice de leur pouvoir temporel d'après l'historiographie médiévale," in *Pays de Loire et Aquitaine de Robert le Fort aux premiers Capétiens* (Poitiers: Société des Antiquaires de l'Ouest, 1997), 117-43.

the meetings. The report later drawn up by Gerbert of Aurillac is larded with extracts from the councils.[34] Episcopal *scientia* thus depended in large part upon consultation of written documents.

4. Government and participation in government

Service to the king

This is the area for which we have the most information, since the books and articles dealing with the bishops show them continually in action at court and in service to the king. There is no use reiterating what has already been said about the German princes and their dependence on the emperor, a point to which we will return briefly. Beginning in the Carolingian period, the king governed by regularly calling together his magnates—counts, bishops, and abbots—while important decisions normally were taken *cum consilio episcoporum*. Councils and counsel thus could easily blend together. When Charlemagne convened four councils in his empire in 813, and when Louis the Pious did the same in 829, they intended to discuss the affairs of the Church, which included the concerns of the Empire in general: faith, justice, the respect due to the king, the minting of coins, or the defense of dogma. Likewise, the so-called "general" *Admonitio* of 789 remained influential for centuries to come.

The importance of nearness to the king is particularly clear when we look at the chancery. The notaries, chaplains, archchaplains and archchancellors appointed by the Carolingians were often clerics destined for the episcopacy or, in the case of the highest posts, bishops and archbishops. In cases of interregna, regencies, or other difficult moments in the history of the German monarchy, an archbishop invariably occupies a central position at court. This holds true for France as well, albeit in more discreet fashion.

Councils and Synods

The bishop was not alone. He was assisted at the diocesan level by his immediate entourage, and at the level of the kingdom by his episcopal brethren.

---

[34] Michel Parisse, "Les évêques de France et le pape, à la lumière des actes du concile de Saint-Basle (991)," in *Gerbert moine, évêque et pape: d'un millénaire à l'autre* (Aurillac: Association cataliennne, 2000), 171-94, especially 173.

Within the diocese and in the city, the bishop had a whole staff of clergy at his disposal, including the cathedral canons and his chosen officials, as well as the archdeacons, who traveled throughout the diocese in his stead. Later he created a chancery to redact his documents. If he followed the dictates of canon law, he called a diocesan synod twice a year. There he welcomed the clergy working in the city, abbots and monks, priests, and important laity, took care of religious and profane business, and often issued charters or presided over court cases. While the episcopal entourage corresponded to the courts of counts and dukes, which were comprised of their closest vassals and family members, the bishop's court was grander, for it brought together both clergy and laity and dealt with a broad range of subjects. Questions of an economic nature, for example, such as those regarding the temporal holdings of the church, were just as important and urgent as questions concerning dogma or worship.

At a higher level, the bishops continued the collegial practices of the apostles in regular or special councils. Editors like Mansi and Hefele have brought together all of the sources for the known councils, but there were many others besides. Indeed, the charters often reveal meetings of prelates unknown from other sources. For example, in 986 the bishop of Nevers gave four altars to the chapter of Saint-Cyr in his city. Seven bishops—representing the archbishops of Reims, Sens, and Lyon—served as witnesses, brought together for reasons that now escape us.[35] This is not an exceptional example at all, and reinforces how knowledge of the charter evidence provides us with a better sense of the daily relationships between the bishops in a region or province. At any rate, this collegiality created a sense of mutual support. We can see this very well at the Council of Verzy, when the thirteen bishops charged with judging their colleague Arnulf of Reims took numerous precautions, aware that any condemnation of Arnulf reflected upon them as well.

The episcopal network revealed its importance during the councils of the Peace of God. Although these are well known and the object of extensive study, they offer us yet another chance to show how the bishops, in concert with the lay princes, participated actively and decisively in governing a territory.[36] The prel-

---

[35] Paris, BN lat. 17130, no. 1.

[36] The most recent study of this question is Dominique Barthélemy, *L'an mil et la paix de Dieu. La France chrétienne et féodale, 980-1060* (Paris: Fayard, 1999), with numerous references in the bibliography to previous work on this subject. It should be noted that the author defends a point of view which does not preclude us from reaching other conclusions about the matter.

ates and dukes shared in the initiative, while the counts followed. With regard to their varied scope, the decisions of these councils recall the Carolingian capitularies, which had disappeared by the end of the ninth century. Historians do not fail to stress that in France the initiative of the bishops made up for the lack of royal power. By contrast, in the Empire the close alliance between bishops and the sovereign, and the effectiveness of their centralized power, made Peace councils useless.

When all is said and done, a comparison of the lay with the ecclesiastical princes easily convinces us of the superiority of the second over the first, for they exercised power in all of the areas that a sovereign did—indeed, in almost more than the king, even though the latter's unction, coronation, and the divine grace invoked in his very title gave him quasi-sacerdotal privileges and the right to intervene in religious affairs.

The bishops in France and Germany

While much more could be said about bishops in general, we know that considerable differences existed between the bishops of different regions. Therefore, let us now look more closely at the two episcopacies that I know best: those of France and the Empire.

1. Recruitment

Germany, which has been extensively studied and the subject of lengthy debate, represents well-explored territory for the historian. With very few exceptions, the German bishops were entirely under the control of the sovereign. This was the case with regards to their election, the confirmation of those elections, and their service to the king, service that involved personal assistance as well as the provision of agricultural products and manpower. Between 950 and 1050 there thus existed what has been called the "imperial church," although Timothy Reuter has rightly criticized this concept as too systematic and idealized.[37] The prelates of the empire around the year 1000 were great figures, and many of them attract our attention: the archbishops Heribert of Cologne, Willigis of Mainz, Egbert of Trier, and Gisilher of Magdeburg, as well as bishops such as

---

[37] Timothy Reuter, "The 'Imperial Church System' of the Ottonian and Salian rulers: A Reconsideration," *Journal of Ecclesiastical History* 33 (1982): 347-74.

Notker of Liège, Bernward of Hildesheim, Burchard of Worms, and Ansfrid of Utrecht.

Most often these bishops were trained for their tasks in the cathedral chapters or monasteries. They occupied positions of responsibility such as chaplain, notary, or chancellor, sometimes at the chapel of the king himself. In addition, they were constantly enriched by royal donations of land and counties, rights and privileges which made them princes as powerful as the dukes and counts, with the additional power provided by their spiritual functions. This episcopacy was truly impressive; the renown enjoyed by the bishops dwarfed that of the dukes and even more of the counts, who are hardly worthy of our attention. Their splendid patronage of the arts, visible today thanks to the impressive exhibitions organized by German historians over the last few decades, further accentuated the superiority of a German Church possessed of enormous resources, some of which survive even today.

In the case of France, on the other hand, we must distinguish between two very different zones. On the one hand was the region in which the king acted directly; on the other, the area that largely escaped his control. In fact, the king exercised direct power over at best only a third of the bishoprics in his kingdom, i.e. those situated to the north and west.[38] Within this region he could effectively oversee the election of bishops, call them into council, solicit their aid, and consider them as adjuncts to his governance. By contrast, in the west and the south, from Normandy to the Pyrenees, the bishops were either individually or in small groups under the thumb of regional magnates: the dukes of Normandy and Aquitaine, the count of Anjou, local seigneurs. Here the episcopate did not succeed in emancipating itself, and instead belonged to laypeople who treated churches as if they were their own belongings. The desire to control church and monastic property obliged these lay lords to control episcopal elections. Under these conditions the definition of the bishop provided earlier in this essay does not really hold, for his and his society's needs were different. This is why the qualities of intelligence and moral rectitude did not have the same importance. In these regions there were sometimes uneducated bishops, married bishops or bishops with concubines, bishops ready to be manipulated politically. The examples that are always cited to show the need for reform and the problems of simony and nicolaitism are bishops from western France (such as those of Le

---

[38] See the map in Marcel Pacaut, *Louis VII et les élections épiscopales dans la royaume de France* (Paris: J. Vrin, 1957).

Mans and Nantes) or from the south. The case of Fulcran of Lodève is thus an exception.

By contrast, there are hardly any examples of bad bishops on royal territory, with the exception of simoniacs. The bishops in those regions were of a different caliber. Clearly the king could not name prelates who were all from his family, as the seigneurs of the Midi were able to do. He thus chose from local families, but according to his lights, and thus was able to create a higher-quality episcopate. There are few examples of bishops from the Midi or the west who made much of a mark; by contrast, the king had at his service some very important men: the archbishops of Reims, Sens, and Bourges, the bishops of Orléans, and several other remarkable individuals.[39]

2. The formation and the length of the episcopacy

It is useful to examine the methods of episcopal formation pursued by the two sovereigns and their bishops. There were forty bishoprics in Germany. The average length of episcopal tenure in the tenth and eleventh centuries was sixteen years, but for the prelates around the year 1000 itself the median was twenty years, if not rather more during the periods just before and after. Moreover, we know that twelve prelates held office for periods of 21 to 25 years; ten of 26 to 30 years; and three of more than 30 years. Only five had their sees for five years or less. These figures are useful, however, only when they are compared to those for the kingdom of France, information which is difficult to come by due to a dearth of sources. We do not know the name of the office holder in about a third of approximately one hundred bishoprics in France, and the duration of episcopal tenures often is impossible to ascertain, even in approximate terms. We have little information for Normandy, Brittany, and southeastern and southwestern France. Comparison thus is possible only for central and northern France, where during the same two centuries the median length of episcopal tenure was about twenty years, i.e. four more than in the Empire. Here too the median rose around the year 1000; we thus may thus note, for example, the episcopacies of over 50 years enjoyed by Fulcran of Lodève, Burchard of Lyon, Adalbero of Laon and Aimeri of Narbonne, and of more than 40 years for Hugh of Rouen, Gautier of Autun, Manasses of Arles, Hugh of Toulouse, Gilbert of Poitiers, Gébuin of

---

[39] For the prelates in the entourage of King Robert, see Christian Pfister, *Études sur le règne de Robert le Pieux (996-1031)* (Paris: F. Vieweg, 1885).

Châlons, and Hildegard of Beauvais. In Germany the only analogous case is that of Ulrich of Augsburg, who was bishop for 50 years.

What can we learn from these general observations? No doubt bishops died at the same age in both countries. Thus we must conclude that men became bishops at a younger age in France, while in Germany they devoted their early years to a variety of other tasks. We can see here one of the effects of service in the royal chapel, which could last for ten to twenty years. But we should not exaggerate this point, because only some of Otto III's bishops came from his chapel. A later assumption of the episcopal see, perhaps at the age of 35 rather than at 30 or 25, meant more mature bishops, men more engaged in public life. In France the bishop took up his office five or ten years earlier; he too had filled some preparatory offices, but for less time. Here, the difference in the authorities responsible for elections, between north and south, and between the dukes and the counts all worked against the establishment of a concerted policy such as that found in the Empire. It would be interesting to make a similar survey of England and Italy, since only a series of such comparative studies will finally permit us to understand the episcopacy as fully as we would like.

3. Freedom of action

At the moment when the imperial church was in full bloom, one of its characteristics was the generous enrichment of episcopal churches and some monasteries by the express will of the king. We need only look at the tables prepared by Leo Santifaller to take stock of the donations of counties, forests, tolls, minting and market rights, and immunities—in short, of everything that would prepare the way for the birth of episcopal principalities.[40] The emperor was rich, and he could distribute the property of the fisc to churches *larga manu*. We know that the situation was quite different in France, where the laity would sooner pillage the property of the church than enrich it, though they too showed their generosity by founding new religious communities. The flip side of royal largesse, as we know, was the claims made by the sovereign on his churches. We need only refer to the *Indiculus loricatorum* of 981, which set out the num-

---

[40] Leo Santifaller, *Zur Geschichte des ottonisch-salischen Reichskirchensystems*, 2nd ed. (Vienna: R.M. Rohrer, 1964), *passim*.

ber of contingents of armed soldiers that each church had to send to Italy to support Otto II's expedition against the Muslims of southern Italy.[41]

Things were far less favorable for the king of France. Hugh Capet and Robert the Pious could not always act as they wished. While they generally succeeded in installing their candidates, they often encountered opposition from other bishops or the faithful, which meant that they had to impose their man by force. Moreover, they attempted to fill sees with candidates from the same region, something with which the emperor was far less concerned. Indeed, he did not hesitate to send a capable individual far away from his homeland (from Saxony or Alemannia to Lotharingia, for example.) The king of France also did not have the means to enrich his bishops like his German neighbor, nor did he receive back the same personal or material *servitia*. The period around the year 1000 thus was one in which the disparities between the two episcopates were particularly stark. The Ottonians retained the Carolingian practice of richly endowing churches; the Capetians did not have the means to do so, and instead focused their attention on the royal crown and state. They prepared, in other words, for centralization—something that did not interest the emperors.

These differences have led Joachim Ehlers to make a new and interesting observation. According to him, with the exception of Burchard of Worms, the German bishops were restrained in their spontaneity and were therefore less creative. In France, on the other hand—certainly from the eleventh century on—the bishops had a freer hand and were able to develop schools and a richer teaching environment.[42] The schools were places of reflection and debate. In the imperial church bishops had fewer possibilities for self expression than they had in the French church. This is why we can cite some French centers of scholarship around the year 1000 but have no corresponding examples in Germany, apart from the cathedral chapters where candidates for episcopal service in the empire were prepared, such as Goslar or Hildesheim. Could the king of France

---

[41] In MGH *Const* I, ed. Ludwig Weiland (Hannover: Monumenta Germaniae Historica, 1893), no. 436; on this, see Karl-Ferdinand Werner, "Heeresorganisation und Kriegführung im deutschen Königreich des 10. und 11. Jahrhundert," in *Ordinamenti militari in Occidente nell'alto Medioevo* [Settimane 15] (Spoleto: Centro Italiano di studi sull'alto Medioevo, 1968), 791-843.

[42] Joachim Ehlers, "Die Reform der Christenheit. Studium, Bildung und Wissenschaft als bestimmende Kräfte bei der Entstehung des mittelalterlichen Europa," in *Deutschland und der Westen Europas im Mittelalter*, ed. Joachim Ehlers [Vorträge und Forschungen 56] (Stuttgart: Thorbecke, 2002), 197-99.

have created a royal church like that found in the Empire? Perhaps, but only in his own territory, since for him a different conception of the state applied.

By Way of Conclusion . . .

The Gregorian reform violently attacked "false prelates", i.e. those tainted by simony and nicolaïtism. But were these individuals really so bad? Simony more or less existed everywhere, and shocked no one except in its most extreme forms, such as the outright purchase of an episcopal see. Most of the time it was part of family transactions, an act of clout. Likewise, nicolaitism, when it existed, bothered no one. Many priests had a wife or concubine. Certainly the canons did too; why not the bishops, if perhaps less visibly? People who had a different attitude towards sexual mores than ours did not gauge the effectiveness of the bishop on the basis of his sexual adventures, but rather of his political effectiveness, his impact on the diocese, and his foundations or restorations of religious communities. Before Leo IX, the bishop was a powerful and wealthy nobleman, the overseer of religion and an advisor to princes, with no real superior in ecclesiastical matters. Much was expected of him, but since there was no control over his choices or his actions, he did what he wanted.

In their monumental *Histoire de l'Eglise*, Fliche and Martin argue that the Gregorian reformers snatched the Church from the hands of the laity in order to give it a certain *libertas*. We could, however, formulate this differently: the real reform was effected by the bishops, when they gave up their pretensions to being laymen rather than churchmen, princes rather than prelates.

Chapter Two
Bishops, Rites of Passage, and the Symbolism of State in Pre-Gregorian Europe
Timothy Reuter

Across Europe at the time of the first millennium (and for some time before and after), dioceses were not mere administrative subdivisions of the church, but vehicles of being and consciousness: in a word, communities.[1] They were not communities in an ecclesiastical sense alone. Episcopal *vitae* of the period, and other sources, show the inhabitants of dioceses, both clerical and lay, acting as group solidarities on all kinds of occasions. Indeed, dioceses looked a lot more regnal, a lot more "state-like", than did most kingdoms at the time. They had a capital city which usually also had metropolitan functions ("metropolitan" in the sense used by geographers, not that used by church historians). They had a ruler in their bishop, who at this stage did not have serious competition in the government of the diocese from his chapter. Those born and baptised in the diocese, together with those—both clergy and laity—who had lawfully "immigrated" with a testimony from the bishop of the diocese from which they had come that their "papers were in order," constituted the group of what might be called the "subjects" of the diocese;[2] pilgrims passing through, who in theory were also supposed to have their papers in order, were in a sense foreign tourists. Dioceses even had territories, though we should be careful about making excessive claims for the degree of territoriality exhibited by tenth- and eleventh-century dioceses. As with kingdoms, we are dealing with what German historians call a *Personenverband*, a network of persons, to which we should add "juristic persons" like churches and monasteries in the case of dioceses, rather than the later *territorialer Flächenstaat*, a state defined by a spatially-conceived territory.[3] Robert

---

[1] For a preliminary exposition of this view, see Timothy Reuter, "Ein Europa der Bischöfe: das Zeitalter Burchards von Worms," in *Burchard von Worms 1000-1025*, ed. Wilfried Hartmann (Mainz: Gesellschaft für mittelrheinische Kirchengeschichte, 2000), 1-28; for the concept of the 'imagined community' on which this approach is based, see Benedict Anderson, *Imagined Communities: Reflections on the Origin and Spread of Nationalism*, 2nd ed. (London: Verso, 1991).

[2] See Reuter, "Ein Europa der Bischöfe," 13-16, for details.

[3] The distinction was thus formulated by Theodor Mayer; the criticisms by Susan Reynolds, *Fiefs and Vassals* (Oxford: Oxford University Press, 1994), 26-27, are pertinent, but the distinction still seems to me to be worthwhile if used for Weberian ideal types. Matthew Innes, *State and Society in the Early Middle Ages: The Middle Rhine Valley, 400-1000* (Cambridge

Brentano's beautiful study of thirteenth-century Rieti offers an elegant account of how the implicit territoriality of early medieval theory was turned into hard administrative practice at a comparatively late stage;[4] this is an example drawn from central Italy, but it is probably valid for other parts of Europe as well.

The fact that bishoprics had rulers has, of course, not gone unnoticed by historians. But they have concentrated very heavily on the "who-whom" aspects of episcopal rule, in particular on the question of how people got to be bishops and on the prosopography of episcopal careers,[5] and still more on the question of who decided which person was going to be appointed.[6] Indeed, it is precisely this latter element of external control which has played the major role in historians' discussions, and we have a well-established typology: strict royal control of elections was an established norm in the *Reich* and in Anglo-Saxon England, probably also in northern Spain, while west Francia and Italy showed a tendency for this to be taken over by local and sometimes competing elites.[7] Both forms of control were in the end denounced by the late-eleventh-century reformers, and the horror stories of bishoprics for sale and of unsuitable appointments fill our textbooks.

But to concentrate on this element is to risk ignoring a much more important feature of of episcopal office in this period. Regardless of why a particular

---

and New York: Cambridge University Press, 2000), 254-63 distinguishes, perhaps more helpfully, between 'interpersonal' and 'bureaucratic' structures—a distinction which applies as much to bishoprics as to kingdoms, considered as 'states'.

[4] Robert Brentano, *A New World in a Small Place: Church and Religion in the Diocese of Rieti, 1188-1378* (Berkeley: University of California Press, 1994), 81-141.

[5] This is particularly true of Germany: see Josef Fleckenstein, *Die Hofkapelle der deutschen Könige*, vol. 2, *Die Hofkapelle im Rahmen der ottonisch-salischen Reichskirche* [MGH Schriften 16/2] (Stuttgart: Anton Hiersemann, 1966); Herbert Zielinski, *Der Reichsepiskopat in spätottonischer und salischer Zeit (1002-1125)* (Stuttgart: Franz Steiner, 1984); and Albrecht Graf Finck von Finckenstein, *Bischof und Reich: Untersuchungen zum Intergrationsprozess des ottonisch-frpühsalischen Reiches (919-1056)* [Studien zur Mediävistik 1] (Sigmaringen: Thorbecke, 1988), with reference to prosopographical studies of bishops elsewhere in Europe.

[6] Again, for Germany in particular, cf. Reuter, "'Imperial Church System';" Josef Fleckenstein, 'Problematik und Gestalt der ottonisch- salischen Reichskirche', in *Reich und Kirche vor dem Investiturstreit. Vorträge beim wissenschaftlichen Kolloquium aus Anlaß des 80. Geburtstag Gerd Tellenbach*, ed. Karl Schmid (Sigmaringen: Thorbecke, 1985), 83-98; and Rudolf Schieffer, *Der geschichtliche Ort der ottonisch-salischen Reichskirchenpolitik* [Rheinisch-Westfälische Akademie der Wissenschaften, Geisteswissenschaften, Vorträge G 352] (Opladen: Westdeutscher Verlag, 1998).

[7] Reuter, "Ein Europa der Bischöfe," 23-24.

bishop came to be chosen, he entered into a clearly defined office with expectations determined far more by the community and traditions of the diocese than by his original backers, whoever these were.[8] The community consisted not only of that group of clerics in the process of evolving into cathedral chapters at this time, but of all clerics within a diocese. It and its associated traditions found literary expression via the authors of *gesta episcoporum*—Adam of Bremen is probably the best-known example, though his work is somewhat later—and of the *Lives* of bishops whose composition flourished in some (though not all) parts of pre-Gregorian Europe;[9] the fact that episcopal biography flourished in the *Reich* and in Anglo-Saxon England but not in France or Italy or Spain at this time still requires explanation. But these literary evocations of community and tradition, though certainly influential, probably found a less wide audience than a number of significant sequences of symbolic action which embodied them.

Here again, the parallels with kingdoms are very striking. For some decades now medieval historians have been aware of the significance of "signs of rulership and the symbolism of state" (to cite the title of Percy Ernst Schramm's groundbreaking set of studies)[10] in the definition and self-representation of medieval secular rulership in the construction of regnal communities—secular in the post-Gregorian sense of being set apart from or even opposed to the spiritual hierarchy of the church, although up to and indeed beyond the period we are talking about the rulers of kingdoms were neither unambiguously lay nor unam-

---

[8] Reuter, "'Imperial Church System'," 357-58; cf. also Janet L. Nelson, "National synods, kingship as office, and royal anointing: an early medieval syndrome," in *Politics and Ritual in Early Medieval Europe* (London: Hambledon Press, 1986), 242 n. 4, on the importance of the episcopal ordination as a rite of passage "in aggregating individual to role."

[9] See most recently Stephanie Haarländer, "Die Vita Burchardi im Rahmen der Bischofsviten seiner Zeit," in *Burchard von Worms*, ed. Hartmann, 129-60; *idem* (as Stephanie Coué), *Hagiographie im Kontext*; and Walter Berschin, *Biographie und Epochenstil im lateinischen Mittelalter, IV: Ottonische Biographie, erster Halbband, 920-1070* (Stuttgart: Anton Hiersemann, 1999).

[10] Percy Ernst Schramm, *Herrschaftszeichen und Staatssymbolik*, 3 vols. [MGH Schriften 13] (Stuttgart: Anton Hiersemann, 1955); see also *idem*, "Das Grundproblem dieser Sammlung: Die 'Herrschaftszeichen', die 'Staatssymbolik' und die 'Staatspräsentation' des Mittelalters," in *Kaiser, Könige und Päpste. Gesammelte Aufsätze zur Geschichte des Mittelalters*, 4 vols. (Stuttgart: Anton Hiersemann, 1968-71), 1: 30-60, and "Grundbegriffe des Bereichs: Herrschaftszeichen und Staatssymbolik," in *ibid.*, 4: 682-705. For commentary, see Janos M. Bak, "Medieval symbology of the state: Percy E. Schramm's contribution," *Viator* 4 (1973): 33-63, and *idem*, "Introduction: Coronation studies—past, present, and future," in *Coronations: Medieval and Early Modern Monarchic Ritual*, ed. Janos M. Bak (Berkeley: University of California Press, 1990), 1-15.

biguously secular figures. Historians also have been aware of the process of exchange between royal or imperial signs and symbolism on the one hand and papal signs and symbolism on the other, not least because of a much-cited article by Schramm himself.[11] The contribution of episcopal ordination rites to the development of royal and imperial inauguration rituals has also been noted.[12] Yet although these things might have prompted us to do so, we have in fact not given *episcopal* "signs of rulership and symbolism of state" nearly so much attention. Royal crowns, sceptres, swords, orbs, thrones and other regalia have been examined not only as works of art but also for their *function*; episcopal staffs, rings, crosses, copes and thrones have remained, by and large, the territory of archaeologists and art historians. We have editions of some of the most important royal and imperial coronation *ordines*,[13] but at best preliminary studies of episcopal ordination rites. Similarly, while royal palaces have been studied not only for their architecture but also their functionality, the study of contemporary episcopal palaces, though not exactly neglected, is much less well advanced than that of their royal counterparts.[14]

---

[11] Percy Ernst Schramm, "Sacerdotium und Regnum im Austausch ihrer Vorrechte: imitatio imperii und imitatio sacerdotii. Eine geschichtliche Skizze zur Beleuchtung des Dictatus papae Gregors VII.," in *Kaiser, Könige und Päpste*, 4: 57-106.

[12] Janet L. Nelson, "Kingship, law and liturgy in the political thought of Hincmar of Rheims," in Nelson, *Politics and Ritual*, 143-46.

[13] *Die Ordines für die Weihe und Krönung des Kaisers und der Kaiserin (Ordines coronationis imperialis)*, ed. Reinhard Elze [MGH *Fontes* 9] (Hannover: Hahn, 1960); *Ordines coronationis Franciae: Texts and Ordines for the Coronation of Frankish and French Kings and Queens in the Middle Ages*, vol. 1, ed. Richard A. Jackson (Philadelphia: University of Pennsylvania Press, 1995). On episcopal rites, see Gerald Ellard, *Ordination Anointings in the Western Church before 1000 A.D.* (Cambridge, MA: Medieval Academy of America, 1933); Michel Andrieu, "Le Sacre épiscopal d'après Hincmar de Reims," *Revue d'histoire ecclésiastique* 48 (1953): 22-73. Cornelius Bouman's *Sacring and Crowning* (Groningen: J. B. Wolters, 1957) is concerned primarily with the development of royal ordination, but is also useful on episcopal rites. The best introduction to the larger complex of episcopal inauguration rituals is Odilo Engels, "Der Pontifikatsantritt und seine Zeichen," in *Segni e riti nella chiesa altomedievale occidentale* [Settimane 33] (Spoleto: Centro Italiano di studi sull'alto Medioevo, 1987), 707-70; for the underlying liturgy and theology see also Antonio Santantoni, *L'ordinazione episcopale: storia e teologia dei riti dell'ordinazione nelle antiche liturgie dell'occidente* [Studia Anselmiana 69: Analecta Liturgica 2] (Rome: Editrice Anselmiana, 1976), and Bruno Kleinheyer, "Ordinationen und Beauftragungen," in *Gottesdienst der Kirche: Handbuch der Liturgiewissenschaft*, ed. Hans Bernard Meyer *et al.* vol. 8, *Sakramentliche Feiern II* (Regensburg: Friedrich Pustet, 1984).

[14] See now Miller, *The Bishop's Palace*. Michael Thompson, *Medieval Bishops' Houses in England and Wales* (Aldershot: Ashgate, 1998), has virtually nothing to say on episcopal *domus* or *palatia* before the Norman Conquest.

These reflections are valid for the history of bishoprics throughout the medieval period, and to fill the gap in scholarship which they reveal completely would require a major programme of research. The present chapter is merely intended to show how reflections on "signs of rulership and the symbolism of state"—here primarily the latter—in an episcopal context can reshape our view of how bishops were perceived and perceived themselves around the millennium, a period for which the very rich narrative and hagiographic sources allow us to examine developments in considerable detail. I have chosen to concentrate on key moments at the beginning and end of pontificates: as we shall see, both the funeral of the deceased bishop and the installation of his successor were accompanied by elaborate sequences of symbolic actions,[15] sequences which stressed the element of diocesan community and the bishop's function as ruler, protector, *pater patriae*. Other sequences of symbolic actions will be touched on, but no more.

The death of a bishop in this period was an important public event. Death being what it is, episcopal deaths could not easily or self-evidently be "staged". Nevertheless, when bishops were able to do so they died in public, surrounded by their clergy, as did for example Brun of Cologne and Dunstan of Canterbury.[16] Death, where foreseeable, had its own dramaturgy and appropriate locations: Meinwerk of Paderborn, on receiving a (false) prophecy that he would die in five days, gave his possessions away and laid himself down to die, while Hildeward of Halberstadt took care to die "in the room in which two of his predecessors had died," according to Thietmar of Merseburg.[17] Once they had died, the procession of the funeral cortege was a significant rite of community, and in

---

[15] I have set out a methodology for distinguishing 'symbolic actions' from the subset of such actions commonly called 'ritual' in "*Velle sibi fieri in forma hac*: Symbolisches Handeln im Becketstreit," in *Form und Funktion öffentlicher Kommunikation im Mittelalter*, ed. Gerd Althoff (Sigmaringen: Thorbecke, 2001), 202-4, and in "*Pastorale pedum ante pedes ipsius apostolici posuit*: Dis- and reinvestiture in the era of the Investiture Contest," in *Belief and Culture in the Middle Ages: Studies presented to Henry Mayr-Harting*, ed. Richard Gameson and Henrietta Leyser (Oxford: Oxford University Press, 2001), 208-9.

[16] Ruotger, *Vita sancti Brunonis*, c. 44 (246-49); *Vita Dunstani* ("B"), c. 38, in *Memorials of Saint Dunstan*, ed. William Stubbs [Rolls Series 63] (London: Rolls Commissioners, 1874), 50-52.

[17] *Vita Meinwerci episcopi Patherbrunnensis*, ed. Franz Tenckhoff [MGH *SSRG* 59] (Hannover: Hahn, 1921), c. 187 (107-8); Thietmar of Merseburg, *Chronicon*, ed. Werner Trillmich [*AQDGM* 9] (Darmstadt: Wissenschaftliche Buchgesellschaft, 1957), IV.26 (142). See also for Thietmar the valuable translation by David Warner, *Ottonian Germany: The* Chronicon *of Thietmar of Merseburg* (Manchester: Manchester University Press, 2001), 170.

the episcopal *Vitae* of the period rich and poor alike were frequently depicted as lining the roads in mourning while the bishop's corpse was borne into the city for the funeral cermonies and burial in the cathedral. Here is a detail- rich but nevertheless typical example, taken from Wulfstan of Winchester's *Life of St Æthelwold*. Æthelwold died at the episcopal estate of Beddington, some 100 km from Winchester, in 984, and Wulfstan describes his funeral as follows:

> It is not possible to say what a countless multitude flocked to his funeral. From every direction had assembled rich and poor alike from neighbouring towns and *burhs* vying to say their last farewell to their shepherd. It was with grief and bitterness at heart that they all followed behind the bier, precious with its incomparable treasure, armed with the holy gospels and crosses, decked with veiling cloths, protected on each side by lit candles, hymns to God and chanted psalms. When the procession came next day into Winchester, the whole city with one accord met the body. Here you might have seen wailing troops of monks, there pale-faced companies of virgins; here you might have heard the voices of the clergy singing on high, there the groans of the weeping poor and the wailing of the shrieking needy, who could not bear to lose their shepherd's presence, and poured endless tears and cries to heaven. So the man of God was led in heavenly funeral to the church of the blessed apostles Peter and Paul, and to his bishop's seat. The solemnities of vigils and masses complete, he was buried in the crypt to the south of the holy altar, where, as he told me himself, a sign from heaven had long ago shown that he should rest.[18]

---

[18] Wulfstan of Winchester, *The Life of St Æthelwold*, ed. Michael Lapidge and Michael Winterbottom (Oxford: Oxford University Press, 1991), c. 41 (62-65): "Iam uero dici non potest quanta ad exequias eius hominum multitudo conuenerit. Vndique certatim ex uicinis oppidis et castellis simul in unum diuites et pauperes, ultimum uale pastori suo dicturi, confluxerant. Omnes cum dolore et amaro animo sequebantur feretrum incomparabili thesauro preciosum, sacrosanctis euangeliis et crucibus armatum, palliorum uelamentis ornatum, accensis luminaribus et hymnis caelestibus atque psalmorum concentibus hinc inde uallatum. Quibus sequenti die Wintoniam ingredientibus, obuiam corpori tota simul ciuitas unanimiter occurrit. Hinc eiulantes turbas conspiceres monachorum, inde pallida agmina uirginum, hinc audires in excelso uices psallentium clericorum, inde gemitum flentium pauperum et ululantium uociferantium egenorum, qui, pastoris sui praesentia se priuari non sustinentes, dabant infinitos lacrimarum clamores ad caelum. Perductus est ergo uir Dei cum caelestibus exequiis in ecclesiam beatorum apostolorum Petri et Pauli ad sedem suam episcopalem, et expletis uigiliarum missarumque sollemniis sepultus est in cripta ad australem plagam sancti altaris, ubi eum requiescere debere, sicut ipsei nobis retulit, olim sibi caelitus ostensum est."

There are a number of features in this account which need to be stressed. First, as already noted, the end of the pontificate culminated in a public ceremony, a slow procession of the funeral cortège through the diocese to the diocesan "capital", accompanied by representative figures from the diocese (and, as we shall see from examples to be introduced shortly, often by neighbouring bishops as well). Second, at the point where the funeral procession entered the city it was greeted in a ceremony which mirrored the *adventus* ritual used for greeting kings, and also bishops on their first entry into their city: instead of the joyous celebration of *laudes* and hymns, we have carefully staged public mourning, but the ceremony was essentially the same.[19] Third, the dead bishop was brought to the site of his "seat" or throne, and following a "state funeral" he was buried in a suitable place within the cathedral itself. Just as kings and great aristocrats used their family monasteries as mausolea, in which the assembled bodies of past genenerations concentrated family *memoria*, so the presence of past bishops gradually accumulated across the decades around the high seat of the bishop currently presiding, who in due course would join his colleagues there to watch over his successors.

Further examples will illustrate these points in more detail. About forty years later we have a report from the *Life* of Burchard of Worms describing the bishop's death and burial in 1025:

> His *milites* [i.e. the aristocratic vassals of the see] were present at his exequies, distinguished and honourable men, who bore his body to all the monasteries [of the city] and at the end to the see [meaning the cathedral]. There it was received with honour by all the brothers, and was laid out with the usual rites. On the next day it was buried with reverence in the same church on the west side of the choir, in front of the altar dedicated to St Lawrence.[20]

---

[19] On this see now David A. Warner, "Ritual and Memory in the Ottonian *Reich*: The Ceremony of *Adventus*," *Speculum* 76 (2001): 264-66. Warner's study appeared in the final stages of my preparing this article for publication, and we appear to have arrived independently at a very similar point of view.

[20] (Ebbo of Worms), *Vita Burchardi episcopi*, c. 25, ed. Georg Waitz in MGH *SS* IV (Hannover: Hahn, 1841), 846: "Aderant in exequiis eius sui milites, viri venerabiles et illustres, corpusque eius per omnia monasteria cirumferentes, ad sedem principalem tandem detulerunt. Ibique ab universis fratribus venerabiliter acceptum, solitics custodiebatur officiis. Postera

Here again there were features which need to be stressed. First we should note the involvement of the great men of the diocese, bound to the bishop and his see by ties of landholding and reciprocity.[21] Second, the procession to each of the monasteries within the city is significant, since here too, as we shall see, we find a mirroring of the rituals used in the installation of bishops.[22]

Thietmar of Merseburg's *Chronicon* offers a number of similar scenes. Archbishop Tagino of Magdeburg died in 1009 at the episcopal fortification of Rothenburg, returning fatally ill from a visit to the king. The body was taken to Frohse (a royal *palatium*); there it was clothed in episcopal vestments and taken to Magdeburg where "it was received with immense grief by all." Thietmar himself, a former canon of Magdeburg and a freshly-elected suffragan of Magdeburg, arrived on the day of the funeral to see Tagino buried on the west side of the choir in front of the entrance to the crypt.[23] Tagino's successor Walthard was elected after the funeral, and accepted after some show of reservation by Henry II. However, soon after his installation Walthard in turn fell ill, and he died at the archiepiscopal palace/fortress complex at the Giebichenstein. The entrails were buried there "between church and chamber," but the corpse was accompanied by Thietmar and others to Könnern, and thence to the monastery of Berge on the outskirts of Magdeburg, and there it was met by "the whole of the clergy, weeping; many Jews also and a multitude of orphans, to whom he had been a father, making known their their pain in lamenting; and we, entering the cathedral with the funeral procession, were received by 'his friends and all the hereditaries,' their hands raised in grief."[24]

---

autem die in eadem ecclesia in choro occidentali, videlicet ante altare sancti Laurentii, honorifice sepultum est."

[21] Timothy Reuter, "Property transactions and social relations," 187-89.

[22] Cf. Warner, "Ritual and memory," 265, with reference to the deaths of Burchard of Worms and Brun of Cologne.

[23] Thietmar, *Chronicon*, VI.61 (310) (trans. Warner, 279): "[Tagino] Ivicansten . . . obiit . . . . Fit oratio a confratribus cum intermixtis fletibus, et Bodo miles ad regem ad haec indicanda mittitur. Corpus autem archiepiscopi at Frasam ipso die venit et ibi sacerdotalibus vestimentis paratum ad sedem suam transfertur et cum ingenti tristicia ab omnibus suscipitur."

[24] Thietmar, *Chronicon*, VI.73 (320) (trans. Warner, 286): "Post haec solutis visceribus et intra aecclesiam atque caminatam sepultis, corpus preparatur et sancto altari presentatur. ibi tum facta pro defunctis memoria, nos ibi cenavimus et corpus eodem die usque ad Coniri prosequimur. In via plangens familia obviavit. Crastino cum ad villam iuxta montem sancti Iohannis sitam venissemus, clerus omnis flens adfuit, et Iudeorum magna et, quorum erat pater, orphanorum multitudo conveniens dolorem lamentando manifestat; et nos in ecclesia

The ceremonies of installation are less well and less frequently recorded,[25] but enough still survives for us to construct a picture of the kind of thing which happened and of the kinds of solidarity which were invoked. Thietmar, following the account of Tagino's death just discussed, describes how his successor Walthard's election, inthronisation and consecration took place. The Magdeburg clergy, urged on by Thietmar, decided to make an election in spite of Henry II's prohibition, and chose Walthard. After that they buried Tagino in the western part of the choir before the crypt he had had built; following an exchange of messages with the king, a Magdeburg delegation including Thietmar went to the court, where Henry received Walthard in his bedchamber alone for hours, before Walthard emerged with a ring as a "pledge of the grace to follow." Walthard was enthroned by Arnulf of Halberstadt on the following Sunday at the king's order, and consecrated by Eid of Meissen and four other bishops on the following day, before he traveled "with the customary honour" (presumably an *adventus*) to Berg and then on to his seat in Magdeburg.[26] Thietmar also tells us that inthronisation was separated from the consecration ceremony in his own inauguration.[27]

Moving away from Saxony, in case that should be thought to be in some way an untypical region, we may examine Ademar of Chabannes' account of the installation of Bishop Gerald of Limoges in 1018 following the death of his predecessor Alduin:

> Bishop Alduin's body was brought to Limoges [note once more the *adventus* of the dead bishop]; vigils were held at his seat and he was buried at Saint-Martin. [Adhémar then relates how Gerald, his nephew, succeeded him, and was consecrated at Poitiers by Archbishop Siguin]. After his consecration, Arnald of Périgeux and Grimoard of Angoulême accompanied him to Limoges. First of all they came together

---

maiore cum funere intrantes amici cum hereditariis omnibus, elevatis cum luctu manibus, miserabiliter suscipiunt." The "hereditaries" may refer either to the "great men" of the diocese, as with the account of Burchard's funeral, or possibly, as Holtzmann suggested in his edition (MGH *SSRG*, n.s. 9 (Berlin: Weidmann, 1935), note 4), "hereditary dependents (serfs and vassals) of the church of Magdeburg," though it is difficult to imagine a class-conscious world like Ottonian Saxony lining up serfs alongside aristocratic vassals. On the participation of the Jews, see below at note 39.

[25] See in general Engels, "Pontifikatsantritt," and Warner, "Ritual and memory," 263-64.

[26] Thietmar, *Chronicon*, VI.62-63, 66-68 (310-12, 314-16) (trans. Warner, 280-81, 282-84).

[27] *Ibid.*, VI.40, 42 (286, 290) (trans. Warner, 264-65, 267).

to Saint-Martial and were received by the monks, who accompanied them to Saint-Pierre-du-Queyroix. There he sat on the *cathedra*, and, borne on the shoulders of the people and with the canons singing antiphons, he took the text of the gospel to be read from Bishop Grimoard and was led to the gate of the church of St Stephen with glory. Grimoard gave him the keys to the church and Arnald the bellropes, and both enthroned him in the see of St Martial, and Bishop Arnald intoned the Te Deum in a clear voice. All kissed the bishop as he was seated, and then they celebrated mass . . . . For seven whole days he went in procession in the sanctified stole . . . and each day he celebrated mass.[28]

Gerald's successor Jordan also was consecrated away from the see before being brought in honour to Limoges by the young William the Fat of Aquitaine, acting in his father's absence on pilgrimage, and Arnald of Périgeux.[29]

What are we to make of these sequences of symbolic action? First of all, we should note the way in which funerals mirrored installations. At least on those occasions when a bishop had died outside the cathedral city, his body would be brought in to the city in state, and received by groups representing the diocese and the bishopric: fellow-bishops, clerics, monks, the poor and defenceless but also the church's *milites*. Installation ceremonies followed a very similar pattern: the details vary, but the models were clearly the *adventus regis* on the one hand (appropriate enough given the opening suggestion that the bishop was a kind of

---

[28] *Ademari Cabannensis Chronicon*, ed. Pierre Bourgain, Richard Landes and Georges Pon [*CCCM* 129/1] (Turnhout: Brepols, 1999), III.49 (168): "Delatum est corpus ejus Lemovicam, et apud sedem vigiliis observatum, in ecclesia Sancti Martini sepultum est . . . Post benedictionem, que dominica dies peracta est, comitati sunt eum usque Lemovicam Arnaldus et Grimoardus episcopi. Primum ad sanctum Marcialem venerunt simul, et recepti sunt a monachis. Inde monachi eos duxerunt cum antiphonis usque ad ecclesiam Ciairoensem. Ibi in cathedra sedit, et humeris populi vectus, canonicis antiphonas concinentibus, textum evangelii a Grimoardo episcopo legendum sumpsit, et ita legens et assidue dextera benedicens, ad hostium basilice Sancti Stephani sedens cum gloria deductus est. Grimoardus tradidit ei portas ecclesiae, Arnaldus cordas signorum, et ambo in sede sancti Marcialis intronizaverunt eum, et alta voce 'Te Deum laudamus' Arnaldus episcopus intonuit. Episcopum sedentem osculati sunt omnes, deinde missam celebraverunt de martirio sancti Theoodori, cujus festivitas ipso die agebatur. Per dies septum indutus processit stola sanctificata cum indumentis cum quibus benedictus fuerat . . . et per VII continuis dies per stationem urbis missas celebravit." For the ceremony of *deportatio* described here, see Janet L. Nelson, "The earliest surviving royal *ordo*: some liturgical and historical aspects," in Nelson, *Politics and Ritual*, 354.

[29] Ademar, *Chronicon*, III.57 (178-79).

ruler of a small kingdom) and Christ's entry to Jerusalem on the other.[30] In each case, what we have is a community—even if it is one which was constructed by topos and selection, a point to which we shall return at the end—which received its ruler, either for the first or for the last time, and did so using forms of symbolic action which underlined such a reception. It was by no means the only point at which the community appeared or was constructed; we should reflect on the function of diocesan synods, episcopal feasting, church dedications and relic translations as further significant sites of being and consciousness.[31] But it was certainly one of the most important.

A further point might be termed a "constitutional" one: it is noticeable in all these accounts how enthroning was separated from consecration, often spatially as well as temporally. We may well already be in the territory so well analysed by Robert Benson here, though the conceptual division of the bishop's two bodies of judge and ruler on one hand and fount of sacramental power within the diocese on the other appears in Benson's work to have been largely the result of the post-Gregorian juridification of the life of the church.[32] It would appear that the authors of the pre-Gregorian era took the significance of the division so much for granted that they did not need to provide their readers with reflections on what they thought that the distinction meant; we probably need more work on the normative texts for the pre-Gregorian era to get closer to this aspect of thinking about episcopality.

What does emerge very consistently from these accounts is the symbolism of the bishop's *sedes*. The writers of the pre-Gregorian era shifted effortlessly between the three possible senses of *sedes*: the bishopric itself ("see" in modern

---

[30] The *imitatio Christi* was an inspiration for displays of humility; for the range of gestures available to a bishop on this occasion, including the public display of humility entailed by entering the city with bare feet, see now Klaus Schreiner, "'Nudis pedibus': Barfüßigkeit als religiöses und politisches Ritual," in *Formen und Funktionen öffentlicher Kommunikation im Mittelalter*, ed. Gerd Althoff [Vorträge und Forschungen 51] (Sigmaringen: Thorbecke, 2001), 53-124, at 96-8.

[31] On church dedications see Karl-Josef Benz, *Untersuchungen zur politischen Bedeutung der Kirchweihe unter Teilnahme der deutschen Herrscher im hohen Mittelalter. Ein Beitrag zum Studium des Verhältnisses zwischen weltlicher Macht und Kirchlicher Wirklichkeit unter Otto III. und Heinrich II* (Kallmünz: M. Lassleben, 1975); on the episcopal reconciliation of penitents on Maundy Thursday (when the clergy of the diocese collected the chrism and attended a synod), see Sarah Hamilton, *The Practice of Penance, 900-1050* (Woodbridge, Suffolk: Boydell Press, 2001), 69, 118-21. On these moments of community in general, see Reuter, "Property transactions and social relations," 188.

[32] Benson, *The Bishop-Elect*.

English); the cathedral church; and the throne on which the bishop was installed, signifying his role as "ruler" of the diocese. Though much more work needs to be done on the details of this and its historical development,[33] it is clear that it was not by accident that so many of the inauguration and valedictory rituals for bishops climaxed by bringing the bishop to his *sedes* in the literal sense in order to underline its metonymic significance for the conceptual coherence of his diocese and his rule.

Finally—and this is a point which needs stressing very heavily—it was not of great importance how the particular individual was chosen. Once the choice had been made, the person was swallowed up by the office—we are dealing here with ascribed rather than achieved status. That does not in the least mean that there was no difference between one bishop and another: there clearly was. It means rather that both modern historians, who have stressed the importance of control of appointments (or the lack of it), and eleventh-century reformers, who stressed the importance of correct form in making appointments, have missed the point in significant ways. In pre-Gregorian Europe, once a bishop was appointed, he was, first and foremost, a bishop of his own see; the symbolic actions surrounding appointment stressed this. There were severe limits to how far any cheques drawn on the bank account of obligation before the bishop went through these rites of passage could actually be cashed afterwards. After the success of reformist rigour, on the other hand, the implementation of the canon law slogan "by clergy and people" in practice meant an unprecedented wave of disputed episcopal elections in the twelfth century over much of Europe (though not in England, where for all the formal compromises made in Henry I's reign pre-Gregorian modes of practice remained largely unchanged in the twelfth century). It was precisely at the point where community needed to find expression that it found it most difficult, left to itself, to do so, and most easy to break up into faction. Although it is not the theme of this chapter, we might also here point to the tendency by locals to appoint "safe pairs of hands" and to avoid charismatic leader-figures: Philip Augustus put his finger on the problem when he identified free election by the chapter as the main reason why there were so few saintly bishops nowadays.[34]

---

[33] For a useful beginning, see Engels, "Pontifikatsantritt," and also Hans Ulrich Instinsky, *Bischofsstuhl und Kaiserthron* (Munich: Kösel-Verlag, 1955)

[34] Reuter, "Ein Europa der Bischöfe," 27.

It was also at the point where community came together and found expression that it was most easily denied, and the symbolism of community could of course be subverted in order to do so. At Cambrai, where there had been a long-standing dispute between the bishop and members of the castellanic family for control of the town, we are presented with the following scene on the death of Gerard in 1051. A deputation had gone off bearing the pastoral staff to see the emperor Henry III, in order to report the death of Gerard and to ask for the appointment of Gerard's favoured successor, Lietbert. Lietbert, who had previously organised the resistance of the episcopal party to the castellan John, was himself amongst the delegation. On hearing that Henry had agreed to the appointment, John feared the worst. He put the city into a state of defence, and

> violently invaded the mother church of St Mary and threw out the canons, taking the treasures of the church and whatever he found inside under his control and leaving armed guards inside. He entered the episcopal palace with his soldiers, and brought his wife into the pontiff's bedchamber, having his bedding spread on the pontiff's bed, and ordered that he and his followers should be ministered to at the pontiff's expense.[35]

Indeed, the authors of the *Gesta Episcoporum Cameracensium* were obsessed with the episcopal bedchamber: a similar story to the one just quoted is told also about Charles of Lotharingia, and some early modern extracts from a now lost recension have a story about how Lietbert himself was "traitorously taken captive" in his own bedchamber by a political opponent towards the end of his life.[36] Local opponents of a newly-elected bishop could seek to subvert his legitimacy by denying him *introitus* into the city.[37]

---

[35] *Gesta Lietberti*, c. 5, in *Gesta episcoporum Cameracensium, continuatio*, ed. Ludwig Bethmann in MGH SS VII (Hannover: Hiersemann, 1846), 489: "matrem aecclesiam sanctrae Mariae violenter invasit, et eiectis canonicis, thesauros aecclesiae et quodcumque intus invenit, ditioni suae mancipavit, custodesque suos armatos inibi posuit. Basilicam itaque pontificalem cum militibus suis introiit, et uxorem suam in camera pontificis introducens, stratum suum in lecto pontificali parari feedit, sibique et satellitibus suis de pontificalibus sumptibus precepit ministrare."

[36] For Charles of Lotharingia, see *Gesta episcoporum Cameracensium*, I.101 (442-43); for Lietbert's capture see *ibid.*, 491 n. *, at 492.

[37] Timothy Reuter, "*Filii matris nostrae pugnant adversus nos*: bonds and tensions between German prelates and their milites in the high middle ages," in *Chiesa e mondo feudale nei*

This chapter has tended to offer what are undoubtedly fairly literal (although, it is to be hoped, not naïve) readings of such moments of community, whether affirmed or threatened. Of course, there are problems with such a mode of exposition. We should not forget that we are dealing with literary texts whose modes and conventions of expression we still understand only imperfectly, where the modern historian constantly runs the risks both of confusing the topical (in the sense of "topos-laden") with the typical, and of dismissing the representative as merely topical. Michael Toch, for example, has issued well-founded warnings against assuming too readily that Jews mentioned at bishops' funerals were indeed present in reality; we may well be dealing with the "even the enemies of the faith acknowledged . . ." topos.[38] Here as elsewhere, it is at least possible that we are dealing with symbolic and coded representations rather than naturalistic ones, and, crucially, faced with any particular instance we may be quite unable to tell with certainty which kind of representation we are dealing with. It is also evident that community was being constructed by these accounts of symbolic sequences themselves as well as by the actual symbolic sequences which they purport to represent. But that is the crux for the historian of early medieval Europe. People who want their sources to offer something like video-reportage of the past should not choose the tenth and eleventh centuries to work on. Here we have to live as best we can with the gap between the once-existing past reality "out there" and its fossilised remains in our libraries and archives.

---

secoli X-XII [Miscellanea del Centro di studi medioevali 14] (Milan: Vita e pensiero, 1995), 247-76.

[38] Michael Toch, *"Dunkle Jahrhunderte": Gab es ein jüdisches Frühmittelalter? 3. "Arye Maimon-Vortrag" an der Universität Trier, 15. November 2000* [Kleine Schriften des Arye-Maimon-Instituts 4] (Trier: Arye-Maimon-Institut für Geschichte der Juden, 2001), 14-15.

Chapter Three
The Bishop As Aristocrat: The Case of Hugh of Chalon
Constance Brittain Bouchard

Hugh, count of Chalon and bishop of Auxerre, was one of the most important figures in both the secular and ecclesiasical spheres in Burgundy around the year 1000. The youngest and only surviving son of Count Lambert of Chalon, he served as count of Chalon-sur-Saône in his own right for over fifty years, beginning in 987.[1] In 999 he was elected bishop of Auxerre as well, an office he held for the next forty years until his death in 1039. Auxerre under Hugh was a true episcopal "realm" of the sort discussed earlier by Timothy Reuter, as much under Hugh's authority as was the county of Chalon. Yet in spite of the crucial role he played in both royal and regional politics, and his influence on Cluniac monasticism, he has been very little noted by modern scholars.[2]

I shall here discuss Hugh for the light he sheds on two different scholarly debates, one old, one new, both of which address changes that are supposed to have taken place around the year 1000. The old debate, one that has never been satisfactorily resolved, concerns the extent to which the monastic reforms of the eleventh century were a rejection of a corrupt, lay-dominated ecclesiastical hierarchy, administered by corrupt, lay-dominated bishops.[3] The new debate involves the political "mutations" in France around the year 1000, marked by a sharp weakening of counts' public power, where the Peace of God, organized by the bishops, is considered to be the most vivid example of a response to these changes.[4]

---

[1] For his family, see Constance Brittain Bouchard, *"Those of My Blood": Constructing Noble Families in Medieval Francia* (Philadelphia: University of Pennsylvania Press, 2001), 149-51.

[2] The only previous study of Hugh, a very brief biography, is by Martine Chauney, "Deux évêques bourguignons de l'an mil: Brunon de Langres et Hughes Ier d'Auxerre," *Cahiers de civilisation médiévale* 21 (1978): 389-92.

[3] For an overview of the debate, see John Howe, "The Nobility's Reform of the Medieval Church," *American Historical Review* 92 (1988): 317-39, and Constance Brittain Bouchard, *Sword, Miter, and Cloister: Nobility and the Church in Burgundy, 980-1198* (Ithaca: Cornell University Press, 1987), 87-89.

[4] For this debate see, most recently, Dominique Barthélemy, *La mutation de l'an mil a-t-elle eu lieu? Servage et chevalerie dans la France des Xe et XIe siècles* (Paris: Fayard, 1997), and Patrick J. Geary, "Monastic Memory and the Mutation of the Year Thousand," in *Monks and Nuns, Saints and Outcasts: Religion in Medieval Society*, ed. Sharon Farmer and Barbara H. Rosenwein (Ithaca: Cornell University Press, 2000), 19-36.

Bishops themselves have been curiously little discussed in these contexts, instead being taken as an unexamined part of the background. For example, when Georges Duby first argued for a weakening in counts' power around the year 1000, followed by a rapid increase in the independence of castellans, he used as his chief example the count of Burgundy and Mâcon, who lost much of his power and prestige in wars in which one of his chief opponents was a bishop.[5] The spread of the Peace of God is generally taken as symptomatic of a breakdown of royal and comital authority, but scholarly attention has usually been given to the violence to which the Peace was a response, rather than to the extent to which the Peace was spread by bishops.[6] Further, whether scholars take such monastic reform movements as the spread of the Cluniac *ordo*, as (in one formulation) a harbinger of the Gregorian Reform, or, alternately, as a precursor to the Cistercians, they generally all agree that these movements represented a rejection of the old Carolingian episcopal structures.[7]

In this chapter, I attempt to move bishops back to the center of these debates by focusing upon Hugh of Chalon as a central but unstudied bishop. He was a crucial player in most of the political and ecclesiastical events that marked the beginning of the eleventh century in northern France. I shall argue that, although he might appear to be the archtypically secular bishop from whom the Cluniacs supposedly had to seek exemption and against whom the Gregorians fought, Hugh was also, perhaps paradoxically, an instigator of Cluny's system of a network of dependent priories of a reformed life—what later became known as the Cluniac Order. He also fought successfully against the count of Burgundy and Mâcon, becoming personally responsible, at least in part, for the weakening power of that count: a weakening which has become the foundation for models of a "feudal" transformation after the year 1000.[8] Yet Hugh acted here not in his

---

[5] Georges Duby, *La société aux XIe et XIIe siècles dans la région mâconnaise*, 2nd ed. (Paris: SEVPEN, 1971).

[6] For various scholarly approaches to the Peace of God, see Thomas Head and Richard Landes, eds., *The Peace of God: Social Violence and Religious Response in France around the Year 1000* (Ithaca: Cornell University Press, 1992). Thomas Head recently has attempted to restore bishops to the forefront of the history of the Peace in his "The Development of the Peace of God in Aquitaine (970-1005)," *Speculum* 74 (1999): 656-86.

[7] Barbara H. Rosenwein, *Rhinoceros Bound: Cluny in the Tenth Century* (Philadelphia: University of Pennsylvania Press, 1982), 25-26.

[8] The fullest discussion of this model is that by Jean-Pierre Poly and Eric Bournazel, *The Feudal Transformation, 900–1200*, trans. Caroline Higgitt (New York: Holmes and Meier,

role as bishop, but as count, and he himself could not possibly be described as a weak count.

In addition, although Hugh's accession to the see of Auxerre can scarcely be considered a canonical election by "clergy and people," and although he himself engaged in extensive wars, he was one of the most important of the second generation of "Peace of God" bishops, who first spread the Peace into northern France. Finally, he was a major proponent of the spread of reformed monasticism in the eleventh century. Indeed, Hugh, abbot of Cluny in the second half of the century (1049-1109), the man who did more than any other to spread his monastery's prestige and who presided over the building of the great church of Cluny III,[9] was a nephew of Hugh of Chalon, almost certainly was named for him, and began his own ecclesiastical career under his uncle's patronage in Bishop Hugh's cathedral school at Auxerre.[10] Thus a study of Hugh's career affords new insights into questions about the political and monastic transformations of the eleventh century—including the crucial issue of whether we are even asking the right questions.

The sources for Hugh's career are rich and varied, reflecting his influence in both the political and ecclesiastical events of his day. He is featured prominently in the chronicles both of Ralph Glaber and of an anonymous monk of St.-Bénigne of Dijon;[11] is found repeatedly in the charters of the monasteries of Cluny, of St.-Marcel-lès-Chalon, and of Paray-le-Monial, the latter a monastery founded by his father;[12] and especially is commemorated in the *vita* composed at Auxerre after his death.[13] The cathedral canons of Auxerre had been composing

---

1991). See also Pierre Bonnassie, *From Slavery to Feudalism in South-Western Europe*, trans. Jean Birrell (Cambridge and New York: Cambridge University Press, 1991).

[9] For Abbot Hugh's career, the work of Noreen Hunt is still valuable; *Cluny Under Saint Hugh, 1049-1109* (London: Edward Arnold, 1967).

[10] For the family connection, see Bouchard, *Sword, Miter, and Cloister*, 359-60, 410.

[11] Radulfus Glaber, *Opera*, ed. John France, Nithard Bulst, and Paul Reynolds (Oxford: Oxford University Press, 1989); *Chronique de l'abbaye de Saint-Bénigne de Dijon, suivie de la chronique de Saint-Pierre de Bèze*, ed. Emile Bougaud and Joseph Garnier [Analecta Divionensis 9] (Dijon: Darantière, 1875).

[12] *Recueil des chartes de l'abbaye de Cluny*, ed. Auguste Bernard and Alexander Bruel, 6 vols. (Paris: Imprimerie nationale, 1876-1903); *The Cartulary of St.-Marcel-lès-Chalon, 779-1126*, ed. Constance Brittain Bouchard [Medieval Academy Books 102] (Cambridge, MA: Medieval Academy of America, 1998); *Cartulaire du prieuré de Paray-le-Monial*, ed. Ulysse Chevalier (Paris: A. Picard, 1890).

[13] *Les Gestes des évêques d'Auxerre*, ed. Lobrichon and Goullet, 245-61.

"lives" of their bishops, the *Gesta pontificum Autissiodorensium*, intermittently for close to two hundred years,[14] and Hugh's *vita* is one of the longer ones composed before the twelfth century. It is intriguing to note that his biographer was unsure whether he was more to be admired or deplored.

Hugh was the second in the line of hereditary counts of Chalon (see table 1). In the ninth and early tenth centuries the region was still dominated by counts appointed by the Carolingians, but the dynasty founded around the middle of the tenth century by Hugh's father Lambert survived for the next 250 years, throughout the so-called "feudal" period of French history.[15] Lambert had originally been a viscount, confirmed in his county by one of the last of the French Carolingian kings, but from the time of his son Hugh onward, there was no question but that the county would pass to the next generation via inheritance. Lambert died in 978, and Geoffrey Greymantle, count of Anjou, promptly married Lambert's widow Adelaide. For the next decade young Hugh kept a low profile, and Geoffrey Greymantle may even have hoped that Maurice, the son he had with Countess Adelaide, would end up inheriting Chalon.[16] But when Geoffrey died in 987, Hugh took over his late father's county, and Maurice, still a little boy, seems to have retreated to Anjou.

One of Hugh's most significant activities as count, in the first years after the death of Geoffrey Greymantle, was to restore the religious life to the monastery of Paray-le-Monial. This monastery had been founded by his father a generation earlier, with the assistance of Abbot Maiolus of Cluny, but it almost immediately seems to have fallen into difficulties. It was said at the time that "brotherly love had declined and iniquity increased." Hugh complained in his restoration charter that "this house has not been able to remain in the state that my father founded it." Hugh could not take the decay of Paray lightly; after all, both he and his mother had made gifts to the monks there after Lambert's death, and his fath-

---

[14] Constance Brittain Bouchard, *Spirituality and Administration: The Role of the Bishop in Twelfth-Century Auxerre* [Speculum Anniversary Monographs 5] (Cambridge, MA: Medieval Academy of America, 1979), 5-11.

[15] For the family, see Bouchard, *Sword, Miter, and Cloister*, 307-14, and *"Those of My Blood"*, 24-25.

[16] Bernard S. Bachrach, "Geoffrey Greymantle, Count of the Angevins, 960-987: A Study in French Politics," *Studies in Medieval and Renaissance History* 17 (1985): 23-24.

Table 1

The Counts of Chalon

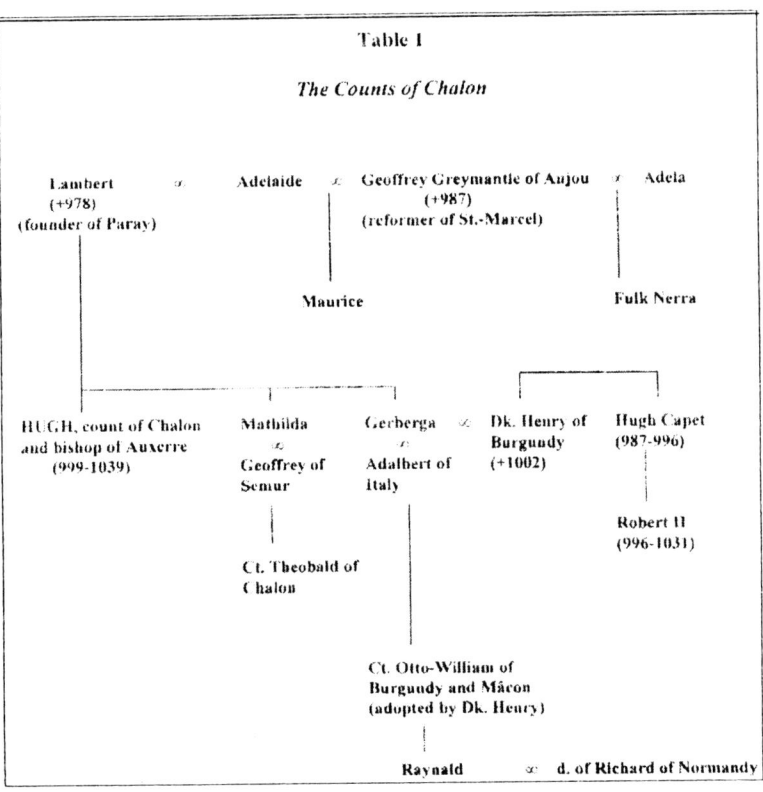

er was buried there. His response to this decline was to give this monastery to Cluny, to become a priory. In doing so, he sought and obtained the consent both of the king and of the king's uncle, Duke Henry of Burgundy. In his charter of confirmation, the king referred to Hugh as his *fidelissimus*.[17]

Cluny was the obvious choice to undertake this restoration. Paray had been founded in the first place with the assistance of the abbot of Cluny, and this highly-regarded monastery was located nearby—one would indeed have to go right by it when traveling from Chalon to Paray. But it needs to be stressed here what a novel idea it was at the end of the tenth century to create a Cluniac priory.[18] The modern vision of Cluny's monastic order, composed of dozens, even hundreds of houses, each following exactly the same way of life and answering to one abbot, owes more to the Cistercian order of the thirteenth century than to Cluny in the tenth. It had of course been common since Carolingian times to make one man abbot of more than one house, if one of the houses needed to be established or reformed—Cluny herself had begun that way, being founded under the direction of Abbot Berno of Baume.[19] But normally after a generation such houses went their separate ways under separate abbots. Paray was different. Hugh gave it to Cluny as a permanently dependent house, to be ruled by a prior but never its own abbot.

Cluny had certainly had dependent cells before this, small churches with a handful of monks, but Paray was a large and well-endowed monastery. Usually in the case of such monasteries, Cluny had reformed them by sending a monk to be the new abbot, rather than submitting them directly to Cluny's abbot. When Abbot Odilo had undertaken to reform St.-Germain of Auxerre and St.-Bénigne of Dijon, a few years before Hugh asked Abbot Odilo of Cluny to reform his family's monastery of Paray, he had done so by sending his monks to become the new abbots of each of these houses.[20] Indeed Heldric, the monk from Cluny who restored the regular life at St.-Germain, might be considered more the head of his own mini-order than part of an overarching Cluniac order, for he also be-

---

[17] *Recueil des chartes de Cluny*, 3: 562-68 (nos. 2484 and 2485).

[18] Rosenwein, *Rhinoceros Bound*, xiii: 17-19.

[19] Constance Brittain Bouchard, "Merovingian, Carolingian, and Cluniac Monasticism: Reform and Renewal in Burgundy," *Journal of Ecclesiastical History* 41 (1990): 365-88.

[20] *Gesta pontificum Autissiodorensium*, 253-55; *Cartulaire général de l'Yonne*, 2 vols., ed. Maximilien Quantin (Auxerre: Perriquet, 1854-60), 1: 158 (no. 82); *Chronique de Saint-Bénigne*, 130-49.

came during his lifetime abbot of Flavigny and of Moûtier-St.-Jean, neither of which was affiliated with Cluny.[21] (All three houses had independent abbots again after Heldric's death.)

The only real precedent in Burgundy for a priory was the monastery of St.-Marcel outside of Chalon, which had also become a Cluny priory some dozen years before Paray did so. In this case, Geoffrey Greymantle, acting count of Chalon along with Countess Adelaide, had given the old and abandoned monastery of St.-Marcel to Abbot Maiolus as a priory, which it then remained for the rest of the Middle Ages.[22] Count Hugh confirmed this reestablishment of St.-Marcel by Cluny's abbot at the same time as he gave Cluny the house of Paray. In the eleventh and twelfth centuries, the monasteries closest to Cluny's abbots, besides Cluny herself, were Paray, St.-Marcel, and La Charité—the latter an old house refounded as a priory fifty years after Hugh's reform of Paray.[23] The special closeness between Cluny and the foundations of the counts of Chalon is emphasized because the same architects were used to build the Romanesque church of Paray as were used at Cluny. Even today the twin towers and absidial chapels of Paray-le-Monial still resemble, in miniature, the monumental church of Cluny III that was destroyed under Napoleon.[24]

Paray and St.-Marcel were not the only monasteries which Hugh helped to reform. In 1018, the bishop of Autun decided to restore the small house of Couches, in his diocese, which he said had been held by "powerful and secular men." In his charter of refoundation—the monastery had shrunk to only one monk—the bishop said that he needed to obtain the consent of the successors of these men, beginning with none other than Hugh of Chalon.[25] Although Hugh had become bishop by this point and signed the refoundation charter as *episcopus*, it was clear that here he was acting as count, for his authority in Autun had nothing to do with his diocese of Auxerre and everything to do with his family's inheritance. Thus Hugh, although a "powerful and secular" lord, was instru-

---

[21] *The Cartulary of Flavigny, 717-1113*, ed. Constance Brittain Bouchard [Medieval Academy Books 99] (Cambridge, MA: Medieval Academy of America, 1991), 147-48.

[22] *The Cartulary of St.-Marcel*, 29-31 (no. 6).

[23] *Cartulaire du prieuré de La Charité-sur-Loire (Nièvre), ordre de Cluny*, ed. René de Lespinasse (Nevers: Morin-Boutillier, 1887), 1-3 (no. 3).

[24] Raymond Oursel and A.-M. Oursel, *Les églises romanes de l'Autunois et du Brionnais* (Mâcon: Imprimerie Protat frères, 1956), 245-52.

[25] *Gallia Christiana*, 4: 76-77 (no. 40); the charter is misdated by the editor.

mental in establishing a kind of monastic reform that would increasingly become the rule in the eleventh century.

Hugh, of course, was more than a powerful secular lord (although it can be noted that his many gifts to Paray, after its restoration, and to Cluny were done with the assistance of his heir Theobold, suggesting that he continued to make them in his capacity as count of Chalon). Later in the same year in which he reformed Paray, Hugh had had himself elected bishop of Auxerre. His succession to office appears at first glance as the kind of abuse of power against which the Gregorian Reform would have to fight. Auxerre in 999 had just been held in succession by two bishops closely tied to the royal court: Heribert, illegitimate son of Hugh Capet, and John, son of Hugh Capet's concubine by a different father.[26] Hugh too, according to his biographer, was put into office at the command of the king. Hugh seems to have been in minor orders as a youth, but his dozen years as count before his episcopal election had been lived as a layman. His biographer tells the rather unedifying story of Hugh stopping at Auxerre on his way to the royal court, pausing at the cathedral to pray, and thinking what a pleasant thing it must be to be bishop in such a see, a wish that almost immediately came true. The biographer said Hugh was elected "in the usual manner," but this usual manner was not with the consent of clergy and people, as would be insisted upon two generations later. Rather, for the biographer the "usual" manner was explicitly with the consent of Duke Henry of Burgundy and King Robert II.[27]

Hugh shortly became personally involved in the Burgundian wars (1002-1005) that broke out after he became bishop. After Duke Henry of Burgundy, Hugh Capet's brother, died in 1002, the fighting over Burgundy became fierce, with the chief combatants King Robert, Duke Henry's nephew, and Otto-William, Duke Henry's step-son. In these wars, Hugh of Chalon took the side of Robert. This support for the king is especially striking because Otto-William was Hugh's own nephew, the son of his sister and her first husband. Hugh's biographer in fact felt compelled to explain why Hugh would have supported the king rather than his relative by evoking the biblical injunctions to "fear God, honor the king" (Peter 2:17) and "let each soul be subject to the powers that be"

---

[26] Bouchard, *Sword, Miter, and Cloister*, 388; Yves Sassier, *Recherches sur le pouvoir comtal en Auxerrois du Xe au début du XIIIe siècle* (Auxerre: Société des fouilles archéologiques et des monuments historiques de l'Yonne, 1980), 25.

[27] *Gesta pontificum Autissiodorensium*, 245-47.

(Rom.13:1). During the protracted fighting around Auxerre, which involved both the king and the count of Auxerre, Hugh remained loyal. In fact, Ralph Glaber commented that Hugh was the only Burgundian lord to favor the king.[28] Once peace was reestablished, Hugh continued to maintain warm ties with the king who had, after all, made him bishop.

Hugh indeed seems to have felt distinct antipathy toward his nephew Otto-William. A generation later, for reasons that are not clear, Hugh went to war against Otto-William's son Raynald, captured him, and refused to release him. Even the appeals of Raynald's father-in-law, the duke of Normandy, who had been the king's and Hugh's ally during the Burgundian wars, did not budge him. Only after the duke launched an army of his own against Hugh—against Hugh's county of Chalon, the Norman chronicler William of Jumièges specifies, rather than against Auxerre—did Hugh relent, make peace, and release his great-nephew.[29]

In spite of—or perhaps because of—this violent streak, Bishop Hugh was frequently selected as a judge in cases which involved Cluny. For example, he helped Cluny obtain compensation when a murder was committed just outside the abbey's gates, and he also persuaded a layman to return to the monks some property that adjoined his own and which he had seized.[30] In addition, Hugh made substantial gifts of his own to Cluny throughout his lifetime, both of land and churches, often accompanied by his nephew and eventual successor in Chalon, Theobold, in preference to the canons of Auxerre.[31] Perhaps his most significant gift was of an abandoned monastery near Chalon, once dedicated to Saints Cosmas and Damian.[32] He also frequently confirmed other laymen's gifts to Cluny, including gifts of both land and churches, from men who held their property from him in fief.[33]

---

[28] Radulfus Glaber, *Historia*, 2.8 (80).

[29] William of Jumièges, *Gesta Normannorum Ducum* 5.16; in *The "Gesta Normannorum Ducum" of William of Jumièges, Orderic Vitalis, and Robert of Torigni*, ed. Elisabeth M. C. Van Houts, 2 vols. (Oxford: Clarendon, 1992-95), 2: 36-38.

[30] *Recueil des chartes de Cluny*, 4: 48-50, 104-5 (nos. 2848, 2905).

[31] For example, *Recueil des chartes de Cluny*, 3: 733-35 (no. 2711) and 4: 125-26 (no. 2924); *The Cartulary of St.-Marcel*, 33-34 (no. 9).

[32] *Recueil des chartes de Cluny*, 3: 733-35 (no. 2711).

[33] For example, *Recueil des chartes de Cluny*, 3: 45-46, 745-46, 752-54 (nos. 1789, 2722, 2729); 4: 46-47, 82-85, 108-9 (nos. 2846, 2888, 2909).

If a highly warlike layman helping establish the Cluniac priory system and acting as secular advocate for the monks seems like something of an anomaly, then Hugh's forty years at Auxerre must be even more so. His activities as a war leader, his highly irregular election, and his intimacy with the king should have foretold a prelate who would dissipate his see's patrimony and allow the religious life of the diocese to stagnate. In fact, however, he proved himself a highly conscientious bishop. He helped build up the patrimony of the cathedral of Auxerre and of his cathedral chapter by giving them property which had fallen into lay hands, but which he recovered, especially property at Varzy and Cosne—located, interestingly, in his diocese but not his county. Under Hugh the early Romanesque cathedral of Auxerre was also built. The Carolingian cathedral, along with much of the rest of the city, had been destroyed in a great fire, doubtless related to the Burgundian wars, although Hugh's biographer did not mention this. Rather, he said that the old cathedral had been built "of delicate material, with few stones," and that Hugh was careful to rebuild in stone. This new church served the diocese for two centuries, until work was begun on the present Gothic structure (and indeed some of the stonework commissioned under Hugh is still visible in the crypt). Hugh himself went on pilgrimage to Jerusalem in 1036, where he worshipped at the church of the Sepulchre, an experience which seems to have inspired some of his own church decorations back at home.[34]

Hugh appears to have kept his personal life one of purity and integrity, and nowhere, even in the chronicles that criticize him, is there a hint of sexual scandal or of offspring. As he was dying, he took the habit at St.-Germain of Auxerre, a house which had been reformed to Cluny's liturgical *ordo* two generations earlier and where bishops of Auxerre were routinely buried.[35] And, as already noted, in spite of his bellicose temper, Hugh was personally responsible for bringing the Peace of God to Burgundy. In the wake of the Burgundian wars,

---

[34] *Gesta pontificum Autissiodorensium*, 255-61. Through a misreading of Hugh's biography, scholars have sometimes stated that Varzy and Cosne were part of his inheritance; see for example Chauncy, "Deux évêques," 389, and Sassier, *Recherches sur le pouvoir*, 24. For a corrective, see Bouchard, *Sword, Miter, and Cloister*, 311-12.

[35] *Gesta pontificum Autissiodorensium*, 261. His death took place on either 3 or 4 November; see *Obituaires de la province de Sens*, vol. 3, *Diocèses d'Orléans, d'Auxerre, et de Nevers*, ed. Alexandre Vidier and Léon Mirot (Paris: Imprimerie nationale, 1909), 239; Jean Lebeuf, *Mémoires concernant l'histoire civile et ecclésiastique d'Auxerre et de son ancien diocèse*, new ed. by Ambroise Challe and Maximilien Quantin, vol. 4, *Recueil de monuments, chartes, titres et autres pièces inédites* (Auxerre: Perriquet, 1855), 19.

amidst calls for restraint, Hugh began assembling the same sort of Peace council that had already proved successful when organized by the bishops of Aquitaine and the Auvergne. It was he who assembled bishops and knights at Verdun-sur-le-Doubs in about 1020 and at Héry a few years later.[36] It is striking to note that the first Burgundian Peace council, that at Verdun, was held in Hugh's county rather than in his diocese, although the second, Héry, *was* held in the diocese of Auxerre. It is also striking that these councils, called with the explicit purpose of restricting violence, were convened by a man who had a long history of violence himself.

It is doubtless due to the curious mix of religious and secular in Hugh's life and activities that his biographer chose to dwell on a rather obscure incident, only a few years after Hugh became bishop, in which he seems to have temporarily abandoned his see. The biographer, without going into detail, said that Hugh had decided that his activities, which would have included the Burgundian wars, now winding down, made him "unworthy of the pontifical dignity." However, again according to the biographer, a certain Pope John urged Hugh not to resign as bishop, absolved him of his sins, and confirmed him in his office as bishop.[37] Since three Johns held papal office during Hugh's episcopacy (John XVII, XVIII, and XIX), it is not altogether clear which one was involved; most likely, however, it was John XVIII (1004-1009), who would have been pope in the aftermath of the Burgundian wars. This whole incident, which is recorded nowhere other than Hugh's biography, seems to have functioned for its author as an attempt to explain and reconcile his subject's disparate roles as bishop and count, but the end result was that Hugh continued to be *both* "episcopus et comes," as contemporary charters generally referred to him.[38]

Hugh, as both lifelong churchman and powerful noble, thus defies all modern ideas of medieval society being divided into separate "orders".[39] Even more im-

---

[36] Charles-Joseph Hefele, *Histoire de conciles d'après les documents originaux*, trans. and aug. Henri Leclercq, 10 vols. (Paris: Letouzey, 1907-38), 4/2: 938-39, 1409-10. For these councils, see also *Gesta pontificum Autissiodorensium*, 251, and Bouchard, *Sword, Miter, and Cloister*, 250 n. 3.

[37] *Gesta pontificum Autissiodorensium*, 249.

[38] For example, *Recueil des chartes de Cluny*, 3: 720 (no. 2692); *Chartes et documents de Saint-Bénigne de Dijon (990-1124)*, ed. Georges Chevrier and Maurice Chaume (Dijon: Bernigaud et Privat, 1943), 79-81 (no. 296).

[39] In fact, very few scholars would support such a schema in light of the work of Georges Duby, who demonstrated the degree to which it was a conscious construction of the eleventh

portantly, he challenges several important paradigms that have been developed about the changes taking place in France in the early years of the eleventh century. The spread of the Cluniac order and the foundations of the Gregorian Reform, it has long been generally assumed, were carried out in opposition to corrupt or greedy bishops, who were hostile to Cluny's exemptions, and also in opposition to the powerful laymen who held church property in their own hands. Yet Hugh, who may not have been corrupt or greedy but was certainly warlike as a bishop, played a major role in spreading Cluny's order, including grants to Cluny's abbot of churches that he had held in his own hands. In fact, Hugh appears in Cluny's charters more often than any other single bishop during the first half of the eleventh century, more even than the monastery's own diocesan, the bishop of Mâcon.

Hugh's very status as an aristocrat, someone accustomed to take command, perhaps should be seen as more likely to position him to lead the way in ecclesiastical reform, than necessarily to stand as an obstacle to such reform. The late tenth- and early eleventh-century establishment of Cluny's priory system and the restoration of many abandoned houses was carried out with the cooperation and indeed insistence of the very leaders of secular society that extreme Gregorianism, two generations later, would number among the enemy. Scholars once debated the extent to which the Cluniacs were the precursors of the program of Gregory VII. In the last generation or so a consensus has been reached that Cluny's reform of local monasteries cannot be considered directly responsible for the later and more developed rhetoric of church and state.[40] But Hugh's example indicates that scholarly understanding of the nature of monastic reform needs to be taken one step further: it was intended to improve the regularity and piety of the life within the cloister, but it was not by any means carried out in opposition to the powerful and worldly. Indeed, without the powerful and worldly, it would not have been possible at all.

Similarly, the Peace of God is often seen as a radical response to the violence that accompanied the weakening of counts and the spread of castellanies in the early eleventh century. Indeed, the Peace has been described as a social revolution, an attempt by the weak to resist those who opposed them. But Hugh here

---

century; *The Three Orders: Feudal Society Imagined*, trans. Arthur Goldhammer (Chicago: The University of Chicago Press, 1980).

[40] H. E. J. Cowdrey, *The Cluniacs and the Gregorian Reform* (Oxford: Oxford University Press, 1970); Bouchard, *Sword, Miter, and Cloister*, 88-89.

seems to be on *both* sides of this perceived divide. As a major fighter in the Burgundian wars, he certainly has to be held responsible for at least some of the violence of his period—even though, it is important to note, his *strength* as a count counters all theories of eleventh-century violence being caused by weakening counts. At the same time, as one of the bishops who first introduced the Peace into northern France, he might seem to be on the side of the oppressed who were fighting back—against, apparently, powerful lords like himself. To conclude, the example of Hugh of Chalon is the example of a bishop at the heart of the major transformations that affected church and society in the years after 1000—and who challenges both older and newer models of how those transformations took place.

Chapter Four
Bishops in the Middle:
Mediatory Politics and the Episcopacy
Sean Gilsdorf

As Gregory the Great famously lamented, the line between "spiritual" and "worldly" concerns was one which bishops were required to cross repeatedly in the performance of their office.[1] At the same time, the case of Hugh of Chalon points out how ambiguous such distinctions could be, particularly in a world where the episcopacy occupied such a central social, cultural, political, and cultic role. In the following pages, we will focus upon a field of social interaction in which the bishop as both "prince and prelate" played a crucial part—that of mediation and intercession (brought together here under the rubric of "mediatory politics").[2] In modern industrial bureaucracies, such mediatory activities, and particularly the position of the "middleman", tend to be evaluated and understood in terms of values such as "impartiality" and "neutrality". As the anthropologist Philip Gulliver has stressed, however, this historically contingent definition is also analytically insufficient. Instead, he suggests that we treat all forms of mediation as "triadic interactions", in which each party influences the outcome, rather than as essentially binary interactions in which the mediating figure is seen as a transparent functionary rather than an interested agent.[3] Such a perspective allows us to recognize episcopal mediation and intercession as an intrinsically political act, one conditioned by ideological imperatives and expectations, but also reflecting the concerns and agendas of a variety of individuals and communities. More particularly, this chapter will explore how the bishop, as a figure structurally, ideologically, and literally "in the middle" of disparate and

---

[1] For a perceptive treatment of this dilemma, and Gregory's solution to it, see R.A. Markus, *Gregory the Great and His World* (Cambridge and New York: Cambridge University Press, 1997), 17-33.

[2] Intercession (sometimes referred to as "intervention") is defined here as advocacy or petition by a group or individual with some other group or individual on behalf of a third party. As such, it is an essentially mediatory practice, a fact indicated as well by the prefix "inter-". The ideology and practice of intercession in the ninth through eleventh centuries are addressed in more detail in my forthcoming study, "*Interveniente ac mediante*: Mediatory Politics in the Early Middle Ages."

[3] Philip Gulliver, "On Mediators," in *Social Anthropology and Law*, ed. Ian Hamnett (London and New York: Academic Press, 1977), 15-52, esp. 35-40.

sometimes competing cultural formations, both became the practitioner *par excellence* of mediatory politics as well as their literal and figurative embodiment.

The bishop's "centrality" within early medieval society was the product of long historical and doctrinal development, and was manifest not only in the bishop's political and ecclesiological importance,[4] but by his role within another and (for contemporaries) more significant network of relations—namely, those which linked human beings to God, realized in the performances of ritual, liturgy, and prayer. Notably, this field of interaction was one structured in an essentially mediated fashion: transactions between humans and God were performed *through* (*per*) a set of divinely ordained practitioners, the clergy. Even prayer, which offers a potential avenue for "personal" interaction with God, was subsumed in the early Middle Ages within this mediatory, vicarious model, as prayer on behalf of the living and the dead was committed to the care of what was essentially an "occupational" category of *orantes*, "those who pray", largely circumscribed by the tenth century within regular monastic and canonical communities.[5]

Within this spiritual economy, however, the bishop occupied a particularly important place, reflective of a tradition of ecclesiastical thought in which the bishop had gradually come to be identified as the mediator not simply between Christians but between this world and the next. In his first letter to Timothy, Paul had taught that "there is one *sacerdos*, one mediator between God and humans, the man Christ Jesus,"[6] a position repeated and advocated by Ambrose, Paulinus, and Augustine, among others.[7] Augustine's fervent defender and follower Prosper of Aquitaine, however, had argued that while "the whole Christian people is a priestly and royal people, the people's rulers [*rectores*] more fully accept the name of *sacerdos*, for it is they who more specially represent the person of the supreme Pontifex and Mediator."[8]

---

[4] See above, chapter one.

[5] See Megan McLaughlin, *Consorting With Saints: Prayer for the Dead in Early Medieval France* (Ithaca: Cornell University Press, 1994), 102-32.

[6] 1 Tim. 2:5.

[7] See e.g. Ambrose, *Explanatio psalmorum xii*, ed. Michael Petschenig [*CSEL* 64] (Vienna: Tempsky, 1919), 39.18; Paulinus of Nola, *Epistulae*, ed. Wilhelm Hartel [*CSEL* 29] (Vienna: Tempsky, 1894), 36.4; and Augustine, *Epistulae*, ed. Alois Goldbacher [*CSEL* 44] (Vienna: Tempsky, 1904), no. 140.

[8] Prosper of Aquitaine, *Expositio Psalmorum*, ed. P. Callens [*CCL* 68A] (Turnhout: Brepols, 1972), 131.16.

In this sense, the *sacerdos* did not displace Christ's mediating function *per se*, but rather performed it in a vicarial sense. In pragmatic terms, however, the *sacerdos* came to occupy the role of mediator between God (Christ) and humanity, a role fulfilled most publically and immediately in the celebration of the liturgy, where the prayer *of* the community was transformed into prayer *for* the community, performed and focused by the priest or bishop. This distinction between pragmatic mediation (performed by the *sacerdos*) and onto-soteriological mediation (performed and embodied by Christ) was explicated in the early ninth century by Hrabanus Maurus, who defined the mass as

> a legation between God and humanity in which the duty [*officium*] of the legate is performed by the *sacerdos*, when he offers the wishes [*vota*] of the people to God through prayer and supplication. It is good that this is done at the time of sacrifice, when the memory of his passion is celebrated—[the passion], that is, of Christ, the mediator between God and humanity, who offered Himself to the Father for us.[9]

In turn, while the reform movements of the eleventh century would make priests and the priesthood the fulcrum not only of Christian ritual life, but of the Christian community as a whole, earlier ecclesiology saw the bishop in a more exalted light—namely, as the priest *par excellence*, the fullest representative of Christ and thus the person who most perfectly bridged the gap between God in heaven and His people on earth.[10] This identification was made explicit in the

---

[9] "Missa autem est legatio inter Deum et homines, cuius legationis officio fungitur sacerdos, cum populi vota per preces et supplicationes ad Deum offert. Et bene hoc tempore sacrificii fit, quando illius passionis memoria celebratur Christi videlicet, mediatoris Dei et hominum, qui semetipsum obtulit Patri pro nobis." Hrabanus Maurus, *De clericorum institutione*, 1.32 (*PL* 107:322).

[10] Perhaps the most effusive statement of episcopal superiority is provided by Rather of Verona in his *Praeloquia*, III.6.12, in *The Complete Works of Rather of Verona*, trans. Peter L.D. Reid (Binghamton, NY: Medieval and Renaissance Texts and Studies, 1991), 102-3. On the reform concept of the priesthood, see Johannes Laudage, *Priesterbild und Reformpapsttum im 11. Jahrhundert* [Beihefte zum Archiv für Kulturgeschichte 22] (Cologne: Böhlau, 1984). Even among reformers, however, there continued to be a clear distinction between the liturgical and pastoral responsibilities (and powers) of the episcopacy and the priesthood; see e.g. Bernold of Constance's *De officio presbyterum*, c. 5 (*PL* 148:1246): "Postquam autem presbyteri ab episcopali excellentia cohibiti sunt, coepit eis non licere quod licuit, videlicet quod ecclesiastica auctoritas solis pontificibus exsequendum delegavit, id est, confectionem chrismatis, consecrationem virginum, reconciliationem poenitentium, et alia hujusmodi, quae statuta Patrum eis intercludunt."

ninth century by Hrabanus, who interpreted chapter 29 of the book of Exodus as an allegory for the hierarchy of priestly orders and their ordination by God. Thus Moses, who gave the priestly garments to his brother Aaron, signified Christ, while Aaron signified "the highest priest, that is the bishop" and Aaron's sons the priests (*presbyteri*).[11] The eucharistic sacrifice and the sacrament of communion, the key moments at which God is joined to His human community, were impossible without the actions and words of the *sacerdos*, whose voice (in the words of Gregory the Great) "opened up the heavens . . . joining heaven to earth and uniting things seen and unseen."[12] Likewise, the bishop's defining role, that of preacher, made him not only the conduit of the divine Word, but the embodiment of that Word—in a real sense, the "voice of God." The bishop thus served not only as a vessel of the Holy Spirit, but as the living point of contact between God and people.

The bishop, however, was understood not only as the mediator between God and humanity, but between human beings and God as well. In the elegant formulation of George Duby, "anointment had placed the bishop right at the point where heaven and earth were joined, between the visible and the invisible. His words were addressed sometimes towards the one and sometimes towards the other, sometimes to persuade, sometimes to coax some kind of benevolence."[13] This latter role was expressed most commonly in the idiom of intercession. Thus Gregory the Great pointed out that a bishop [*antistes*] was chosen to act as "an intercessor with the Lord for the sins of his people,"[14] a duty which, as he wrote in his commentary on the Book of Kings, was a "divine one" for which the *sacerdos* was shown to be suited by the purity of his life.[15] This emphasis upon the bishop-*sacerdos* as intercessor became established in Christian discourse in the following centuries; thus the Frankish noblewoman Dhuoda admonished her son William to "venerate the *sacerdotes* . . . for they are intercessors for our sins, and hold a sacred office [ordo] . . . always beseech and pray that they might deign to

---

[11] Hrabanus, *De clericali institutione*, I.4 (*PL* 107:299-300): ". . . oportet Aaron sacerdotem summum fuisse, id est episcopum . . . Moyses vero huius facti mediator, Christum significat."

[12] Gregory I, *Dialogues*, IV.58 (*PL* 77:425). On this issue see below, pages 157-59.

[13] Duby, *The Three Orders*, 15.

[14] Gregory I, *Registrum Epistularum*, ed. Dag Norberg [*CCL* 140] (Turnhout: Brepols, 1982), I.24.

[15] Idem, *In librum primum Regum expositionem libri vi*, ed. Patrick Verbraken [*CCL* 144] (Turnhout: Brepols, 1963), II.84.

pray and intercede for you with God, who chose them as intercessors here on earth for his people . . . ."[16]

In turn, beliefs and practices about intercessory prayer and the operation of intercession in the "heavenly court" were structurally and pragmatically linked to broader ideologies of social and political order, a binary relationship which was recursive rather than unidirectional in the orientation of its elements.[17] The image of the bishop as intercessor with God for his people was one modelled on, but also informative of, a tradition of episcopal intercession which originated in Late Antiquity, one deeply rooted in the culture of patronage and personal networks that defined late antique aristocratic life. As Peter Brown and others have noted, the rise of Christianity to prominence within the later empire did little to change the basic dynamic: important families continued to dominate their cities and regions, while the emperors sought to enforce an increased authority over government and finance. What did change under Christianity, however, was the composition of the patronal clique. In rural areas in particular, ascetics and "holy men" became important mediating figures not only between the largely poor population and a heavy-handed but distant imperial authority, but between that population and self-styled local *patroni*—a role which Peter Brown has noted consciously evoked the the patronal ideology of the imperial court.[18] The patronal function, however, increasingly came to be filled at an institutional level

---

[16] Dhuoda, *Liber Manualis*, 2nd ed., ed. Pierre Riché [Sources Chrétiennes 225 bis] (Paris: Editions du Cerf, 1991), III.11 (184; 196): "Venerandi sunt sacerdotes, fili, pro eo quod in sorte ministerio Dei sunt electi, quia pro peccatis nostris intercessores existunt, sacrum tenentes ordinem . . . semper roga et ora, ut dignentur pro te orare et intercedere ad Deum, qui eos intercessores populorum elegit in mundo."

[17] The nature of this relationship has been summarized neatly by J.M. Wallace-Hadrill ("The *Via Regia* of the Carolingian age," in J.M. Wallace-Hadrill, *Early Medieval History* (Oxford: Basil Blackwell, 1975), 182): "The Carolingians saw God as King of Heaven. To Him they transferred the essential features, duly magnified, of royal power, and then, as it were, borrowed them back. God thus became not only the source of their power but also their model." Cf. more recently the excellent treatment in Geoffrey Koziol, *Begging Pardon and Favor: Ritual and Political Order in Early Medieval France* (Ithaca: Cornell University Press, 1992), 77-95, and, for the Byzantine world, Henry Maguire, "The Heavenly Court," in *Byzantine Court Culture from 829 to 1204*, ed. Henry Maguire (Washington, DC: Dumbarton Oaks, 1997), 247-58.

[18] See Peter Brown, "The Rise and Function of the Holy Man in Late Antiquity," in *Society and the Holy in Late Antiquity* (Berkeley: University of California Press, 1982), 103-52, and "Arbiters of the Holy: The Christian Holy Man in Late Antiquity," in *Authority and the Sacred: Aspects of the Christianization of the Roman World* (Cambridge and New York: Cambridge University Press, 1995), esp. 73-74.

by bishops, as the episcopacy came to occupy positions of patronage and authority within the cities which formerly had been occupied by secular magnates.[19]

Indeed, the job of bishop now required the same administrative, personal, and political skills as any other high imperial post; in turn, the bishop's increased power and influence made it even more imperative for communities to be governed by a man who was not only devout, but also politically savvy and well-connected. Given this context, it is no surprise that the episcopacy largely became the province of imperial elites, particularly in the West—a new institutional outlet for traditional aristocratic skills and concerns.[20] Thus, in many regards the holders of episcopal sees carried on the Roman traditions of urban leadership and patronage after the imperial power had ceased to be present in their regions.[21] At the same time, however, the religious demands of Christian stewardship and the ideological imperatives of Christian tradition meant that this "ruling elite" pursued different goals and developed new means to achieve them. Bishops' attention to groups normally ignored by secular urban elites, such as the poor, widows, and orphans, stemmed from scriptural injunctions to love and selflessness, casting the socially self-exalting practice of the *patronus* in the new and otherworldly light of *caritas*, "love for the other".[22]

The bishop's intercessory activity, therefore, was not simply a case of the old wine of aristocratic patronage being poured into new Christian skins. It is more useful, rather, to examine episcopal intercession and mediation as a field of performance in which these two major aspects of the bishop's *persona*—roughly

---

[19] Arnaldo Marcone, "Late Roman Social Relations," in *The Cambridge Ancient History*, vol. 13, *The Late Empire, A.D. 337-425*, ed. Averil Cameron and Peter Garnsey (Cambridge and New York: Cambridge University Press, 1998), 338-70; Peter Brown, *Power and Persuasion in Late Antiquity: Towards A Christian Empire* (Madison, WI: University of Wisconsin Press, 1992), 136-52

[20] The connection between the senatorial aristocracy and the episcopacy was particularly close in late antique and early medieval Gaul; this was not the case, however, in other regions of the empire. See Walter Eck, "Der Einfluß der konstantinischen Wende auf die Auswahl der Bischöfe im 4. und 5. Jahrhundert," *Chiron* 8 (1978): 561-85.

[21] For the situation in Gaul, see Martin Heinzelmann, *Bischofsherrschaft in Gallien: Zur Kontinuität römischer Führungsschichten vom 4. bis zum 7. Jahrhundert. Soziale, prosopographische und bildungsgeschichtliche Aspekte* [Beihefte der Francia 5] (Munich: Artemis, 1976), especially sections II and III, and Ralph Mathisen, *Roman Aristocrats in Barbarian Gaul: Strategies for Survival in an Age of Transition* (Austin, TX: University of Texas Press, 1993), 98-100.

[22] Brown, *Power and Persuasion*, 89-103; 152-58.

characterized here as the "political-patronal" and the "spiritual-pastoral"—were indexed to varying degrees. Notably, while one sometimes took a dominant role, the other could never be completely effaced, since both aspects were integral components of the social (and self-) identity of the early medieval episcopacy. The bishop's position "in the middle", partaking of two distinct sets of social and ideological ideals, thus made him a particularly resonant medium for a mode of interaction that allowed the structural and performative negotiation of two distinct axes of social and symbolic power, i.e. the communal and consensual ("horizontal") and the hierarchical and lordly ("vertical").

The complex interplay of "politics" and "ideals" within episcopal mediation and intercession can be seen most clearly in a social forum where bishops were particularly active in the early Middle Ages—namely, negotiation and peacemaking, often subsumed by modern anthropologists under the rubric of "dispute settlement" (or "dispute processing").[23] Central to episcopal peacemaking was the practice of mediation and arbitration, in which the bishop would operate "in the middle" of disputants and seek to end, or at least alleviate, the differences which separated them. As we will see, modern observers have tended to treat such mediation either as a benign manifestation of virtuous intentions, or as the attenuated cousin of more "direct" kinds of negotiation and political interaction. In fact, however, episcopal mediation involved a critical, albeit precarious, balancing of often conflicting normative demands by its practitioners, one best understood not in terms of "neutrality" or "impartiality", but rather as a complex political act.

The theological foundation for episcopal peacemaking was provided by Christ's declaration in the Beatitudes, "Blessed are the peacemakers, for they shall see God."[24] This passage, as Edward James has made clear, was one that resonated in a particularly powerful way through the Late Antique and early medieval episcopacy.[25] The text and its prescriptive offspring, enunciated by later theologians and Church councils, established within the Christian community

---

[23] For a summary of the distinctions between these categories, and the scholarly context in which they have arisen, see John Comaroff and Simon Roberts, *Rules and Processes: The Cultural Logic of Dispute in an African Context* (Chicago: The University of Chicago Press, 1981), 3-17.

[24] Matt. 5:9.

[25] Edward James, "'*Beati Pacifici*: Bishops and the Law in Sixth-Century Gaul," in *Disputes and Settlements: Law and Human Relations in the West*, ed. John Bossy (Cambridge and New York: Cambridge University Press, 1983), 25-46.

what we might call an "ideology of peace". It is in this context that the bishop's peacemaking activity was primarily rooted: the expectation that he himself should be a lover or "cultivator" of peace stemmed from his position as the overseer of a community which, as Christ's teaching made clear, should be ruled by mutual love. In the late fourth-century *Apostolic Constitutions* (based upon a third-century guide to Christian ethics and ecclesiology), disputes were to be settled not by appeals to secular courts or litigation, but by the bishop: "Draw by your instruction those who are angry to friendship, and those who are at variance to agreement. For the Lord says, 'Blessed are the peacemakers, for they shall be called the children of God'."[26] Thus, as Jill Harries has noted, "contemporary legal formalities were underpinned by a distinctively Christian ideology of reconciliation," one which persisted even as Constantine and later Christian emperors attempted to assimilate episcopal and secular processes of adjudication.[27] Furthermore, that mutuality was in fact essential to the very definition of *pax* is indicated by the ubiquitous pairing of the terms "pax" and "concordia", indicating that "peace" described a social situation in which all were united, literally "of one heart" or (to use a lexically cognate expression) "unanimous". The bishop, therefore, was subject not only to a dogmatic imperative (keep the peace), but to an almost ontological one, insofar as his community only truly existed as such insofar as peace and love reigned.

It is in light of this ideological imperative that we can read an account from Gerhard's *Vita* of Ulrich of Augsburg, in which Ulrich and his fellow bishop Hartpert of Chur negotiated peace between Otto I and his elder son, Liudolf, the duke of Swabia. Liudolf, it will be remembered, had joined Conrad the Red of Lotharingia in revolt against his father in 953, prompted both by animosity towards his fellow duke, Otto's brother Henry of Bavaria, and by anxiety over his own chances at royal succession following Otto's second marriage to Queen

---

[26] *Constitutions of the Holy Apostles*, II.46, in *The Ante-Nicene Fathers*, vol. VII, ed. Alexander Roberts and James Donaldson (New York: Scribner, 1926); cf. II.1, where the Beatitudes (including that regarding peacemaking) are used as a template for the desired characteristics of episcopal candidates.

[27] Jill Harries, *Law and Empire in Late Antiquity* (Cambridge: Cambridge University Press, 1999), 193; cf. 211: ". . . the prevalent ideology of the handling of disputes by bishops remained that of mediation and reconciliation, not only because the bishops were true to Christian doctrine but for practical reasons, that they had to govern, for life, the congregations whom they taught as well as judged . . . bishops were a fixture, and their *auctoritas* was dependent on tried and tested rules laid down, not by emperors, but by the Gospels and St. Paul."

Adelheid of Italy in 951.[28] It is in the midst of the rebel campaign against Henry in Bavaria that Gerhard sets the scene:

> When King Otto had entered Alemannia with an army on account of those who sought, together with his son Liudolf, to oppose the authority of his royal power, he set up camp next to the river Iller in the field belonging to the fortress called Tussa [Illertissen]. There his aforementioned son, Liudolf, appeared with another army in order to do battle against him. When they had drawn so close to one another that there remained no doubt in the mind of either side that there would be fighting between them, God's beloved Bishop Ulrich placed his whole faith in God and joined forces with the pious bishop of Chur, Hartpert. He began to send legations between the two sides, exhorting them to peaceful concord lest the people commended to their rulership by God should be led into perdition on account of their misdeeds. And through God's favor the hard hearts of both Otto the father and Liudolf his son were transformed by the constant admonitions and teaching of these venerable bishops. Thus they reached a peace agreement and, having calmed the tempests of war, returned to their own lands in peace.[29]

As Hatto Kallfelz has noted in his edition of the *Vita*, it is not clear to what "agreement" Gerhard is referring. We only know of peace negotiations at the royal *conventus* at Langenzenn in early summer of 954, where Conrad submitted

---

[28] On the circumstances of this rebellion, see Karl Leyser, *Rule and Conflict in an Early Medieval Society: Ottonian Saxony* (Oxford: Blackwell, 1979), 20-21.

[29] "Cum rex Otto in Alamannia propter eos, qui cum Liutolfo, filio eius, dicioni suae regalis potestatis contradicere voluerunt, cum exercitu conversaretur iuxta flumen quod Hilara vocatur, in campo oppidi quod dicitur Tussa, et ibi saepedictus filius eius Liutolfus cum alio exercitu obvius ad pugnandum contra eum deveniret, et cum tanta vicinitate coniuncti essent, ut nulla ambiguitatis spe detenti manerent in utrarumque partium multitudine, ni bellum ab eis committerentur, tunc amabilis Deo Oudalricus episcopus in Deum tota fiducia confidens, assumpto Curiensis aecclesiae Hardperto religioso episcopo, legationes inter eos facere coepit, et ad pacis concordiam exhortare, et ne populus, qui a Deo illis commendatus est ad regendum, pro eorum reatu duceretur ad perditionem. Deo autem annuente, durae amborum mentes, patris scilicet Ottonis et filii eius Liutolfi, de proficus ammonitione et doctrina venerandorum episcoporum in molliciam versus, pactum pacis inter se placitaverunt, et turbine belli mitigato, in sua cum pace redierunt." Gerhard of Augsburg, *Vita Sancti Oudalrici*, c. 12, in *Lebensbeschreibungen einiger Bischöfe des 10.-12. Jahrhunderts*, ed. Hatto Kallfelz [Ausgewählte Quellen zur Deutschen Geschichte des Mittelalters 22] (Darmstadt: Wisssenschaftliche Buchgesellschaft, 1973), 102-4.

to the king, and at Arnstadt in December, after Liudolf's surrender to his father.[30] For our purposes, however, this is less important than the fact that Gerhard chose to depict his episcopal protagonist in the role of mediator. Notably, here we see episcopal mediation as an autonomous activity, engaged in by the bishop (and a partner). In turn, Gerhard presents this mediation as motivated by, or perhaps better construed as, the enunciation of social norms: that is, Ulrich and Hartpert suggest that peaceful behavior is a requisite of responsible Christian rulership. In this context, then, episcopal mediatory activity is portrayed as the enforcement of transcendent values. Moreover, the bishop is presented here as a transformative force, able through his enunciation of such values to bring about profound changes in the hearts of rulers and hence in the lives of subjects.

What this represents, in essence, is a 'displacement' of the social power of the bishop into the realm of the divine. Put another way, it is not the messenger who ultimately is important, but the message itself, i.e. divine precepts or (implicit) expectations. Nonetheless, it is important here to note the difficult balance struck between pragmatic engagement and ideological "deep structures": while the norms are there and need to be followed, it is crucial nonetheless that there be individuals who instantiate those norms verbally and performatively. Normative propositions (dogma) thus inform practice, but at the same time are re-formed through that practice, recalling the recursive relationship between "rules and resources" and practice posited by sociologist Anthony Giddens, where the former are "drawn upon by actors in the production of interaction, but are thereby also reconstituted through such interaction."[31] "Blessed are the peacemakers" encodes an enduring ideological imperative, but it is only through practice that this imperative becomes meaningful. In other words, while the bishops act to bring about peace in accordance with certain ideological dicta, at the same time their very peacemaking defines the social reality to which those dicta should or could apply, and thus the situated meaning of the norms themselves.

Another, equally important perspective upon episcopal mediation is provided by the tenth-century Saxon monk and historian Widukind of Corvey, who affords us a valuable account of the activities of the other key player in the revolt

---

[30] *Ibid.*, 104 n. 83.

[31] Anthony Giddens, *Central Problems in Social Theory: Action, Structure, and Contradiction in Social Analysis* (Berkeley: University of California Press, 1979), 71. Cf. however the comments and critiques of William H. Sewell, Jr., "A Theory of Structure: Duality, Agency, and Transformation," *American Journal of Sociology* 98/1 (July 1992): 1-29, esp. 6-13.

of 953, Archbishop Frederick of Mainz. Widukind's first mention of Frederick, who succeeded Hildebert as archbishop in 937, presents him as a mediator (or more precisely, an intercessor) for Duke Eberhard of Franconia, who in 938 had joined Otto's half-brother Thankmar in a short-lived revolt against their new king. This brief account, we should note, is a positive one, as Frederick (described as "an outstanding man [*vir optimus*] and one most upright in his religious life") urged Eberhard to approach Otto and humbly seek royal pardon for his deeds, advice which Eberhard took and which was rewarded ultimately by a return to royal favor.[32] When, a year later, Eberhard again rebelled against the king, this time in league with Otto's younger brother Henry and Duke Gilbert of Lotharingia, it seemed that the stage was set for a repeat performance. As Widukind tells us,

> The archbishop, who had been sent to Eberhard to establish concord and peace, concluded a mutual agreement and, since he so desired peace, sealed it with his own oath, which he is reported to have said could never be broken by him. The king, however, sent back with the bishop a reply well-suited to his office, namely that he did not wish to be bound by anything that the bishop had done without his [the king's] orders.[33]

The tension between bishop and king suggested here was not unprovoked, to be sure. Indeed, we are told a few lines earlier that Frederick as well as Bishop Ruodhard of Strasbourg had abandoned Otto during the seige of Eberhard's castle at Breisach, "leaving behind their tents and other supplies"—behavior that resulted in their short-lived exile and confinement.[34] Nonetheless, I would suggest that Otto's displeasure with Frederick had more to do with the latter's activities as mediator. This impression is bolstered by Frederick's later activities

---

[32] Widukind of Corvey, *Res Gestae Saxonicae*, II.13, in *Quellen zur Geschichte der sächsischen Kaiserzeit*, ed. Albert Bauer and Reinhard Rau [Ausgewählte Quellen zur Deutschen Geschichte des Mittelalters 8] (Darmstadt: Wissenschaftliche Buchgesellschaft, 1971), 100.

[33] "Summus pontifex missus ad Evurhardum pro concordia et pace, cum esset earum rerum desiderantissimus, pacto mutuo suum interposuit iuramentum, et ideo ab eo non posse desipere fertur narrasse. Rex autem per pontificem officio suo congruentia dirigens responsa, nil ad se pertinere voluit, quicquid episcopus egisset sine suo imperio." *Ibid.*, II.25 (110).

[34] *Ibid.*, II.24 (110): "Nam summi pontifices relictis tentoriis et alia quilibet suppellectili, ipsi etiam defecerunt a fide."

during Liudolf's revolt, and the king's response to them. Notably, it was Otto who, during a sojourn in Franconia, initially called upon Frederick in 953, seeking his counsel after becoming aware of plotting by Liudolf and Conrad. Frederick's response seems to have been to advise the rebels to ask the king for a chance to clear themselves of the charges. While Widukind is not clear on this point, it appears that Otto let them off the hook before returning home.[35] Widukind continues:

> Once he was comfortably back in the company of his allies [*amici*] and his own people, he admitted that he had made an invalid agreement, one into which he had been coerced. He then announced to his son and son-in-law that they must hand over those who had offended against him, or realize that they would certainly become public enemies. The bishop then weighed in [*intercessit*] on behalf of the earlier agreement, urging the king to seek after peace and concord. On account of this the king grew suspicious of him, and he [Frederick] was rejected by the royal allies as well as all the king's counsellors.[36]

Subsequently, Frederick was charged by Otto's brother Henry with "many serious offenses" at a royal *conventus* at Fritzlar.[37] While Widukind does not tell us what happened to Frederick, it seems likely that his later self-exile to a hermitage was prompted by royal political disfavor. Notably, however, Frederick's episcopal city of Mainz allowed Liudolf to enter soon after, barring its gates to the king and provoking a long seige which ended only when Frederick and Conrad, after unsuccessfully trying to persuade Liudolf to surrender, "departed from him and joined themselves to God and king."[38] According to Widukind, it was only with Frederick's death in 954 that the city, along with Franconia as a whole, reverted unequivocally to royal control.

---

[35] *Ibid.*, III.13 (136).

[36] "Nam confortatus amicorum gentisque propriae presentia, irritum fecit pactum, quod coactus inire confessus est, edictumque est filio generoque auctores sceleris puniendos tradere aut certe se hostes publicos nosse. Pactis pristinis pontifex intercessit, tamquam paci et concordiae consulturus. Ob id regi fit suspectus, amicis regalibus consiliariisque omnimodis spernendus." *Ibid.*, III.15 (136)

[37] *Ibid.*, III.16 (138).

[38] ". . . discesserunt ab eo, Deo regique sese iniugentes." *Ibid.*, III.33 (146).

What does the complicated relationship between Otto and Frederick of Mainz tell us about the role of episcopal mediation in early medieval Germany, and about how it was understood? Earlier church historians argued that Frederick's work as bishop, marked not only by his peacemaking activities but also by his efforts to reform monastic life at Fulda and elsewhere, was motivated by "deeply held religious attitudes" as well as by his sense of duty, not only as a prelate but also as the papal legate in East Francia.[39] This view was shared by Josef Fleckenstein, who described Frederick and his successor William as "pastors pure and simple, who viewed the political type of bishop with mistrust."[40] Others, however, dismissed such interpretations in favor of more "political" ones; Friedrich Lotter, for instance, contended that Frederick's monastic reforms were a reaction to Otto's own efforts in this regard, a manifestation of the archbishop's rivalry with, and opposition to, the king.[41] More recently, Michael Frase has suggested that Frederick's image as a rebel and opponent of royal power was due in large part to the hostility of partisan historians, including Adalbert of St.-Maximin and Widukind; instead, argues Frase, Frederick's position was an emphatically neutral one, as befit his clerical and vicarial role as pastor and peacemaker.[42]

The problem with these approaches lies less in their historical analysis *per se*, and more in their tendency to seek univocal explanations for what was in reality a complex social and ideological phenomenon. This is particularly evident in the explicit (and implicit) contrast drawn between "religion" and "politics" as motives or contexts for action, as well as in the identification of mediation and peacemaking as "neutral", and hence apolitical, modes of social practice. As we pointed out earlier, however, a more nuanced and attentive consideration of me-

---

[39] The classic formulation of this position is that of Albert Hauck; see his *Kirchengeschichte Deutschlands*, 3rd. ed., vol. 3 (Leipzig: J.C. Hinrich, 1912), 34-40. On Frederick's activities as papal vicar, see Heinrich Büttner, "Die Mainzer Erzbischöfe Friedrich und Wilhelm und das Papsttum des 10. Jahrhunderts," *Geschichtliche Landeskunde* 3/1 (1966): 2-14.

[40] Fleckenstein, *Die Hofkapelle der deutschen Könige*, 2: 58: "Friedrich und Wilhelm von Mainz waren noch reine Seelsorger gewesen, die dem politischen Typ des Bischofs misstrauten."

[41] Friedrich Lotter, *Die Vita Brunonis des Ruotger* [Bonner Historische Forschungen 9] (Bonn: Röhrscheid, 1958), 119.

[42] Michael Frase, *Friede und Königsherrschaft. Quellenkritik und Interpretation der* Continuatio Reginonis *(Studien zur ottonischen Geschichtsschreibung)* [Studia Irenica 35] (Frankfurt am Main: Peter Lang, 1990), 276-79; as he concludes (279), "Erzbischof Friedrich war zwar ein Befürworter der Anliegen Liudolfs und Konrads, doch trat er nie offen die Seite der Rebellen über. Er versuchte, Neutralität zu wahren."

diation and other forms of dispute settlement requires that we set aside the modern analytical emphasis upon "neutrality" or "impartiality", in favor of an approach in which "third parties" are treated *as* parties in a given dispute or negotiation, rather than simply as transparent media for communication. Serving in a mediating capacity, even in its most "detached" form, one cannot help but affect the content and the direction of the discussion or negotiations at hand. The very practice of mediation, its use by opposed parties, is predicated upon some expectation of "effectiveness" or "success"—i.e., upon the belief that the mediator will *change things* in some way (or more to the point, will change *minds*). For this to happen, the mediator *must* offer something of his or her own to the proceedings.

These general observations are particularly to the point here, since Widukind's narrative makes it very clear that for Otto and his contemporaries, mediation and intercession were distinct *forms of political action*, not simply "resources" or "solutions" for particular disputants. Indeed, Frederick's activities highlight the "interestedness" of imputedly "disinterested" parties, such as mediators or truce-builders. Otto's disavowal of Frederick's peacemaking in 939, and his suspicious reaction to the bishop's support for the "coerced" treaties of a decade later, only make sense in such a context. Mediation, in other words, was understood not only as a positive good, but as a potentially disruptive force, a means by which not only to cement bonds between the king and his subjects, but also to create new ones between the mediator and his enemies. Walter Norden saw this when, in contrast to many other historians, he characterized Frederick as a "politician", one whose politicking centered upon acts of mediation and negotiation.[43]

To be sure, as we saw earlier, episcopal mediation clearly could be (and was) defined or understood as the alleviation of strife, the creation of *pax et concordia* mandated by divine authority, and hence a duty accompanying a God-given office. Acknowledging this fact, however, is itself to acknowledge the "interestedness" of mediation. It may well be the case, of course, that notions of neutrality or impartiality were part of the ideology of peacemaking, or clerical engagement in politics, in the early Middle Ages. Nonetheless, it is important that we acknowledge this fact—i.e., that these were cultural *values* associated with certain actors or fields of action, rather than intrinsic aspects of the action itself. The mediator's activities thus were not simply passive or instrumental, i.e., oriented

---

[43] Walter Norden, *Erzbischof Friedrich von Mainz und Otto der Große* (Berlin: E. Ebering, 1912), 104; cf. Frase, *Friede und Königsherrschaft*, 261.

by the goals of opposing parties. Rather, the mediator had his own agenda, albeit one which was structured by (or more accurately, in accordance with) a set of universalist or at least non-personal concepts. The mediator's goal, then—the realization of a particular social situation and the re-casting of inter-personal relations—was *not* that of the disputing parties, seeking their own personal ends. Instead, effective mediation was defined precisely by the transformation of pre-existing goals and positions, replacing them with a number of imputedly superior ones.

At the same time, pursuing these goals and fulfilling these duties constituted a praxis which could and often did conflict with other possible praxes, themselves founded on equally idealistic or grounded principles. Norden, for instance, has argued that Otto and Frederick's fraught relationship stemmed from a fundamental difference over the definition of *pax*: Frederick sought to establish peace through treaties between equally powerful parties, reaching a "balance of interests between the king and his domestic opponents," while the king saw peace as obedience to his own (God-ordained) authority.[44] As a result, the pursuit of peace according to Frederick's pragmatic definition (an equilibrium of interests) led to conflict with Otto's distinctly separate notion of peace as the satisfaction of an ethical imperative (summarized by the injuction "obey the ruler").

Nevertheless, while this is a compelling argument, it fails to take into account another crucial element in Frederick's performative repertoire—namely, the ethical imperative represented by the ideology of the *beatus pacificus*. Frederick, that is, must make peace because this is what God has said (through the Spirit, through the apostolic succession of the episcopacy, and through the tradition of the canons) that bishops are required to do. In this respect, "deeply held religious attitudes," as Heinrich Büttner has noted, were central to Frederick's conception, and performance, of his episcopal office.[45] Notably, however, this ideological demand itself could sow the seeds of conflict, since praxis generated in accordance with one imperative can contravene the demands of another. In this case, aggressively seeking to pacify and settle with royal enemies ("blessed are the peacemakers") simultaneously comprised a form of disloyalty or disobedience to Otto as *rector per Deum*, and hence to God. Recognizing this fact, I would suggest, can help us both to understand and resolve Adalbert and Widukind's con-

---

[44] *Ibid.*, 104-7.

[45] Büttner, "Mainzer Erzbischöfe," 2.

tradictory appraisals of Frederick as both pious and rebellious, a true servant of God and an opponent of God's anointed king. Frederick and Otto's disagreement, that is, was one in which "piety" and "power" were inextricably linked, reflecting fundamentally different notions about the nature and use of authority.

It is important to remember as well that the "religious attitudes" appealed to by Büttner and others did not exist in a social vacuum, nor did they operate in a unicausal fashion. On the one hand, mediation was an important element in the repertoire of social control and political management available to early medieval rulers, a fact made clear by Otto's own employment of negotiators and go-betweens, both ecclesiastical and lay, in a number of fraught circumstances. At the same time, mediating agents themselves had the potential to effect changes which went beyond the intentions and control of those who employed them. This situation, moreover, was amplified in the case of bishops, whose own agendas as rulers, kinsmen, and friends were overlaid by a complex ideological body of precepts and dogma, norms which simultaneously structured action and were reconditioned by it. As we have seen, Otto's use of Frederick of Mainz likely stemmed from his recognition of this normative code and its political utility—just as his periodic disagreements and struggles with the archbishop were rooted in the fundamentally *partisan* quality of the Gospel's injunction to act as, and be, a "blessed peacemaker."

The ideology of the *beati pacifici* was implicated as well in the other major form of episcopal mediatory activity, that of intercession. This was particularly true in the arena of "crime and punishment," the reconciliation of wrongdoers with the ruler and the reestablishment of *pax et concordia*. As Edward James has shown, bishops (and other clerics) long played important roles in disputes and quarrels, from the rise to power of Christianity in the Roman Empire onward. Alongside their activities as judges and arbitrators in their own right, however, bishops were allowed, and even expected, to work on behalf of the accused and of those seeking pardon or aid. In 419, the emperors Honorius and Theodosius had granted bishops the right to enter prisons, investigate the cases of those inside, and "direct [their] intervention before the competent judge."[46] The survival of this law, together with a series of other Late Roman edicts (the *Sirmondian Constitutions*), in a seventh-century Lyons manuscript alongside Gallican con-

---

[46] *Constitutiones Sirmondianae*, no. 13, in *The Theodosian Code and Novels and the Sirmondian Constitutions*, trans. Clyde Pharr (Princeton: Princeton University Press, 1952), 483.

ciliar legislation provides a striking parallel to the persistance of judicial intervention into the Merovingian period, where (as James demonstrates amply from the works of Gregory of Tours) bishops were often found intervening on behalf of criminals or disputants, usually with the king or some high official.[47] This practice, however, which continued unabated in the centuries which followed, was increasingly presented in the idiom of Christian peacemaking. Thus, after Louis the German suppressed an uprising by his son Louis II in 866, the *Annals of Fulda* report that "the young Louis was reconciled with his father in November at Werla through the mediation of Archbishop Liutbert [of Mainz] and other lovers of peace."[48]

At the same time, it is important to keep in mind that episcopal intercession on behalf of malefactors cannot be separated from the bishop's patronal role. Such intercession was not simply a matter of good intentions: it depended for its efficacy upon the position and the "pull" of the intercessor himself, and it is clear in many cases that the person for whom a bishop interceded was bound to him by affective or official ties—as his cleric, his suffragan, his relative, or his *amicus*. When Ernest, the brother of Margrave Henry of Bavaria and a member of the uprising led by the king's brother Brun of Augsburg, was captured by Henry II's men in 1003, Adalbold of Utrecht recorded that many of those close to the king advised that he be killed as an example to others. Archbishop Willigis of Mainz succeeded in saving Ernest from death, we are told, because "he held the highest position from which to ask the king for anything."[49] Thietmar of Merseburg's account of this same event, moreover, reveals yet another aspect of successful intercession: Willigis, we are told, had the death sentence cancelled not only by his "humble intercession", but by a payment "with which the king was pleased."[50]

---

[47] See James, "*Beati Pacifici*." On the manuscript, see Mark Vessey, "The Origins of the *Collectio Sirmondiana*: A New Look at the Evidence," in *The Theodosian Code: Studies in the Imperial Law of Late Antiquity*, ed. Jill Harries and Ian Wood (London: Duckworth, 1993), 192-97.

[48] *The Annals of Fulda*, trans. Timothy Reuter (Manchester and New York: Manchester University Press, 1992), a. 866 (56).

[49] Adalbold of Utrecht, *De rebus gestis S. Henrici imperatoris*, c. 38 (*PL* 140:101).

[50] Thietmar, *Chronicon*, V. 34 (230): ". . . presentatoque regi captivo capitalis sententia a iudicibus decernitur, quae Magontinae archipresulis Willigisi intercessione supplici et, quae regi placuit, redemptione amovetur."

What was significant, therefore, was the way in which a "universalist" ideology founded upon canonical and scriptural precedent was imbricated with the strategic and highly "particularist" practices of patronage and alliance-making. Intercession for the accused and the condemned, in other words, was more than simply the instantiation of a moral imperative. It was a form of political action, one which required not only an awareness of the balance of power and authority, but also access to the resources required to gain acquiescence to one's requests. These resources, moreover, were not just material ones: social and cultural "capital", as well as spiritual and ritual power, could be employed by intercessors in striking ways. Perhaps the most intriguing instance of this is provided by Thietmar of Merseburg, in his account of Jaromir of Bohemia's victory over Boleslav and his subsequent acclamation as duke in September of 1004.[51] Henry II, an ally and *amicus* of Jaromir, was present at Prague for the duke's acclamation, and asked Bishop Gottschalk of Freising to prepare a sermon for the occasion. As reported by Thietmar, however, Gottschalk's sermon turned out to be an exhortation to the king himself: after calling upon Henry to recognize that his power and actions were gifts from God, he then beseeched the king to cultivate the virtue of mercy, "the sole butress of salvation" [*quae unicum est salutis presidium*], both because it befitted a person of his stature and power and because it was necessary to avoid the torments of hell.

This was only a prelude, however, to Gottschalk's main message: to free the rebellious margrave Henry of Schweinfurt, Ernest's brother, and receive him back into the royal grace:

> I implore you, most beloved lord [*senior karissime*], in the name of and for the love of him who forgave his debtor the ten thousand talents that he owed (that is, the circumcised Jews for violating his precepts): have mercy upon Henry, once a margrave and now (so I hope) a true penitent; loosen his bonds and grant your grace to him, so that with a lighter heart you might today ask God to "forgive us our debts."[52]

---

[51] *Ibid.*, VI.13 (256-58)

[52] "'Te,' inquiens, 'obtestor per nomen et amorem eius, qui suo debitori decem milia talentorum, id est Iudeis recutitis suorum transgressionem preceptorum, indulsit, Heinrici quondam marchionis, nunc autem, ut spero, vere penitentis, senior karissime, miserearis, vincula solvas et gratiam dones, ut eo liberiori animo hodie Deum interpelles: dimitte nobis debita nostra'" (258).

Upon hearing the bishop's words, we are told, Henry was moved not only to tears, but also to promise to follow Gottschalk's counsel as soon as he returned home.

This short episode, among other things, reveals both what the act of intercession entailed, and the diverse forms which it might take. To be sure, it is difficult to know whether intercession often (or ever) took the form of a sermon, as Thietmar describes it here. Nonetheless, it is telling that Thietmar found the episcopal sermon, exhortatory and highly public in nature, as a plausible context in which to couch a plea for mercy and grace. What is highlighted here is the degree to which acts of intercession could also be acts of *admonition*, in which the intercessor exercised a measure of moral suasion, if not explicit "political power", with the ruler. While Thietmar himself was a bishop, and his work is filled with expressions of support and approval for churches and clerics who strove to defend their position and their autonomy, it is still safe to assume that this dynamic of exhortation and persuasion was an important one in the practice of intervening with the ruler.

As these examples indicate, while episcopal intercession on behalf of wrongdoers was framed, at least in part, by the bishop's duty to be a *pacis cultivator*, his activity as an intercessor was situated largely within what we have labelled the "political-patronal" realm of episcopal identity. This can be seen more clearly when we consider the numerous cases in which bishops intervened, usually with the ruler, on behalf of petitioners seeking land, rights, and offices (especially ecclesiastical ones). As Rudolf Schetter has shown in his monographic study of intervention clauses in Ottonian and Salian diplomata, bishops throughout the period tended to intervene for individuals and institutions within what we might describe as their local clientèle: subordinate clerics, regional *milites*, dependent religious houses, suffragan bishoprics, and the like.[53] The cultivation and maintenance of this patronal circle would seem to be the rationale behind intercession on behalf of candidates for episcopal or other office. Thus, to give only a few examples, Bertulf became bishop of Trier in 870 through the intervention of his uncle, Adventius of Metz;[54] Erp, the provost of Bremen, suc-

---

[53] Rudolf Schetter, *Die Intervenienz der weltlichen und geistlichen Fürsten in den deutschen Königsurkunden von 911-1056* (Bottrop: Postberg, 1935), 27-53.

[54] Regino of Prüm, *Chronicon*, ed. Friedrich Kurze [MGH Scriptores rerum Germanicarum in usum scholarum separatim editi 50] (Hannover: Hahn, 1890), a. 869 (98).

ceeded Brun of Verden in 976 through the intercession of Adaldag of Bremen;[55] and Tagino of Magdeburg persuaded Henry II to appoint the Magdeburg cleric Thietmar to the vacant see of Merseburg in 1009.[56]

In each of these cases, the episcopal intercessor "went to bat" for "his" candidate, one tied to him by familial bonds of blood or of community. It was the existence of such bonds between petitioner and intercessor that led diplomatists like Bresslau and Kerr to categorize similar instances of intercession as "private" in nature, as opposed to "political" ones in which the critical relationship was deemed to be that between the intercessor and the ruler.[57] Yet this distinction is of dubious value even at a heuristic level, due not only to its overly narrow definition of "political" practice, but also to its failure to recognize the *multirelational* and processual nature of intercession. To return to our earlier metaphor, what is essential in intercession is not only stepping up to the plate, but hitting the ball. The personal and symbolic resources that allowed this to take place in early medieval society, however, were an index not only of the bishop's autonomous status and influence, but of his imbrication within the network of relationships radiating outward from the ruler, measured in terms of *Königsnähe* or "nearness to the king."[58] This "nearness", in turn, was in part a reflection of the episcopacy's intimate ties to the royal court and chapel, the nexus of face-to-face, patronal politics in the kingdom, in which the highest offices were filled by bishops and which produced a number of bishops from among the ranks of its clerical personnel, particularly from the reign of Otto I onwards.[59] Thus, as we saw earlier in the case of Willigis, Adventius' intercession on Bertulf's behalf was rendered effective not only by his wealth, but also by his special relationship with Charles the Bald. Likewise, Thietmar's account makes it clear that while Tagino may have supported his candidate due to patronal affection, it was

---

[55] Thietmar, *Chronicon*, III.6 (90-92)

[56] *Ibid.*, VI.39 (284).

[57] See Harry Bresslau, *Handbuch der Urkundenlehre für Deutschland und Italien* (Leipzig: Veit, 1889), 793.

[58] See in particular Gerd Althoff, "Verwandschaft, Freundschaft, Klientel. Der schwierige Weg zum Ohr des Herrschers," in *Spielregeln der Politik im Mittelalter. Kommunikation im Frieden und Fehde* (Darmstadt: Wissenschaftliche Buchgesellschaft, 1997), 185-98, as well as the brief but valuable comments of Karl Leyser, "Ottonian Government," in *Medieval Germany and Its Neighbors, 900-1250* (London: Hambledon Press, 1982), 98-99.

[59] On episcopal appointments, see Fleckenstein, *Die Hofkapelle der deutschen Könige*, 2: 52-58.

his position as a royal *familiaris*, and thus his access to the ruler, which enabled him to hear of another possible candidate and to dissuade the king from choosing him.[60]

At the same time, however, the intercessor's *Königsnähe*, while an important prerequisite for the success of those who used him, was no guarantee either of success or of good faith. This was made maddening clear when the people and clergy of Magdeburg elected the *magister scholae* Ohtric to succeed Archbishop Adalbert in 981, and sent a legation to Italy to announce their choice to Otto II and remind him of his promise to allow free election to the see. When they arrived, they sought out Giselher of Merseburg, "who had great influence with the emperor," told him of their mission, and asked for his aid. Giselher conveyed their request to Otto II, only to turn around and beg that he be appointed instead—an act which, despite the obvious canonical impediments to it, took place once the Roman judges and Pope Benedict VII gave their approval.[61]

Despite the obvious animus which Thietmar of Merseburg, the author of this account, had for Giselher (the man responsible for effectively eliminating the diocese of Merseburg until its restoration by Otto III), his narrative gives us a clear picture not only of the expectations of those seeking intercession on their behalf, but also of the strategic use (or misuse) to which the intercessory process and the role of intercessor could be put. Another episode related by Thietmar (who likely was a witness to the events) nicely highlights this strategic aspect of intercession, as well as the way in which intercession could function as a political resource, this time to the advantage of the Magdeburg community.[62] In 1004, the archbishop of Magdeburg died, creating a vacancy in one of the most important sees in the kingdom. Henry II had chosen as his candidate for the see the royal chaplain Tagino, and sent Bishop Arnulf of Halberstadt to get approval for the appointment from the cathedral chapter in Magdeburg. Upon his arrival, however, Arnulf was told that the chapter had chosen its own candidate, the provost Walther, in accordance with its royally-confirmed right to free election. Walther, speaking for the chapter, now asked Arnulf for his *intercessio* with

---

[60] "Rex autem in Franckenvort audita morte episcopi [March 1009] memoriam pro eo debitam precepit fieri. Iam vero tum quorundam instinctu mentem suam a me ad meliorum convertebat; voluit enim Ethelgero cuidam bene merito honorem huic impendere. Quod cum regis familiaris Thagino rescivit, summopere rennuit et cum assidua supplicacione eo me cum gratia regis per Gezonem prepositum vocavit."

[61] *Ibid.*, III.13 (98-100)

[62] *Ibid.*, V.40-41 (234-36).

Henry, so that the king would approve *him* as archbishop instead of Tagino. When subsequently Arnulf informed the king of what had occurred, Henry was compelled to send for Walther in person, only gaining his *licentia* and that of his "consocii" after "multumque ei promittens."

As represented here by Thietmar, in other words, intercession was in effect a strategic resource sought by Walther and the chapter in their conflict with the ruler. In turn, the use of intercession (for it seems that Arnulf did in fact speak on Walther's behalf) forced the king to *negotiate* for Walther's support and "promise many things to him". This episode thus is revelatory at a number of levels. First, the "recruitment" of an intercessor here was strikingly opportunistic. In contrast to the strategies and patterns seen earlier, Walther took what was available and used it. Second, intercession here was clearly understood as the appropriate mode not only of petition, but also of negotiation. Walther and the chapter, as Thietmar portrays them, were fixed in their opposition to Henry's plans, and used Arnulf as the vehicle for their complaints. Third, "intercession" here constituted a *transformation* of relationships: Arnulf, originally the king's representative, was made into the provost's advocate, and the provost, formerly the king's opponent, was made his ally. Fourth, this transformation suggests, although we have no explicit evidence, that the bishop of Halberstadt was amenable to the chapter's claim. While this can be read as an instance of the old diplomatic category of "political intercession"—Arnulf, after all, was a trusted messenger of the king and thus "had the ruler's ear" —such an interpretation is inadequate for the reasons outlined earlier. That is, not only does it fail to account for the *intercessor's* rationale in serving such a role, it also passes over in silence why the chapter would have chosen to approach him (one could well imagine that other royal messengers may (or may not) have been appealing options; why was Arnulf in particular chosen here?)

Worth considering here as well is the larger context of Henry's kingship, which was based in Bavaria (where he, his father, and his grandfather had held ducal office), even though he made clear efforts to maintain and expand his presence in the Liudolfing heartland of Saxony. Arnulf, in this context, can be seen as part of a Saxon mileau with affective and pragmatic ties to other Saxon bishops and clergy. It is notable, moreover, that this was not the only instance reported by Thietmar in which Henry refused a cathedral candidate; in 1008 he passed over Adalbero (his brother-in-law) as bishop of Trier in favor of Meingaud,[63] while in 1013 he refused to approve the election of Otto as archbishop of Hamburg, spurning the "fidos intercessores" who had approached him and choosing instead his chaplain Unwan.[64] As Timothy Reuter has pointed out, this pattern of refusing local candidates reached its high point under Henry II. At the same time, however, this episode also illustrates Reuter's point that even under an activist ruler like Henry, royal control over episcopal elections was neither uncontested nor total; indeed, even when the local chapter failed to have its choice approved, "often the unsuccessful candidate would be promised a later bishopric," as seems to have been the case at Magdeburg.[65] Intercession in this case, therefore, was more than just a way to demonstrate patronage or to acknowledge the demands of social hierarchy: it was a recognized and craftily employed element in the repertoire of ecclesiastical and aristocratic politics.

As we have seen, the bishop's role and image as mediator and intercessor in the late Carolingian and Ottonian world were not new. Intercession and mediation were occupational expectations of the episcopate that arose in Late Antiquity and resonated with a broader conception of the bishop-*sacerdos* as a mediating figure between heaven and earth. Each bishop therefore was bound by traditional expectations and ideals, ones which he and his contemporaries strove to fulfill. At the same time, the mediatory activities of the episcopacy took place within, and helped to shape, a tight-knit but fractious aristocratic polity. Within this political landscape, the bishop's intercession, and even more so his work as a mediator, were authoritative, or at least political, acts. Intercession and mediation thus were more than simple instantiations of hierarchical political and social ideology; rather, they were social interactions subject to strategic manipulation, through which social relations both were created and cultivated. This is important, for it exposes the complex relationship between ideology and praxis that defined (and defines) the field of mediatory politics—the contrast between an ideology of hierarchically stable relations of dependence and authority, and a praxis which was inherently unstable, contingent, strategically oriented, and subject to change. As this chapter has shown, bishops at the turn of the first millennium occupied a social, historical, and ideological position which made them particularly open to, and effective at, the kind of mediatory politics that could bring these seemingly discordant elements into harmony.

---

[63] *Ibid.*, VI.35 (280).

[64] *Ibid.*, VI.89 (336-38).

[65] Reuter, "'Imperial Church System'," 350-51.

Chapter Five
The Bishop As Cultural Medium:
Berthold of Toul, Byzantium, and Episcopal Self-Consciousness[†]
William North and Anthony Cutler

Historians long have recognized the crucial role played by the *Reichskirche*, or imperial church, in Ottonian rulers' ability to control and administer their increasingly far-flung empire.[1] Indeed, so much has the edifice of Ottonian kingship seemed to rest upon ecclesiastical foundations that scholars have at times run the risk of reifying what were, in fact, fluid, complex, and contingent relationships of power, patronage, and personality.[2] In recent years, as scholars have more precisely and subtly characterized the changing shape and meaning of the church within the Empire over the course of the tenth and eleventh centuries,[3] carefully assessing the literary and visual representations of the prelates who manned it,[4] they have been able to give sharper definition to the role of the Ot-

---

[†] William North would like to thank his colleagues Jackson Bryce of the Classics Department at Carleton College and Anne Groton of the Classics Department at St. Olaf College for offering their informed assessment of the inscription's poetic worth, and Anthony Cutler his colleague Brian Curran for reconsideration of the passage in Gori Passeri cited in note 26. The authors would also like warmly to thank the staff of Dumbarton Oaks and its fellows, in particular Holger Klein, now of the Department of Art History and Archeology at Columbia University: by a happy chance, the three of us were together there in the spring of 1998, when this chapter was first conceived.

[1] For the strongly institutional approach to the *Reichskirche*, see the classic studies of Santifaller, *Zur Geschichte des ottonischen-salischen Reichskirchensystems*; Oskar Köhler, "Die ottonische Reichskirche: Ein Forschungsbericht," in *Adel und Kirche. Festschrift für Gerd Tellenbach dargebracht von Freunden und Schülern*, ed. Josef Fleckenstein and Karl Schmid (Freiburg: Herder, 1968), 141–204; Josef Fleckenstein, "Zum Begriff der ottonisch-salischen Reichskirche," in *Geschichte, Wirtschaft, Gesellschaft: Festschrift für Clemens Bauer zum 75. Geburtstag* (Berlin: Dunker und Humblot, 1974), 61–71; and *idem*, "Problematik und Gestalt."

[2] Particularly important here is the incisive and illuminating critique in Reuter, "'Imperial Church System'." Cf. the response by Josef Fleckenstein, "Problematik und Gestalt," 84, 95–98.

[3] E.g., the recent study of the episcopacy in Swabia and Bavaria by Bührer-Thierry, *Evêques et pouvoir dans le royaume de Germanie*, and the rich collection of essays in *Die Salier und das Reich*, ed. Stefan Weinfurter, 3 vols. (Sigmaringen: Thorbecke, 1991), esp. vol. 2, *Die Reichskirche in der Salierzeit*. See also above, especially chapters 1 and 4.

[4] See in general the fundamental study of Oskar Köhler, *Das Bild des geistlichen Fürsten in den Viten des 10., 11. und 12. Jahrhunderts* [Abhandlungen zur mittleren und neueren Geschichte 77] (Berlin: Verlag für Staatswissenschaften und Geschichte, 1935), along with C.

tonian bishop as a figure mediating between king and nobility, court and locality, ecclesiastical and secular spheres of life.[5] Likewise, they have come to appreciate the ways in which the imperial church, and the episcopate in particular, constituted one of the most important social contexts for cultural production and exchange around the year 1000. Through the bishops' service in the *Hofkapelle*,[6] the king's council, and the army, as well as routine and spontaneous occasions of ecclesiastical assembly and action, Ottonian bishops became living conduits of culture, transmitting ideas, ideals, and objects between the various cultural milieus of the Empire. As the potential field of the bishop's influence and action increased, so did episcopal rivalry, cultural as well as political: prelates now strove to distinguish themselves before their subjects, their peers, and, most of all, their kings in the hope of winning the greater honor, power, and other rewards—material, spiritual, and social—that such distinction might bring.[7]

That episcopal collaboration and competition left their mark on all aspects of Ottonian politics can be easily observed in the contemporary chronicles of Widukind of Corvey or Thietmar of Merseburg. Yet it is now becoming clear that bishops' activities also informed Ottonian artistic production and sensibilities in intricate and fascinating ways and that episcopal inspiration, both intellectual and material, stand behind some of the most notable artistic efforts of the era. As recent work on Egbert of Trier (977–93) and Bernward of Hildesheim (993–1022) has clearly demonstrated, Ottonian prelates played a powerful role in shaping the visual culture of the Empire as a whole.[8] At the same time, these

---

Stephen Jaeger, *The Origins of Courtliness: Civilizing Trends and the Formation of Courtly Ideals, 939–1210* (Philadelphia: The University of Pennsylvania Press, 1985), esp. 19–48, with further bibliography. For an analysis of episcopal *vitae* as examples of *pragmatische Schriftlichkeit*, i.e., literary representations designed to meet specific contemporary needs, see now Stephanie Coué, "Acht Bischofsviten aus der Salierzeit— neu interpretiert," in *Die Salier und das Reich* (as note 3), vol. 3, 347–413 (a summary of her *Hagiographie im Kontext*), and her more recent and extensive study (as Stephanie Haarländer), *Vitae Episcoporum*.

[5] See above, chapter four. Cf. the synthetic studies of Zielinski, *Der Reichsepiskopat in spätottonischer und salischer Zeit*, and Finck von Finckenstein, *Bischof und Reich*.

[6] On this, Fleckenstein, *Die Hofkapelle der deutschen Könige*, vol. 2 remains fundamental.

[7] On the place of *familiaritas* as a valuable social resource, see the comments of Karl Leyser in "Ottonian Government," esp. 99: "Since the migrant ruler was the government and communications between him and the regions, the *patriae*, were often uncertain, slow and expensive, to have friends who were near him and had his ear, was all important. The *familiaritas* of an emperor was a gift of God."

[8] The essays and images assembled in the recent exhibition catalogues on Egbert of Trier and Bernward make this role particularly clear: *Egbert, Erzbischof von Trier, 977–993: Gedenk-*

studies have shown that the bishops employed available resources to produce artistic and architectural works aimed at achieving the distinctly local and personal goals of enhancing status or memorializing the past.[9]

Bishops thus have emerged ever more clearly as crucial and complex figures in Ottonian cultural production. On the one hand, as high-ranking prelates, they could and did bring together the human, material, and ideological resources necessary for the making of objects worthy of their God, their saints, and their kings. On the other, as members of an imperial elite often enjoying access to the imperial court and required to travel more frequently and more widely than contemporaries of lesser status, they were vital agents in the active redistribution of ideological and material capital to the diverse regions of the Empire and its integration into local cultural economies. In a word, they were key middle-men and impresarios in the cultural economy of the Ottonian world.

Exploration of the role of the bishop as cultural impresario has hitherto tended, for obvious reasons, to be restricted to such exceptional figures as Egbert of Trier and Bernward, the indefatigable artist-bishop of Hildesheim,[10] or focused on well-known monuments.[11] This chapter, in contrast, seeks to broaden the evidential basis for assessing the cultural aspirations of the Ottonian episcopate through the identification and discussion of a new player in the field: Bishop Berthold of Toul. Similarly, through an investigation of the episcopal practice of inscribing objects, and the inscription upon one Byzantine ivory in

---

enschrift der Diözese Trier zum 1000. Todestag, ed. Franz Ronig [Beiheft zur Trierer Zeitschrift für Geschichte und Kunst] (Trier: Rheinische Landsmuseum Trier, 1993); and *Bernward von Hildesheim und das Zeitalter der Ottonen. Katalog der Ausstellung, Hildesheim 1993*, 2 vols., ed. Michael Brandt and Arne Eggebrecht (Hildesheim: Bernward Verlag, 1993), with earlier bibliography.

[9] On Egbert's artistic activity, see below, chapter six, as well as Thomas Head, "Art and Artifice in Ottonian Trier," *Gesta* 36/1 (1997), 65–82.

[10] See notes 8 and 9. On Bernward of Hildesheim, Francis Tschan's study of the bishop's career and artistic production remains valuable: *Saint Bernward of Hildesheim*, 3 vols. (Notre Dame: University of Notre Dame Press, 1942, 1951–52). For a more recent assessment, see Bernhard Gallistl, "Byzanz-Rezeption und Renovatio-Symbolik in der Kunst Bernwards von Hildesheim," in *Byzanz und das Abendland im 10. und 11. Jahrhundert*, ed. Evangelos Konstantinou (Cologne: Böhlau, 1997), 129–60.

[11] Adam Cohen's study of the Uta Codex presents a model of this kind of investigation: *The Uta Codex: Art, Philosophy, and Reform in Eleventh-Century Germany* (University Park, PA: Pennsylvania State University Press, 2000). The second volume of Henry Mayr-Harting's *Ottonian Book Illumination*, rev. ed. (London: Harvey Miller 1999) adopts a similar, monument-driven approach with regard to book illumination.

particular, we highlight the appearance of a new dimension of the Ottonian episcopate's self-consciousness and habits of self-representation—the bishop's desire to commemorate not so much his piety as his performance as *arbiter elegantiarum*.

Byzantine Ivories, Ottonian Attitudes

The prevailing scholarly approach to the use of Byzantine artifacts within the Ottonian and Salian Empire has tended to emphasize in these appropriations westerners' admiration for, emulation of, and, finally, competition with the cultural and artistic superiority of the Rome of the East.[12] Such an approach has led scholars often to undervalue, whether implicitly or explicitly, the creativity and skill of local artisans and almost reflexively to connect developments in many areas of Ottonian art with the benevolent presence of a Greek Muse.[13]

More recently, however, some scholars have shifted their focus away from questions of influence and borrowings and have tried instead to understand the functions and meanings of Ottonian objects when viewed on their own terms. The resulting studies have consistently suggested that Ottonian attitudes toward these objects and their associations with Byzantium were considerably more complex and polyvalent than has been traditionally assumed. Byzantium, far from being considered a source of inviolable treasures and an unchallenged aesthetic, seems rather to have been regarded as but one of many rich sources of artistic inspiration and raw material—Greco-Roman, late antique, Carolingian, and Islamic—all of which Ottonian artists and patrons exploited, combined, and adapted to create new objects that would adequately express the aims and self-

---

[12] For a survey of Byzantine objects in circulation in the Ottonian Empire, see Arne Effenberger, "Byzantinische Kunstwerke im Besitz deutscher Kaiser, Bischöfe, und Klöster im Zeitalter der Ottonen," in *Bernward von Hildesheim*, ed. Brandt and Eggebrecht, 1: 145–59, with earlier literature.

[13] While the broadest description of this position is Otto Demus, *Byzantine Art and the West* (New York: NewYork University Press, 1970), earlier and influential statements in the same vein are to be found in the works of Wilhelm Koehler, Ernst Kitzinger, and Kurt Weitzmann cited (and criticized) by Anthony Cutler, "Misapprehensions and Misgivings: Byzantine Art and the West in the Twelfth and Thirteenth Centuries," *Medievalia* 7 (1981), 41–77. On Italy in particular, see *idem*, "La 'questione bizantina' nella pittura italiana: una visione alternativa della 'maniera greca'," in *La pittura in Italia: L'altomedioevo*, ed. \Carlo Bertelli (Milan: Electa, 1994), 335–54. A radically new paradigm for the study of East–West relations is proposed by Robert S. Nelson, "Byzantine Art and the West: An Asymmetrical Relationship," in *Actes du XXe Congrès international des études byzantines* (Paris, forthcoming).

consciousness of a new and would-be universal empire and its ruling elite.[14] The way to a more nuanced understanding of the meaning of Byzantine objects in the Ottonian world lies, therefore, in the careful analysis of the nature and function of these objects as integral elements of often complex assemblages. To do so, scholars must set aside often inflated assumptions about the cultural and ideological meaning of Byzantium in the Ottonian world and instead base their conclusions on the visible and palpable evidence for the Ottonians' actual use of objects from the East.

One such amalgam has recently been analyzed: the careful and intelligent use made by Bishop Sigibert of Minden (1022–36) of a tenth-century triptych to embellish the covers of two liturgical books—a lectionary and an epistolary.[15] Taken together, the decision to dismantle the Byzantine original, the careful technical execution of the ivory's dissection, and the sophisticated nature of Sigibert's appropriation of the resulting plaques for his own needs offer a more authentic paradigm of the artistic relationship of Byzantium and the West. Neither passive recipients gazing in wonder nor inept barbarians ravaging civilized art, Ottonian patrons and artisans emerge instead as savvy, skilled, and self-confident men who appreciated objects of quality, eagerly acquired them, and knew how to analyze and manipulate their techniques of production and modes of signification. Moreover, they seem to have done so uninhibited by the modern attitude of artistic essentialism that demands reverence for the object in its original state and thereby restricts its subsequent possessor to acts of display, preservation, and admiration.[16] Sigibert of Minden's loving and purposeful manipulation of his treasure suggests, in contrast, that by the early eleventh century, the Ottonians looked critically upon the glories of Byzantium that came into their

---

[14] See, for example, Hiltrud Westermann-Angerhausen, "Spolie und Umfeld in Egberts Trier," *ZfKg* 50 (1987), 305–36; Head, "Art and Artifice in Ottonian Trier;" and, most recently, Karen R. Mathews, "Expressing Political Legitimacy and Cultural Identity through the Use of *Spolia* on the *Ambo* of Henry II," *Medieval Encounters* 5/2 (1999), 156–83.

[15] Anthony Cutler, "A Byzantine Triptych in Medieval Germany and Its Modern Recovery," *Gesta* 37/1 (1998), 3–12.

[16] In other words, the Ottonians do not seem to have participated in the modern cult of the original, in which an object's value depends heavily on its uniqueness. One corollary of this attitude, as we shall see, is the lack of any declaration that they were re-using older pieces to which, by whatever means, they had access. On this larger question, which to some extent contrasts the viewpoint of the historian with that of the art historian, see Anthony Cutler, "Reuse or Use? Theoretical and Practical Attitudes towards Objects in the Early Middle Ages," in *Ideologie e pratiche del reimpiego nell'alto medioevo* [Settimane 46] (Spoleto: Presso la Sede del Centro, 1999), 1057–83.

hands with eyes that keenly perceived the full range of semiotic opportunities afforded by these eastern exotica and with minds that did not flinch from capitalizing upon them.

The Berlin Hodegetria

One Constantinopolitan ivory that passed through Ottonian hands is the plaque depicting Maria Hodegetria now in the Museum für Spätantike und Byzantinische Kunst in Berlin (fig. 1).[17] This was once the central member of a triptych, as is shown by the holes in the frame originally drilled for the attachment of a cornice and base at the ends of which pivoting wings would have been set.[18] The upper and lower portions of the frame would therefore have remained concealed while those at left and right would have been exposed only when the wings were opened. The removal of those wings—presuming that they were detached after, rather than before, the object arrived in the West—would have been the first step in its transformation into the main feature of a book cover. (Despite a widely held belief, there is no evidence that ivory appliqués were used this way in Byzantium). This secondary use is signaled by the smaller holes in the corners of the ground where they are overshadowed by a frame on all sides proportionally wider than is normal on Byzantine plaques. Exploiting this unusual expanse, the Ottonian craftsman incised a double frame, the better to set off an elegant Latin inscription that took advantage of the regular spacing of the five original peg holes and constituted the final and, from our present point of view, most telling stage in the conversion of the trophy. We, of course, gaze upon the eastern artifact with eyes that see it in a different, but perhaps no less appreciative, light than those who performed the conversion.

In terms of technique, the plaque that resides today in Berlin is closely related to the Romanos ivory in the Cabinet des médailles, datable to between 944

---

[17] The most recent study is that by Gudrun Bühl in the catalogue *Meisterwerke aus Elfenbein der Staatlichen Museen zu Berlin* (Berlin: Staatliche Museum zu Berlin-Preussischer Kulturbesitz and Braunschweig: Herzog Anton Ulrich-Museum, 2000), no. 7, with earlier bibliography, where the Latin inscription with which we are concerned is not associated with a known individual but correctly assigned to the eleventh century.

[18] For a surviving example and discussion of the various methods of triptych construction in Byzantium, see Anthony Cutler, *The Hand of the Master: Craftsmanship, Ivory, and Society in Byzantium (9th–11th Centuries)* (Princeton: Princeton University Press, 1994), 149–50 and plate VI.

and 949.[19] Particularly within the central roundel containing the Mother of God the plaque (eight millimeters thick at the frame) has been shaved down until it is translucent; a similar, almost gossamer-like quality characterizes much of the ground of the ivory in Paris.[20] Uncommon as this painstaking step is, it is matched in rarity by the presence of deep undercutting, most obvious in the area between Mary's neck and the hood of her *maphorion*, and behind the hand with which she gestures toward the Child. Many further resemblances connect the two plaques, but in this context it is more useful to concentrate on the iconography and ornament of ivories that depict the Hodegetria ("She who shows the way"). Her full-length figure on the magnificently preserved central portion of a triptych in Utrecht (Fig. 2),[21] although it cannot be dated as precisely as the Romanos plaque, may have the advantage of being the handiwork of the same craftsman who produced the Berlin plaque. Along with a host of other similarities, the arched eyebrows, the heavy eyelids, the ample folds of the *maphorion* across Mary's neck, and the virtual identity of her right hand with that on the Berlin ivory—to say nothing of the physiognomic resemblances between the two versions of Christ—are evidence of the hand of one master and, more broadly, of Byzantine carving skill at its highest level of attainment.

The Berlin plaque, then, can be fairly related to some of the finest examples of tenth-century Constantinopolitan carving, even as it departs in several respects from the customary manner of presenting the half-length Hodegetria. Normally she and her son are shown unidentified and unaccompanied by other figures (as in fig. 4, below),[22] whereas on the Berlin ivory they are surrounded by a unique openwork net of double lozenges and a resultant tondo that itself subtends smaller medallions enclosing the busts of Sts. John the Baptist, Peter, Paul, and Thomas. This selection of figures may represent the original destination of the plaque or the particular devotion of its first owner, but, whatever the

---

[19] *Idem*, "The Date and Significance of the Romanos Ivory," in *Byzantine East, Latin West: Art-Historical Studies in Honor of Kurt Weitzmann*, ed. Christopher Moss and Katherine Kiefer (Princeton: Department of Art History and Archaeology, 1995), 605–13.

[20] Such reductions often resulted in breakage, an untidiness usually removed by modern collectors and dealers who severed the figures from the ground. For two examples of the half-length Hodegetria treated in this manner, see Cutler, *Hand of the Master*, figs. 197 and 98.

[21] See the entry by Arne Effenberger in *Bernward von Hildesheim*, ed. Brandt and Eggebrecht, no. II-18 (54–56), who dates the ivory to the second half of the tenth century (as is generally agreed) and hypothesizes its transmission through Ottonian hands.

[22] For a variety of examples, see Cutler, *Hand of the Master*, 174–84 and figs. 195–209.

explanation for their presence, the zig-zag medallions[23] that enclose them are found on other major creations in ivory, such as an undated but probably late tenth-century triptych in the Vatican[24] and the Cortona cross-reliquary which names the emperor Nikephoros (II; 963–69).[25]

According to early scholarly investigation, this latter ivory reached its Italian destination shortly after the Fourth Crusade.[26] In the case of the Berlin ivory, however, both the epigraphy of the inscription upon the frame and the ivory's obvious use as the adornment for the cover of a book—an aesthetic of ornamentation more characteristic of the tenth and eleventh centuries than the thirteenth—suggest that it arrived in the West long before that time.[27] But the cen-

---

[23] For whatever reason, a deliberate attempt to excise these frames was made at some point. That they are not merely "abgebrochen," as Goldschmidt and Weitzmann observed, is evident from the fact that they are severely damaged, even while they are lower than the plaque's main frame; by contrast, the double-lozenge border of the Hodegetria and its inhabitants are unworn despite their projection beyond the main frame. See Adolph Goldschmidt and Kurt Weitzmann, *Die byzantinischen Elfenbeinskulpturen des X. bis XIII. Jahrhunderts*, 2 vols. (Berlin: Bruno Cassirer, 1931–34), vol. 2, no. 50.

[24] *The Glory of Byzantium: Art and Culture of the Middle Byzantine Era, A.D. 843–1261*, ed. Helen C. Evans and William D. Wixom (New York: Metropolitan Museum of Art, 1997), no. 79 (Ioli Kalavrezou). The use here of the lozenge as a band of ornament as well as for the periphery of medallions is repeated on the back of the wings of the Borradaile triptych in the British Museum. See Cutler, *Hand of the Master*, fig. 242.

[25] Cutler, *Hand of the Master*, 213 and plates I, II, and esp. fig. 232.

[26] Philippus de Venutis, *De cruce Cortonensi dissertatio* (Livorno: J.P. Fantechi, 1751); Anthony Cutler, "From Loot to Scholarship: Changing Modes in the Italian Response to Byzantine Artifacts, ca. 1200–1750," *Dumbarton Oaks Papers* 49 (1995), 254, 285. The provenance of the Berlin ivory is a more complicated affair. It is first recorded, but without any indication of its whereabouts, by the antiquarian G.B. Passeri in his supplement to Antonio Gori, *Thesaurus veterum diptychorum consularium et ecclesiasticorum*, 3 vols. (Florence: Caietani Albrazzini, 1759), III, 21–23 and pl. V, an engraving which reads as St. Andrew the inscription identifying the Prodromos. Gori had apparently passed no notes on the object to Passeri, who indulged in a farrago of error and irrelevance, misreading the last word of Berthold's text ("nitenti" for *decenti*) and expatiating at length on a Byzantine *mosaic* panel, described as being in Florence, that he says resembles the ivory. Cutler was misled by Passeri's comments in "From Loot to Scholarship," 261 n. 163, producing remarks that he now withdraws. The Berlin plaque may not have been in Italy before it reached Fabriano and the collection of Count Girolamo Possenti. It is clear from the detailed record of a visit to this collection by J.O. Westwood, *A Descriptive Catalogue of the Fictile Ivories in the South Kensington Museum* (London: Eyre and Spottiswoode, 1876), 372–76, that Possenti acquired his ivories over the course of fifty years rather than by inheritance; the Berthold plaque, however, was in this collection before 1841, when it was described as "Greco-Latina" by Camillo Ramelli, *Visita al Museo di Avori in Fabriano* (Fabriano, 1841), 7.

[27] Our thanks to Ihor Sevcenko and Brigitte Bedos-Rezak for their assessment of the approximate dating of the Latin inscription. See also the judgment of Bühl, *Meisterwerke*, no. 7.

tral evidence for the western context of the Berlin plaque's use lies in the content of the Latin inscription, written in hexameters of some merit, carefully laid out in capital letters without abbreviations around its broad frame, and allocated over its four sides in such a way as to respect the principal caesura in each verse. It reads:

PRESULIS IMPERIIS
BERTOLDI CLAUDITUR OMNIS
TEXTUS EVANGELII
REDIMITUS HONORE DECENTI.
By Bishop Berthold's command,
The text of the entire Gospel is enclosed,
Garlanded with fitting honor.[28]

The inscription contains five precious pieces of information. First, it notes the plaque's use on the cover of a gospel book. This is confirmed by the presence of the holes drilled in the corners of the image space between the medallions and the inner corners of the frame (see fig. 1) through which the plaque would have been attached to a wooden book cover. Second, it clearly indicates the identity of the person commissioning this act of use: *presul Bertoldus*, a name and title that point clearly toward a member of the ecclesiastical hierarchy of the German empire. Third, it clarifies the relationship of this individual to the actual work of art: Berthold commissioned but did not execute the project. Fourth, the careful sizing and spatial allocation of the elegant inscription that made abbreviation or distorted letter forms unnecessary suggest that this Berthold had access to a skilled craftsman, and surely one experienced in ivory carving. Finally, the concluding line of the inscription—composed, as it almost certainly was, in consultation with, if not actually by, the bishop himself—offers the viewer insight into Berthold's own estimate of his achievement. In garlanding (*redimitus*) the gospel book with this ivory, he has bestowed upon the book a *honos* that was fitting in several respects. The beauty of the plaque, first of all, clearly denoted the inestimable worth of the book's subject and content. Likewise, the depiction of Mary, John the Baptist, and apostles provided a suitable visual context for the

---

[28] The use of *honor* here is particularly apt, inasmuch as its semantic field includes meanings ranging from dignity or distinction to beauty or grace, all of which would be appropriate in this context.

Gospel narrative itself, while the layout of the four apostles in the corners may have offered a visual echo of medallions depicting the four evangelists, for these often adorned contemporary book covers.[29] It was indeed a *honos decens*.

The Invisible Impresario: Bishop Berthold of Toul (996–1019)

Who was this Berthold who held episcopal rank and had access to both a fine Byzantine ivory and a craftsman capable of the quality of work evinced by the loving execution of the text? Despite the clues offered by the inscription, scholars have hitherto refrained from conjecture; Goldschmidt and Weitzmann, for instance, preferred to leave his identity a completely open question.[30] A survey of the standard biographical dictionaries and medieval prosopographies explains their hesitation, for possible candidates—ranging from Bishop Berthold of Hildesheim in the early twelfth century to Berthold of Zähringen, abbot of Wilten near Innsbruck in the mid- to late twelfth century, to a thirteenth-century Berthold who was patriarch of Aquileia—all lived significantly later than the period when the plaque was originally carved. The well-attested applications of Byzantine ivories relatively soon after their arrival in the West[31] suggest that the bishop named in the inscription was likely active in the very late tenth or early eleventh century. The last quarter of the tenth century witnessed a golden age in East–West relations, an *entente cordiale* nourished by marriage negotiations, military aid, and lavish gifts.[32] It therefore seems most likely that *presul Ber-*

---

[29] It is likely that the author of the inscription intended *honos/honor* to oscillate between its more literal and poetical meanings of honor and beauty, respectively. For noting the visual echo of the Berlin plaque's four apostle-bearing medallions and the medallions bearing the symbols of the evangelists (such as adorn figs. 3 and 7), William North would like to thank his colleague George Shuffelton. In this view, the wreathed apostles adorning the corners (identified only in small Greek letters that would have been, for most viewers, illegible) would essentially be "read" as the evangelists because of their quaternity and their layout.

[30] Goldschmidt and Weitzmann, *Die byzantinischen Elfenbeinskulpturen*, no. 50.

[31] Thus the Dormition ivory used on the covers of the Gospels of Otto III in Munich and a host of other examples; see *ibid.*, nos. 1, 22, 25, 65, 66, 106, 125, 129, 133, 134 and *passim*, as well as note 15 above.

[32] Most famously, the negotiations and gift-exchanges associated with the marriage between Theophano and Otto II, on which see now Odilo Engels, "Theophano, the Western Empress from the East," in *The Empress Theophano: Byzantium and the West at the Turn of the First Millennium*, ed. Adalbert Davids (Cambridge: Cambridge University Press, 1995), 28–48; and Hans Wentzel, "Das byzantinische Erbe der ottonischen Kaiser: Hypothesen über den Brautschatz der Theophanu," *Aachener Kunstblätter* 40 (1971): 11–84, and 42 (1972): 11–96.

toldus held high religious office somewhere within the German empire during the late tenth or, at the latest, the early eleventh century.

There is one Berthold known to us who fits all of these criteria, although his name rarely appears in the standard reference works and general historical surveys of the Ottonian and Salian periods.[33] Extant prosopographical and historical evidence, however, supports the hypothesis that the *Bertoldus ignotus*, whose command shaped the fate of the Hodegetria plaque, was none other than Bishop Berthold of Toul, ruler of his diocese from 996 to 1019.

Because of the almost complete lack of charter evidence from the period of Berthold's episcopacy,[34] the majority of our knowledge about his character and interests depends upon the *Gesta* of the bishops of Toul, a work written by a cleric or monk of Toul in the early twelfth century who, in composing his glowing portrait of Berthold, seems to have drawn on documents, his own observations of local buildings, and a still vital oral tradition.[35]

This classic study has been properly criticized by Arne Effenberger, "Byzantinische Kunstwerke," as too ready to assign too many objects to Theophano's advent. As late as 1002 relations between Byzantium and the German kings remained amicable. For a discussion of Henry II's apparently cordial reception of Byzantine legates at Frankfurt in 1002, see Werner Ohnsorge, "Die Legation des Kaisers Basileios II. an Heinrich II.," *Historisches Jahrbuch* 73 (1954): 65–67.

[33] The episcopal list at the end of Hauck, *Kirchengeschichte Deutschlands*, vol. 3, 1000, contains one of the few mentions of Berthold in a general reference work. The *Lexikon des Mittelalters*, for example, omits any reference. An Archbishop Bertaldus of Besançon was deposed at the synod of Mainz in the autumn of 1049 (see Jaffé-Loewenfeld, no. 4188, for the text); this Bertaldus may be the same archbishop whose ignominious expulsion from Besançon was vividly recounted by Thietmar of Merseburg in his *Chronicon*, VII. 28 (384). Neither of these figures, however, is a particularly good candidate for possessor and patron of the Berlin Hodegetria.

[34] Only one charter remains from Berthold's episcopacy. On the charters and chancery of the Toul bishops in general, see Michel Parisse, "Importance et richesse des chartes épiscopales: Les exemples de Metz et de Toul, des origines à 1200," in *À propos des actes d'évêques. Hommage à Lucie Fossier*, ed. Michel Parisse (Nancy: Presses Universitaires de Nancy, 1991), 19–44, esp. 34–41. We have not been able to consult the thesis of Andreas Schoellen, *Les actes des évêques de Toul des origines à 1069* (Thèse du doctorat, Université de Nancy, 1985). In a letter of 5 September 2000, however, Professor Parisse confirmed the lack of both contemporary charter evidence and studies on Berthold's episcopacy. On the forgery of an imperial privilege granted to Berthold in 1011, see Rainer Maria Herkenrath, "Das Diplom Kaiser Heinrichs II. für Bischof Berthold von Toul," *DA* 28 (1972): 537–42.

[35] On the textual history of the *Gesta*, see Joachim Dahlhaus, "Zu den Gesta Episcoporum Tullensium," in *Papstgeschichte und Landesgeschichte: Festschrift Hermann Jakobs*, ed. Joachim Dahlhaus and Armin Kohnle (Cologne: Böhlau, 1995), 177–94. For an extended look at the *Gesta*'s *Tendenz*, see now Hans-Werner Goetz, *Geschichtsschreibung und Geschichtsbewußtsein im hohen Mittelalter* (Berlin: Akademie Verlag, 1999), 304–11. On the develop-

The author begins by alerting his reader to the fact that Berthold was of Swabian origin and had "most noble parents." Having made himself "outstanding in religion" as the disciple of Bishop Adalbero II of Metz,[36] Berthold was elected by the chapter of Toul and appointed bishop by decree of Otto III in 996, a career path that already suggests access to court circles and royal favor.[37] Diligent in instructing his clergy, affable in his disposition, and prudent in affairs, Berthold—or rather his textual portrait—conforms in every respect to that of the model Ottonian prelate.[38] Yet most important to the author of the *Gesta*—and, one may argue, within the social memory of the diocese—was Berthold's role as the restorer, amplifier, and embellisher of Toul's sacred spaces. Thus the author exclaimed:

> Who can make plain with any reasonable expression how prudent and cautious he was in disposing all his affairs, what kind and how many ornaments he acquired for his church, with what buildings he expanded the cloister of his clergy, with what benefits he increased his see?[39]

---

ment and characteristics of the genre of the *Gesta episcoporum* more generally, see Sot, *Gesta episcoporum, Gesta abbatum*.

[36] Further evidence for the closeness of the relationship between Berthold and Adalbero may be gleaned from these bishops' shared use of the monastic reformer William of Volpiano to reform monasteries within their dioceses. On this, see Radulfus Glaber, *Vita Domini Willelmi Abbatis*, c. 9 and 11, in idem, *Opera*, ed. and trans. France *et al*. 276 and 284. On Adalbero as a monastic reformer, see now John Nightingale, *Monasteries and Patrons in the Gorze Reform: Lotharingia c. 850–1000* (Oxford: Oxford University Press, 2001), 71–86. For an extended discussion of monastic reform in Toul prior to Bishop Berthold's tenure as bishop, see ibid., 109–68.

[37] *Gesta episcoporum Tullensium*, ed. Georg Waitz in MGH *SS* VIII (Hannover: Hahn, 1848), c. 36 (642): "Nam votis utriusque fidelium ordinis, aspirante clementia divinae maiestatis, triumphatoris invicti, domini videlicet Ottonis tercii augusti, decreto statuente, domnus Bertoldus nobilissimis Alemannorum natalibus ortus, in sancta religione conspicuus, per Dei providentiam electus, in hac sede est 5. Idus Octobris [996] pontifex ordinatus." On his election, see Eugène Martin, *Histoire des diocèses de Toul, de Nancy et de Saint-Dié*, vol. 1, *Des origines à la réunion de Toul à la France* (Nancy: A. Crépin-Leblond, 1900), 182, with further references. Although he is not mentioned in the *Gesta*, the importance of Berthold's mentor, Bishop Adalbero II of Metz, in supporting his promotion both in Toul and at court should not be undervalued.

[38] On which see Jaeger, *The Origins of Courtliness*, 28–48.

[39] *Gesta Episcoporum Tullensium*, c. 36 (642): "Quis autem queat ullo rationis affatu pandere, quam prudens et cautus fuerit in omni sua re disponenda, quae et quanta suae ecclesiae acquisierit ornamenta, quibus aedificiis claustrum sui cleri adornaverit, quibus emolumentis suam sedem amplificaverit?"

Later, when describing the bishop's construction of the monastery of the Savior in the Vosges, he offered the general assessment that Berthold had enriched the foundation "most fittingly with diverse ecclesiastical adornments."[40] When he came to recount the improvements that the bishop had wrought in the interior of his cathedral, however, the author of the *Gesta* was more specific: "He polished the vaults with wondrous beauty, he adorned the high altar incomparably with the gleam of gold and gems, and he acquired innumerable kinds of vessels, the beauty and multitude of which were beyond any reckoning."[41]

This chronicler was not the only one to associate Berthold with the material enhancement of the church of Toul. The late eleventh-century life of Pope Leo IX (formerly Bruno of Toul) also portrayed Berthold, Leo's early spiritual father and master, as "that pursuer of genuine honor and man more wondrous than his predecessors who ennobled the city of Toul with the sons of the nobility and truly expanded its treasures and honor in diverse forms. . . ."[42] Sketching a similar portrait of Berthold as an ambitious and acquisitive prelate only in order to condemn it, the twelfth-century author of the *Book on the Successors of St. Hildulf at Moyenmoutier* described Berthold as a man "particularly set upon worldly honor, second to none in the building of new and outstanding structures, and . . . a wily oppressor of the common people and monasteries."[43] Berthold's

---

[40] *Ibid.*: "Cenobium quoque in honore sancti Salvatoris in saltu Vosago construxit, quod diversis ecclesiasticis ornamentis decentissime locupletavit. . . ." The use of the superlative "decentissime" in the context of decoration resonates strikingly with the "redimitus honore decenti" of the Berlin ivory's inscription. Could the author have been inspired by the ivory on the cover of the cathedral's gospel book to associate Berthold with the idea of fitting adornment?

[41] *Ibid.*, c. 6 (643): "Valvas suae sedis miro polivit decore, altare summum incomparabiliter exornavit auri ac gemmarum fulgore, innumerabilia vasorum adquisivit genera pulchritudine et multitudine nullo precio taxanda."

[42] *La Vie du Pape Léon IX (Brunon, évêque de Toul)*, ed. Michel Parisse [Les Classiques de l'Histoire de France au Moyen Age 38] (Paris: Les Belles Lettres, 1997), c. 2 (10): "Qui videlicet Bertoldus genuinae honestatis sectator mirabilis prae suis decessoribus Leucam urbem filiis nobilium nobilitavit, in diversis speciebus thesauros eius et decus valde ampliavit, aedificiis quamplurimis decoravit. . . .." This comment refers to the presence of noble youths preparing for ecclesiastical careers, including Bruno himself, who were likely sent to Toul because of the reputation of its school.

[43] *Chronicon Mediani monasterii, alias Liber de successoribus S. Hildulfi in Mediano monasterio*, ed. Georg Waitz in MGH *SS* IV (Hannover: Hahn, 1841), c. 12 (91–92): "Successor vero eius in pontificatu extitit Bertoldus natione Suevus, honestati seculi praecipue intentus, in constructione atque eminentium fabricarum nulli secundus, in solitis legibus oppressor

acquisitive urge also appears later in the *Gesta*, but this time as an aspect of the bishop's personality that had inspired later episcopal action. In describing Bishop Udo, who succeeded Bruno in the see of Toul, the author of the *Gesta* claimed that Udo had modeled his own zeal for acquisition on the *mores* of his great predecessor Berthold, an act of *imitatio patrum* that appears fully realized in "multiplying the church's adornments and revenues."[44]

In sum, Bishop Berthold was remembered in Toul as a man of ambition, with an eye for beauty, a taste for precious ornament, and the ability to muster the resources to satisfy both. What were these resources? Although the acquisition of new lands and rights naturally provided the long-term economic foundation for Berthold's embellishment of his church, it was his *familiaritas* at the courts of Otto III and Henry II that would have been his most important asset, especially in the acquisition of an object like the Berlin Hodegetria plaque.[45] As noted above, Berthold's ascent was remembered to have had the court of Otto III as one of its way stations.[46] Unfortunately nothing further is known of the nature and duration of the relationship between the prelate and this emperor. Yet in evaluating Berthold's rise to power, one should not underestimate the potential significance of his six years as bishop under Otto III.

Berthold's amicable relationship with Henry II, by contrast, has left considerably more traces. The author of the *Gesta*, for example, recorded three occasions on which the bishop obtained properties, tolls, or valuable hunting and mining rights from Henry.[47] Berthold also played an active role in ecclesiastical

---

vulgi et monasteriorum versutus qui Mediano coenobio irrecuperabilem calamitatem intulisse dinoscitur."

[44] *Gesta episcoporum Tullensium*, c. 43 (645): "Studebat etiam [Udo] mores domni Bertoldi in multiplicandis reditibus et ornamentis ecclesiae suae sedis pro posse imitari. . . ."

[45] Effenberger, "Byzantinische Kunstwerke," provides a useful overview of the kinds of Byzantine objects that entered Ottonian royal episcopal treasuries and their patterns of distribution. In his life of Bishop Bernward of Hildesheim, Thangmar offers explicit evidence for the role of Otto III's court as a center for the study, and perhaps acquisition, of exotica from other regions of the world: "Picturam vero et sculpturam et fabrilem atque clusoriam artem, et quicquid elegantius in huiusmodi arte excogitare poterat, numquam neglectum patiebatur, adeo ut ex transmarinis et ex Scotticis vasis, quae regali maiestati singulari dono deferebantur, quicquid rarum vel eximium reperiret, incultum transire non sineret"; *Vita Sancti Bernwardi episcopi*, c. 6, in *Lebensbeschreibungen einiger Bischöfe des 10.-12. Jahrhunderts*, ed. Kallfelz, 282.

[46] See note 37.

[47] *Gesta Episcoporum Tullensium*, c. 36 (642): "Idem impetravit ab imperatore Heinrico et bannum venationis super Mosam fluvium, a Segintensi comitatu usque Sorciacum. Ipse reim-

affairs under Henry II, participating in both the reforming synod at Thionville in 1004[48] and in the synod at Frankfurt in 1007,[49] at which Henry realized his dream of transforming Bamberg into a bishopric. Berthold may also have been among the "bishops of the Moselle region" who, according to Adalbold's *Life of King Henry II*,[50] showed early support for the new king by attending his coronation in 1002.

The bishop of Toul's access to royal favor is further confirmed, albeit somewhat indirectly, by the author of the chronicle of the community of Moyenmoutier mentioned earlier. As he narrated the monastery's financial woes during Berthold's episcopacy, the author claimed that the community's well-meaning abbot, eager to regain a valuable piece of land that had escaped the community's control, sought the advice of the bishop of Toul on the strategy to use when approaching the emperor. Treacherously, Berthold advised him to offer the emperor a *servitium* far beyond the monastery's means, only then to press his own claims to the property once the monastery had acquired it. Whether a true account or not, the logic of the narrative depends on Berthold's acknowledged reputation as a man who knew the emperor's court, mind, and favor.[51]

None of this evidence, of course, explicitly confirms the award of a Byzantine ivory plaque to the bishop of Toul by a generous Ottonian king, and one would not expect it to do so, given the relative paucity of information on what

---

petravit ab eodem imperatore reddi ecclesiae suae villam in Halsacio sitam quae vocatur Berchem, et theloneum et districtum minae. Adquisivit . . . a praefato imperatore quicquid in Caulei villa videbatur habere." On the authenticity of Henry's grant of hunting rights on the Maas to Berthold (who is called *venerabilis* in the charter), see Herkenrath, "Das Diplom," 537–41, with an edition of the charter at 541.

[48] Martin, *Histoire des diocèses*, 188, citing Constantine of St. Symphorian, *Vita Adalberonis II episcopi Mettensis*, ed. Georg Pertz in MGH SS IV, (Hannover: Hahn, 1841), c. 37 (672): ". . . accurrente etaim domno Bertaldo Leuchorum venerabili pontifice, qui quod sic leniter dulcissimeque ab eodem enutritus sit, donec ad apicem pontificatus proveheretur. . . ."

[49] See MGH *Const* I, ed. Ludwig Weiland (Hannover: Hahn, 1893), 59–61.

[50] Adalbold of Utrecht, *De rebus gestis S. Henrici imperatoris*, c. 11 (*PL* 140: 92). Martin, *Histoire des diocèses*, 188, rightly emphasizes the ambiguity of this passage.

[51] *Chronicon Mediani monasterii*, 92: ". . . praefatus abbas tempore Heinrici principis ratus sibi divinitus offerri occasionem repossendi praedii Bercheim ab iniquis diu possessi, suasu praedicti Bertoldi enorme servicium exibuit imperatori." Interestingly, to fulfill this obligation, the abbot was obliged to strip *omne ornamentum* from the crosses, candelabras, the resting place of St. Hildulf, and the monastery's reliquary. There is no indication of what was done with these pieces, but it is not unreasonable to imagine that they were acquired by Bishop Berthold.

must have been an almost constant stream of precious gifts flowing between the king, his ecclesiastical and lay magnates, and monastic institutions.[52] But the available evidence shows both that Berthold of Toul was well-positioned within the network of royal patronage to receive such a gift and that he was a man who, via the acquisition of precious materials, had successfully realized a number of ambitious artistic projects within his diocese.

That Berthold would have been able to acquire the Hodegetria plaque at some point during his episcopacy seems entirely plausible. And during the kingship of Henry II, who has been called "the greatest patron of the arts among the Saxon and Salian emperors," such an acquisition is made even more likely by the fact that Henry is known to have dispersed many such precious objects from his treasury.[53] Furthermore, Henry is recognized for his regular use of late antique, Carolingian, and Byzantine ivories.[54] For example, on the covers of gospel books donated to the cathedral of Bamberg and to the palace chapel at Aachen, respectively, his craftsmen deployed a magnificent Carolingian plaque depicting the Crucifixion, the Women at the Tomb, and the Resurrection (fig. 3) and the central member of a tenth-century Byzantine triptych depicting the Hodegetria (fig. 4). Two further tenth-century Byzantine plaques representing the Hodegetria and applied to book covers are also associated with Henry II and his Bamberg craftsmen.[55] As is well known, sixth-century ivories, perhaps from the

---

[52] A transaction of this sort seems more likely to have been the occasion of the Hodegetria's acquisition than the residence at Toul of Greek monks, emigrés who seem to have begun arriving during the episcopate of Bishop Gerard (963-94). On their presence and the liturgical arrangements made to accommodate them, see Patricia M. McNulty and Bernard Hamilton, "Orientale lumen et magistra latinitas: Greek influence on Western Monasticism (900-1100)," in *Le millénaire du Mont Athos, 963-1963: Études et mélanges*, vol. 1 (Venice: Editions de Chevetogne, 1963), 199 and 214.

[53] Peter Lasko, *Ars Sacra, 800-1200*, 2nd ed. (New Haven: Yale University Press, 1994), 123. Henry II's artistic patronage has recently received further treatment in *Kaiser Heinrich II. 1002-1024*, ed. Josef Kirmeier, Bernd Schneidmüller, Stefan Weinfurter, and Evamaria Brockhoff (Bamberg: Konrad Theiss Verlag, 2002), esp. 52-92.

[54] This, of course, is not to suggest a focus on this one material. The vertical enamel plaques depicting Christ, the apostles, and the evangelists that surround the Carolingian ivory on the front of Henry's gospel book (Munich, Bayerische Staatsbibliothek, Clm 4452; fig. 3), which are referred to in its peripheral inscription, seem originally to have adorned a Byzantine crown or diadem. See Olle Källström, "Ein neuentdecktes Majestätsdiadem ottonischer Zeit," *Münchner Jahrbuch der bildenden Kunst*, ser. 3, 2 (1951): 61-72.

[55] See *Heinrich II.*, ed. Kirmeier et al, 341-44 and nos. 172 (cover of Bamberg, Staatsbibliothek, Misc. Lit. 1) and 173 (Bamberg, Historisches Museum, pl. 3/1). On the Byzantine crafting of these ivories, see Cutler, *Hand of the Master*, 181-82.

treasury of Otto III, were newly installed on the ambo which Henry installed in the royal chapel at Aachen.[56] Nor was the king's munificence with ivory limited to explicitly imperial foundations, for, as Thietmar of Merseberg rejoiced to recollect:

> King Henry increased our church with many useful things, and liturgical objects above all. . . . He gave us a gospel book adorned with gold and an ivory plaque (*eburnea tabula*), a golden chalice well encrusted with gems with a paten, and a *fistula*.[57]

Henry, in other words, was a king with access to ivory plaques, ancient and modern, and an established practice of awarding them to ecclesiastical foundations. It therefore seems reasonable to conjecture that Berthold, an early and enduring supporter of Henry's reign and ecclesiastical policy and a known beneficiary of the king's patronage in other respects, received the Hodegetria plaque as a token of Henry's esteem or reward for service rendered.

Whether he was awarded the ivory already mounted in a book cover, as a single plaque, or as part of a triptych, the wings of which remain as yet unidentified or lost, Berthold's past experience and contemporary milieu would have equipped him to put such a gift to good use. While still serving Bishop Adalbero II in Metz, he would have been exposed to some of the finest products of the local school of ivory carving,[58] as well as to contemporary works such as the Crucifixion plaque now in the Metz Museum that has been attributed to Berthold's superior, Adalbero (fig. 5). From the Adalbero Crucifixion (or its sponsor), Berthold could also have learned that it was a bishop's prerogative to inscribe, and thereby memorialize, his name in ivory: on the window at the base of the cross his mentor had had carved *Adalbero crucis xpi servus*.[59]

---

[56] On the *ambo*, see the fundamental study by Ilene Forsyth, "Art with History: The Role of *Spolia* in the Cumulative Work of Art," in *Byzantine East, Latin West*, ed. Moss and Kiefer, 153–62; and Mathews, "Expressing Political Legitimacy," 159–62.

[57] Thietmar, *Chronicon*, VI.102 (350): "Henricus enim rex ecclesiam nostram multis utilitatibus adauxit, in primis divino apparatu; et de omnibus curtis, quas in Thuringia et in Saxonia habuit, duas nobis tradidit familias. Evangelium auro et tabula ornatum eburnea et calicem aureum atque gemmatum cum patina dedit et fistula, cruces duas et ampulas ex argento factas et magnum calicem ex eodem metallo cum patina simul ac fistula dedit."

[58] On the Metz workshops, see Lasko, *Ars Sacra*, 35–40, 59–62, and note 63.

[59] For a brief discussion of this piece and the problems of attribution, see *ibid.*, 114.

Additional evidence suggests other endeavors involving ivory that should be assigned to the time of Berthold's episcopate. A fragment of a long overlooked handwritten label on the back of a well-worn ivory plaque depicting the Crucifixion and the Women at the Tomb, now housed in the Cathedral treasury at Nancy (fig. 6), establishes that it arrived there from the cathedral of Toul.[60] Although the date of this ivory is still debated, it has recently been assigned on stylistic grounds to the period around 1010.[61] If this dating is correct, it is likely that the Nancy plaque, which is believed to have been part of the cover of a luxurious Carolingian lectionary,[62] should also be associated with the episcopacy of Berthold of Toul, whether as a gift to him or his church or his own commission.

Equipped with both object and inspiration, and bishop of a see in the artistically vibrant Middle Rhine region, Berthold would have been ideally positioned socially and geographically to realize his own agenda for the Berlin Hodegetria. He might have turned, for example, to the artisans of Metz, his former home and Toul's ecclesiastical neighbor. As bishop of Toul and suffragan of the archbishop of Trier, Berthold would also have had access to workshops and craftsmen who had become skilled in ivory carving under the patronage of Egbert, archbishop from 977 to 993.[63] That contemporaries could and did turn to such regional artistic centers, and to Egbert's Trier in particular, for the production of luxury objects intended for local use is clearly attested in a series of letters written by Gerbert of Aurillac to Egbert on behalf of Archbishop Adalbero of Reims that trace the course of such a commission—a cross—from the moment of the

---

[60] Jacques Choux, "Plaque de reliure d'un évangéliaire carolingien de la cathédrale de Toul," *Annales de l'Est* (1958): 65–67; reprinted in *La Lorraine chrétienne au moyen âge: Recueil d'études* (Metz: Editions Serpenoise, 1981), 327–29. The fragmentary label (at 328) now reads: "couverture / missel de / [cathé]drale de Toul." The deluxe manuscripts of Toul's cathedral were dispersed at the time of the French Revolution.

[61] Lasko, *Ars Sacra*, 121–22 and n. 59. See also Ulrike Surmann, "Der Meister der Wiener Gregortafel," in *Egbert, Erzbischof von Trier, 977-993*, ed. Ronig, 2: 207 and note 8, with earlier literature.

[62] Choux, "Plaque de reliure," 328–29.

[63] On ivory carving in Egbert's Trier, see Ulrike Surmann, *Studien zur ottonischen Elfenbeinplastik in Metz und Trier* (Witterschlick and Bonn: M. Wehle, 1990), and *idem*, "Der Meister der Wiener Gregortafel," 207–29.

initial request to the rendering of thanks and praise for a job well done.[64] The archbishop first asked Egbert to employ his great skill and artistry to "ennoble our meager matter" with the addition of glass and the artisan's elegant craft,[65] later adding that he hoped that the cross had been "elaborated through your knowledge."[66] His hopes were fulfilled, and when, late in 988, he wrote again to Egbert to inquire after his health, he made explicit the meaning of such artistic collaboration: "Thus does our holy society remain one, feeling the same thing. Nor are we alone in perceiving your affection for us. They, too, sense it who gaze with great delight upon the admirable work of the cross which you elaborated at our request. In it the pledge of friendship desires eternity for itself."[67] Episcopal affection also found its expression in the decoration of book covers; a letter from late 987 records that Adalbero had also turned to his colleague in Trier for the improvement of a sacramentary, asking that it be "very handsomely decorated in gold."[68]

Trier thus emerges from Gerbert's correspondence as a recognized regional center in the late tenth century for the luxury adornment of both books and objects; and what was known to and possible for the archbishop of Reims would have been all the more so for the bishop of the nearby diocese of Toul. More importantly, such artistic commissions are revealed in the letters to be not simply possible but indeed an integral element of the economy of episcopal friendship. It is clear, therefore, that as bishop in Toul Berthold would have had knowledge of and access to several important centers of artistic production

---

[64] *Epp.* 104, 106, 126, in Gerbert of Aurillac, *Correspondance*, ed. Pierre Riché and Jean P. Callu [*Les Classiques de l'Histoire de France au Moyen Age* 35] (Paris: Les Belles Lettres, 1993), 1: 254–55, 258–59, 302–3.

[65] *Ibid., Ep.* 104 (254): "Exiguam materiam nostram magnum ac celebre ingenium vestrum nobilitabit, cum adjectione vitri, tum compositione artificis elegantis." The phrase *adjectione vitri* probably refers to the addition of enamel work.

[66] *Ibid., Ep.* 106 (258): "Et quoniam per Verdunum iter nobis est, eo crucem vestra scientia, ut speramus, elaboratam, si fieri potest, kl. novemb. dirigite."

[67] *Ibid., Ep.* 126 (302): "Sic sancta societas unum et idem sentiens manet. Nec nos soli dulcem affectum vestrum circa nos sentimus. Sentiunt et illi qui admirabile opus cruces a vobis nostro nomini elaboratae, non sine magna oblectatione conspiciunt, in quo pignus amicitiae aeternitatem sibi affectat."

[68] *Ibid., Ep.* 108 (262): "Sit etiam is qui relator nostrorum librorum esse debet, sacramentalis auro decentissime insigniti lator . . . ." The use of the term *decentissime* is noteworthy for its resonance with the Berlin Hodegetria's *honore decenti*, a convergence in language suggesting that contemporary prelates thought about the decoration of their books and other objects in terms of "that which was fitting."

skilled in the working of ivory. Furthermore, he participated in an episcopal culture that looked upon such exchanges as a normal and desirable way of communicating esteem and demonstrating *amicitia*.

While the workshop where Berthold had the ivory plaque inscribed cannot be located with certainty, what we can know for certain, again from the *Gesta* of the bishops of Toul, is that these bishops actively commissioned works of art. His immediate successor Hermann, although unable to rival Berthold's acquisitions of land, was remembered for having commissioned a "chalice of wondrous beauty" to be made from "no small quantity of gold," as well as silver crowns intended for distribution to each abbot along with many *pallia* of diverse kinds.[69] Likewise, we recall that Berthold himself adorned the high altar of his cathedral with gold and gemstones, a project that clearly required skilled craftsmen.[70] In other words, whether at Trier, Metz, or elsewhere, the early eleventh-century bishops of Toul made active and well-attested use of what were probably local workshops and craftsmen, capable of producing high quality work in gold, silver, and textiles. To add ivory to this list seems logical, given the record of carving in this material at Trier in the late tenth century.

The available evidence thus supports the identification of our unidentified Bertoldus with Berthold of Toul. He possessed the social connections, status, and career that would have offered many opportunities to obtain an ivory such as the Berlin Hodegetria. Furthermore, he came of age as a cleric and ruled as a bishop in a cultural milieu that would have afforded him the personal experience as well as the material and technical resources necessary to adapt the Berlin plaque to his own artistic and ideological ends. Finally, and most important, Berthold was part of a group of bishops that included Adalbero of Metz, Egbert of Trier, Bernward of Hildesheim, and Notker of Liège,[71] who pursued the artis-

---

[69] *Gesta episcoporum Tullensium*, 643: "Is quamquam nichil praediorum suae ecclesiae adquisierit . . . tamen eam diversis pro posse suo decoravit ornamentis. Nam sedi domus sancti Stephani contulit non minimam auri quantitatem, de quo disposuerat fieri miri decoris calicem. Singulis etiam abbatiis suae dioceseos argenteas adtribuit coronas, amplians eas palliorum diversitate numerosa." It should be noted that Hermann's gift of gold to the see of the house of St. Stephen had come in the form of an ornate chalice (as is indicated by the pluperfect tense of *disposuerat*).

[70] See above, note 41.

[71] Art historians have long assigned to Notker's episcopate (972–1008) the ivory plaque that bears his name; see Adolph Goldschmidt, *Die Elfenbeinskulpturen aus der Zeit der karolingischen und sächsischen Kaiser (VIII.–XI. Jahrhundert)*, vol. 2 (Berlin: Bruno Cassirer, 1918), 6 and nos. 4, 50–57. This dating has been questioned, however, by scholars who note the in-

tic enhancement of both their dioceses and the Ottonian Empire with heightened energy, creativity, and self-consciousness.[72]

An Epigraphic Community

That the modern scholar can even begin to associate Berthold of Toul with the Berlin Hodegetria depends entirely upon Berthold's decision to add those lines of self-reflexive verse to the frame of the ivory plaque. While the full contemporary significance of these verses remains to be demonstrated, before undertaking such a demonstration it is worth pausing a moment to consider the epigraphic means employed by the Ottonian carver to celebrate Berthold's act. First, the inscription must be understood as a statement written for and addressed to a specific audience, namely, those who would hold, or at least admire from afar, the magnificent manuscript on which the ivory is set, namely, Berthold's own clergy and his episcopal successors. Second, it should be seen as an arrogation of the visual capital of the ivory's surface, a *prise de possession*, and thus an assertion of power.[73] Once marked with this inscription, the ivory's association with Berthold could be neutralized only by risking damage to the object itself. At the same time, Berthold's willingness to inscribe the plaque, and thereby to rewrite its significance, indicates that he did not fetishize the artifact. The inscription does not focus the viewers' attention on the content or quality of the

---

congruity of the surrounding inscription, which describes a Notker oppressed by the burden of sin, and the halo surrounding the head of the figure intended to represent the bishop. For discussion and relevant literature, see Lasko, *Ars Sacra*, 171–75, esp. 171–73, who prefers a date of *ca.* 1100.

[72] The bishops' heightened sense of themselves as cultural impresarios for both Church and Empire is best glimpsed, of course, in Thangmar's *Vita Bernwardi*, esp. c. 6. Here Thangmar praises Bernward's efforts to acquire and to produce the finest work possible in manuscript illumination, sculpture, metalwork, and architecture as "divine": it is activity that honors Christ even as it fills the Hildesheim treasury. Just as monks are to pray without ceasing, so Bernward seems to "create without ceasing." Yet his creations were meant to honor not solely the Church, as Thangmar notes, drawing on Matthew 22:21 ("Render unto Caesar the things that are Caesar's, and unto God, the things that are God's"), but also the *imperium* of the Ottonians: "Et cum in Christi gazophilacio quaeque idonea scivit fideli devotione congereret, non minus tamen caesari sua iuxta euangelium persolvebat. Nam tercio Ottoni imperatori affectuosissimo animo pro scire ac posse obsequebatur."

[73] On the political functions of public inscriptions in Italy from the eleventh century onward, see Armando Petrucci, *La scrittura: Ideologia e rappresentazione* (Turin: G. Einaudi, 1986); trans. Linda Lappin as *Public Lettering: Script, Power, and Culture* (Chicago: The University of Chicago Press, 1993).

ivory itself nor does it do more than allude to the content of the manuscript between the book covers: *omnis textus evangelii* is the grammatical subject of the sentence, but it is graphically enfolded within phrases that emphasize who the patron was and what he had done (*Presulis imperiis Bertoldi . . . redimitus honore decenti*). In short, the inscription speaks of the patron and the way he has used, not reused, the object.

Berthold's decision to use his precious Byzantine ivory as a field on which to register his claim to possess book and cover was a subtle assertion of power. In doing so, he offered tangible evidence of his confidence that his episcopal power and the memory of it would prevent his gift from becoming a victim of destruction or theft. For as fellow bishops and even popes well knew and anxiously remembered, their manuscript treasures were vulnerable to a wide range of adverse fates. A passage in the *Liber pontificalis* on the gifts of Pope Benedict III (855–58), for example, records that the pope:

> saw that the holy church had suffered the theft or loss of the cover of that volume in which the readings from the apostle Paul's true preaching, and the epistles of the other apostles and prophets are set out in order. . . . He became greatly anxious and worked energetically to prepare another volume of like worth. To it he ordered that Greek and Latin readings be added. . . . Decorating it with silver panels of wondrous workmanship, he freely presented it to the Roman church.[74]

Given such perils, the manner and substance of Berthold's offering evince his belief that the gift would remain in Toul in perpetuity, secure through the ages owing to the stability of the ecclesiastical order of which he was a part.

Yet, timeless as the newly adorned volume may have seemed to the Bishop of Toul and his peers, the inscription, like the plaque on which it is written, inevitably bears the marks of its time. To interpret such signs is the domain of epi-

---

[74] See *Benedictus III*, in *Le Liber pontificalis*, ed. Louis Duchesne (Paris: E. Thorin 1892), 2: 147: "tectum scilicet voluminis in quo constant vere predicationibus, Pauli videlicet apostoli, et aliorum epistolas atque prophetarum ordinabiliter constitute lectiones . . . raptum vel perditum a sancta ecclesia fuisse percipiens, captum cum magna vehementer sollicitudine, oc [sic] tale dignum similiter volumen praeparare studuit, in quo grecas et latinas lectiones . . . scriptas adiungi praecepit, mire que operationibus tabulis argenteis decenter adornans sancta ecclesiae Romanae libenter optulit." The translation given here is that of Raymond Davis, *The Lives of the Ninth-Century Popes* (Liverpool: Liverpool University Press, 1995), 185.

graphy, a discipline often devoted to matters of dating,[75] which, however, also has the capacity to establish an artifact's place in a cluster of related objects—an "epigraphic community". It would be farfetched, of course, to suppose that those trained to carve inscriptions on ivory (or to inscribe texts in other materials) did so with the deliberate aim of relating their handiwork to that of others. Nonetheless, the specificity of their epigraphic creations, e.g., the characteristic shape of letter forms and the arrangement of particular graphic signs—precisely because they were the product of ingrained habit—offer the interested observer a too little tapped means of tracing an object's adornment to a given cultural milieu.[76]

Berthold's inscription can be usefully compared to those on other Ottonian works. A simple, somewhat abraded cross, for example, is evident in the inscription on the ivory bookcover given by Henry II to the cathedral at Bamberg (fig. 3). Crosses traditionally marked the beginning of texts, and one is found in this position at the start of Berthold's inscription (fig. 1). But in the cantons of Berthold's cross there are four dots. This device is found earlier, at the beginning of the dedication inscription on the reverse of the Byzantine cross-reliquary in Cortona,[77] twice on the coronation page of Henry II's sacramentary in Munich produced at Regensburg between 1002 and 1014,[78] and once on the John page of the lectionary that the abbess Uta presented to her convent at Niedermünster

---

[75] We too have exploited the letter forms for this purpose. See note 27.

[76] Epigraphy is thus, we would argue, a valuable, if hitherto largely neglected, source of "clues" for determining the context of an object's production or adornment, a form of evidence to be employed alongside the more frequently analyzed stylistic and formal elements of an object's imagery and decoration or a manuscript's script. For stimulating reflections on this method in general, see the wide-ranging discussion of Carlo Ginzburg, "Clues: Roots of an Evidential Paradigm," in *Clues, Myths, and the Historical Method*, trans. John and Anne Tedeschi (Baltimore: The Johns Hopkins University Press, 1986), 96–125. On the state of the field of medieval epigraphy, see now Robert Favreau, *Épigraphie médiévale* [*L'atelier du médiéviste* 5] (Turnhout: Brepols, 1997).

[77] Cutler, *Hand of the Master*, color pl. II.

[78] Munich, Bayerische Staatsbibliothek, Clm 4456, fol. 11; see Cohen, *Uta Codex*, fig. 40. The crosses precede the inscriptions at the top of the mandorla above Christ and again in the lower frame beside Henry's right foot. The cantoned cross appears earlier as a device intended to draw attention to the name of Archbishop Everger of Cologne (985–98) on the dedication page of his lectionary; Cologne, Dombibliothek, MS Col. Metr. 143, fol. 3v. See Peter Bloch and Hermann Schnitzler, *Die ottonische Kölner Malerschule*, vol. 1 (Düsseldorf: Schwann, 1967), 13 and color pl. I. Everger had himself depicted in proskynesis, his hands reaching out to the facing leaf where Peter and Paul—their names written in defective Greek—acknowledge his presence.

about a decade later.[79] Given that the device is missing from the bookcover given to Bamberg, and equally absent from the inscription of Henry II's ambo in the palace chapel at Aachen,[80] it is clear that the cantoned cross was not a sign that appeared automatically on splendid objects produced for this king. But other features connect these works with Berthold's inscription.

The letter G in EVANGELII, upside down but perfectly legible, has a notably curved internal "tail" (fig. 1). In shape it resembles the G in COGNOSCERE in the upper border of Henry's dedication on the book cover in Munich (fig. 3), and the same letter is seen in SURGE along the top of his ambo in Aachen.[81] Further, although we are citing letter forms in metal (where epigraphic evolution need not have marched in lockstep with developments in ivory carving), similar curlicues are discovered in the words REGINA and GISELA as repeatedly incised in gold on the altar cross commissioned by Queen Gisela, Henry's II sister, on the tomb of her mother who died in 1006.[82] Further study might yield further associations or reveal additional lines of influence.[83]

Epigraphic conventions employed on the Berthold ivory thus provide a rich, and hitherto untapped, kind of evidence for its relationship with other contemporary works and centers of production. Furthermore, this ivory offers a model of how, when the specific formal character of an inscription is studied in conjunc-

---

[79] Munich, Bayerische Staatsbibliothek, Clm 13601, fol. 89v, at the start of the peripheral inscription in the lower left corner; see Cohen, *Uta Codex*, color pl. 12.

[80] See note 56 above.

[81] For illustrations see the works cited in note 53 above. It is worth remarking that a more luxuriant curl occurs within the G of SURGE in the band below the restored evangelist in the bottom row of plaques and a variant in PROGENIEM above the (original) Mark in the uppermost row. Because of the uncertainty that attaches to the date of the Notker ivory in Liège (cf. note 72 above), we refrain from adducing the form of the letter used there in GENU.

[82] Lasko, *Ars Sacra*, pl. 185; for the same words, with the same letter forms, on the reverse of the cross, see *Schatzkammer der Residenz München: Katalog*, 3rd ed., ed. Herbert Brunner (Munich: Bayerische Verwaltung der staatlichen Schlösser, Garten und Seen, 1970), no. 8 (40), fig. 4. In another epigraphic community—across the border in Capetian France—this form of the letter occurs on the seal of King Robert II as early as 997. See Germain Demay, *Inventaire des sceaux de Normandie* (Paris: Imprimerie nationale, 1881), iv, a reference for which we are grateful to Brigitte Bedos-Rezak.

[83] Thus, for example, the R's with their raised "legs" (PRESULIS, IMPERIIS, etc.) in the Berthold inscription and its be-serifed S's find close counterparts on the diptych in Berlin showing St. Martin and the introduction of church music into the liturgy. See Surmann, "Der Meister der Wiener Gregortafel," 218 and fig. 16, who tentatively assigns this ivory to Trier at the end of the tenth century. But the rounded form of other letters (notably the U in CIUITAS) diverges radically from the angular V on Berthold's plaque.

tion with its content, epigraphy can shed new light on the ways in which medieval objects, especially those resulting from acts of material appropriation, were made to play specific roles in the realization of larger ideological programs. For example, Berthold of Toul and Bernward of Hildesheim each had carved on a Byzantine ivory a message that was presumably of great personal importance. Berthold, in an elegant inscription on an exceptionally precious ivory, all but ignored the image of the Hodegetria and apostles and instead proclaimed his role in the ivory's refashioning. Bernward, in contrast, in an inscription on a much inferior plaque, invoked the threefold powers (TRINA POTESTAS) of those depicted on the plaque—Christ, the Virgin and St. John the Baptist—whom he supplicates, to look kindly upon him (SIS PIA QUESO TUO BERNWARDO) (fig. 7). Thus, while both prelates used the inscription to associate object and self *in aeternum*, the distance between the bishop of Toul's formal record of his own achievement as a patron of elegant adornment and the bishop of Hildesheim's memorial to his pious devotion, is writ large, and literally, upon their ivories.

Objects, Inscriptions, and Episcopal Self-Consciousness

In his invasive designs upon his Byzantine treasure, Berthold was, of course, no isolated case. He shared his passion to mark ivory exotica with a number of his fellow bishops and contemporaries, the most important being his episcopal mentor, Adalbero II of Metz, and colleagues like Bernward and perhaps Notker of Liège. As is well known, the commemoration of the patron or donor of an object was a widespread practice in early medieval art, especially in manuscript illustration. Yet the practice of inscribing the patron's name on the object—at least to judge from extant exempla—was rarely applied to ivory plaques after consular diptychs ceased to be produced in the mid-sixth century.[84] Any words that were inscribed were intended to function as labels, identifying figures depicted and thereby drawing the viewer's attention to the content of the image rather than to the person responsible for its existence.

By contrast, the epigraphic decisions of these late Ottonian bishops seem to represent a marked change in attitude. Rather than leave the object unmarked

---

[84] Not surprisingly, this is most evident in the case of ivories with imperial images such as the plaque in Milan showing Otto II and Theophanu (Lasko, *Ars Sacra*, fig. 127). There are, of course, exceptions such as the Milan *situla* (*ibid.*, fig. 125) where the inscription indicates the name of the patron, Archbishop Gotfredus (975–80), as well as the occasion for which it was made, a reception of the (same?) emperor.

and therefore mute as to its patron, bishops used their ivories to celebrate the fact of their possession and permanently to record their own names. Thus, on the Crucifixion ivory attributed to Adalbero II of Metz (fig. 5), a small inscription wreathing a window (with Adalbero looking out?) at the base of an ornate column both identified the ivory's patron and articulated explicitly the nature of the bishop's piety: "Adalbero, servant of the cross of Christ." Likewise, on the ivory used on the front cover of his Precious Gospels (fig. 7), Bernward, as noted above, inscribed an invocation that transformed the plaque, regardless of any conceivable future situation, into an enduring simultaneous commemoration of both his devotion to Mary, John the Baptist, and Christ and his ability to acquire and dispose of such an object. If the inscription is contemporary, Notker of Liège may have intended to register a similar metamorphosis when he had inscribed: "Behold! I, Notker, a man oppressed by the weight of sin, bow down to you on my knee, you who terrify all things by your will."[85]

The decision by these prelates to inscribe their own names into their ivory treasures created a decisive break in the object's semiotic history and particular visual power.[86] Once inscribed, the ivory was no longer able to serve as a timeless tableau of piety that could be shifted from one context to another without disruption in its visual semiotics, as it had been to a large extent when originally removed from its anonymous setting in a Byzantine triptych. Instead, the inscription permanently conjoined object and patron and thereby established a specific context of use, requiring the viewer to see the ivory, regardless of current owner and current site, as the possession of the bishop who had once owned, dedicated, and transformed it. By including their names in the inscriptions and thereby embedding their persons into the very being of the object itself, these Ottonian bishops thus sought to guarantee that their acts of patronage,

---

[85] See note 71. "EN EGO NOTKERUS PECCATI / PONDERE PRESSUS / AD TE FLECTO GENU QUI TERRES / OMNIA NUTU."

[86] On such breaks, particularly as they occur in the exchange of cultural artifacts, see the illuminating remarks and examples of Igor Kopytoff, "The Cultural Biography of Things: Commoditization as Process," in *The Social Life of Things: Commodities in Cultural Perspective*, ed. Arjun Appadurai (Cambridge: Cambridge University Press, 1986), 64–91, especially 73–77. The inscription of a personal name on the ivory can be seen as a form of "terminal commoditization," rendering the object efficacious in commemorating only one specific owner.

and hence their authority, would be recapitulated, and thus revivified, with each new beholder.[87]

At the same time, they sought to insure that the precious results of their imagination, wealth, and power could not be claimed by others. This can be observed plainly in the inscription on metal on the back of Bernward's Precious Gospels (fig. 8), a cover that replicated, symptomatically, the schema of a Byzantine Hodegetria (e.g. fig. 2). There, surrounding the depiction of the standing figure, he summoned God and the Virgin to become appreciative viewers of his masterpiece: "Look kindly, O God and your nourishing mother, upon the outstanding work made by the craft of Bishop Bernward."[88] Expressing far from humble claims about the quality of the object in its final state and, implicitly, the measure of divine appreciation that was therefore its due, Bernward's inscription called the viewer to witness as the bishop created and dedicated his precious creation anew.

Such an inscription likewise guaranteed that the Precious Gospels, or any other such creation, would not simply become part of the anonymous, albeit glorious, artistic patrimony of a diocese. Artistic and literary elements combined to maintain the presence of the patron. Thus, Archbishop Adalbero of Reims, whose appreciation of the artistry of Egbert of Trier has already been noted, sought to insure that a precious chalice would forever be reckoned to his credit by commissioning the following distich, presumably for inclusion in the decorative scheme: "With this [cup] thirst and famine are put to flight. Hasten to it all ye faithful. Thus does Bishop Adalbero share these treasures among his peo-

---

[87] In their capacity to re-evoke a specific episcopal persona and the historical moment of their act of power, these inscriptions function in a way similar to that which seals come to have. For thought-provoking reflections on seals as a materialization of individual presence, see now Brigitte Bedos-Rezak, "Medieval Identity: A Sign and a Concept,"*American Historical Review* 105 (2000): 1489–1533. In the words of this author (at 1527), "seals embodied the real presence of the individuals who affixed them . . . .. The ego of the author–donor–sealer and his mark are not so much within the text but in consubstantial relationship to it." See also below, chapter seven.

[88] "HOC OPU[S] EXIMIU[M] / BERNWARDI P[RE]SULIS ARTE / FACTU[M]. CERNE D[EU]S. MATER ALMA TUA." It is interesting to note the parallel between the *Bernwardi presulis arte* and the *presulis imperiis Bertoldi* of the Berlin Hodegetria inscription. On Bernward's "Kostbaren Evangeliar," see most recently Holger Klein, "Aspekte der Byzanz-Rezeption im Abendland," in *Byzanz: Die Macht der Bilder*, ed. Michael Brandt and Arne Effenberger (Hildesheim: Staatliche Museen zu Berlin-Preussischer Kulturbesitz, 1998), 122–53 at 131–32 and figs. 127–36.

ple."[89] That without such precautions the memory of such donations was much less stable is nicely exemplified in the case of a Roman cameo depicting the apotheosis of Germanicus, of particular interest here because it pertains to Toul. According to tradition, it is said to have been given to the monastery of Saint-Èvre in this city by Cardinal Humbert, a native of Lorraine and former monk of Moyenmoutier, who may have acquired it when he headed Pope Leo IX's embassy to Constantinople in 1054.[90] Yet, in the absence of an inscription to this effect, Humbert's reputation as benefactor and donor of a specific element to the diocese's artistic riches hangs by tenuous threads of tradition. The epigraphic practices of Bernward, Berthold, and others, by contrast, sought to insure that the growth of the diocese's artistic glory would be a history of specific individuals and actions authenticated in no small measure by the objects themselves.

In the context of such aesthetic and commemorative ambitions, the inscription on the Berlin Hodegetria seems very much at home: "By command of Bishop Berthold / The text of the entire Gospel is enclosed / Garlanded with fitting honor." Like Bernward, Berthold used the inscription to transform the ivory into a record of his own relationship with the object. Yet there is an important difference. Berthold's contemporaries, and his mentor Adalbero, had designed their inscriptions so as to play off the religious content of the images and thereby emphasize the virtues of piety and humility in their relationship with the object. Their epigraphic activity thereby retained, at least in part, the traditional role played by inscriptions on ivory plaques: that of identifying the image and directing the viewer's gaze to the depicted figure or scene. In Berthold's inscription, by contrast, the specific visual content of the ivory itself has been completely neglected; indeed, his inscription leads the reader away from meditation upon the devotional images within the frame and, instead, prompts the viewer's mind to recapitulate the historical moment of the object's commission and to appreciate the final product: the fittingly, because episcopally, bound gospel book. In essence, Berthold consciously appropriated his Hodegetria plaque to announce his authority as bishop and his role as a cultural impresario, while at the same time commemorating his act of largesse (and hence power) and good taste

---

[89] Gerbert. *Ep.* 90 (212): "Distichon in calice. Hinc sitis atque fames fugiunt, properate fideles./ Dividit in populis has praesul Adalbero gazas."

[90] Ernst Babelon, *Catalogue des camées antiques et modernes de la Bibliothèque nationale* (Paris, 1897), 137–40. no. 225, and pls. LXII, LXXIII; Cyril Mango and Marlia Mango, "Cameos in Byzantium," in *Cameos in Context: The Benjamin Zucker Lectures,* ed. Martin Henig and Michael Vickers (Oxford: Ashmolean Museum, 1993), 62.

(and hence aesthetic authority). Through Berthold's inscription, in other words, a portion of the ivory's aesthetic capital was fundamentally reallocated to commemorate his act of artistic patronage itself.

In its explicit celebration of the act of patronage itself and treatment of the material object, Berthold's inscription offers valuable additional evidence for a dimension of Ottonian episcopal self-consciousness that often remains invisible to historians: the bishop's own estimation of his action as a cultural entrepreneur. Such evidence suggests that, far from being passive, even awestruck, possessors of precious objects and exotica, Ottonian bishops like Berthold of Toul, Sigibert of Minden, Egbert of Trier, Adalbero II of Metz, and Bernward of Hildesheim were adept managers of the semiotic and artistic resources available to them and often keenly aware of their own status as key figures in the aesthetic economy of the Empire. It was their power, their piety, and their creativity that brought together ideas, precious materials, and craftsmen to create works worthy of their God and their churches. In the case of ivories like the Berlin Hodegetria, these bishops—whether through careful dismantling and reintegration into broader artistic programs or by manipulating vision, meaning, and memory through inscribed words—collected, co-opted, and compelled the glories of Byzantium and the West to affirm to themselves and to posterity their power as bishops, their creativity and generosity as patrons, and their vital role as *arbitri elegantiarum* in the entity that Maurice Godelier cunningly called "the Holy German Empire."[91]

---

[91] Maurice Godelier, *The Enigma of the Gift*, trans. Nora Scott (Chicago: The University of Chicago Press, 1999), 203.

Fig. 1. Hodegetria, second half of tenth century. Berlin, Museum für Spätantike und Byzantinische Kunst. Photo © Staatliche Museen zu Berlin, Museum für Spätantike und Byzantinische Kunst.

Fig. 2. Hodegetria (detail), second half of tenth century. Utrecht, Rijksmuseum Het Catharijneconvent. Photo © Museum Catharijneconvent.

Fig. 3. Crucifixion ivory (c. 870) on the cover of the Pericope Book of Henry II (before 1014). Munich, Bayerische Staatsbibliothek, MS Clm. 4452. Photo © Bayerische Staatsbibliothek.

Fig. 4. Hodegetria ivory (second half of tenth century), on the cover of the Aachen Gospels. Aachen, Domschatz. Photo by Ann Münchow, © Domkapitel Aachen.

Fig. 5. Ivory of Bishop Adalbero of Metz, 984-1005. Metz, Musée d'art et d'histoire. Photo © Musées de la Cour d'Or, Metz.

Fig. 6. Ivory with Crucifixion and Women at the Tomb, c. 1010 (?). Nancy, Cathedral treasury. Photo from Adolph Goldschmidt, *Die Elfenbeinskulpturen aus der Zeit der karolingischen und sächsischen Kaiser (VIII.-XI. Jahrhundert)*, vol. 1 (Berlin: Bruno Cassirer, 1914), plate 137.

Fig. 7. Front cover of Bernward of Hildesheim's "Precious Gospels" (c. 1000-1010), with Deesis ivory (late tenth century). Hildesheim, Domschatz. Photo © Dom-Museum Hildesheim.

Fig. 8. Rear cover of Berward of Hildesheim's "Precious Gospels". Hildesheim, Domschatz. Photo © Dom-Museum Hildesheim.

Chapter Six
Modelling the Bishop:
Egbert of Trier, Gregory the Great, and the Episcopal Image
Hiltrud Westermann-Angerhausen

Archbishop Egbert of Trier has been a central figure in studies of Ottonian art and culture for more than a century; indeed, the first studies of the staff of St. Peter (now in Limburg) and the so-called Egbert Psalter[1] remain as important for scholars today as the two volumes edited by Franz Ronig on the millennial anniversary of Egbert's death, volumes which sum up much of what we know about the times and personality of this important Ottonian bishop.[2] Yet Egbert of Trier has tended to be seen quite differently by art historians and historians. To the former, Egbert is one of the leading artistic patrons of his time, and the first such patron before the year 1000 whom we can definitively associate with a whole range of high-quality works of representative art. The extraordinary group of manuscripts, book covers, and reliquaries that he commissioned himself or had made in Trier for the empress Theophanu are paradigmatic examples of Ottonian art, making Egbert a pivotal figure for art historians.

On the other hand, historians tend to pity Egbert more than praise him. Egbert's marginal status during his episcopal tenure, both in terms of his family connections and his political alliances, has made him seem less successful than other bishops like Willigis of Mainz or Bernward of Hildesheim.[3] As the son of Count Dietrich of Holland, who owed allegiance to both the French and German crowns, Egbert was sent (essentially as a noble hostage) to the imperial court, where he served in the chancery. He thus received a profound political education under the watchful eye of Otto I's brother Brun, who was not only imperial chancellor but also archbishop of Cologne and "archduke" of Lotharingia.

It was against this backdrop that Egbert was made archbishop of Trier in 977; six years later, he sided with Theophanu's adversaries after Otto II's death and actively supported the cause of Duke Henry "the Quarrelsome" of Bavaria, who had kidnapped the young Otto III shortly after the latter's coronation at Aachen

---

[1] H.V. Sauerland and Arthur Haseloff, *Der Psalter Erzbischof Egberts von Trier. Codex Gertrudiana in Cividale* (Trier: Gesellschaft für nützliche Forschungen, 1901).

[2] *Egbert, Erzbischof von Trier*, ed. Ronig.

[3] See Wolfgang Seibrich, "Egbert als Metropolit und Erzbischof von Trier," in *ibid.*, 2: 187-95.

and claimed the regency for himself. For historians, Henry's surrender at Rara in 984, and his return of Otto III to his mother and grandmother (Adelheid), was tantamount to the end of Egbert's political career. This has led some people to suggest that the archbishop's political failures were compensated for by his dedication to the arts. Franz-Reiner Erkens, for instance, has argued that Egbert gained his fame solely through his support of the arts, while Wolfgang Seibrich has concluded that Egbert's straitened political options turned him into an assiduous artistic patron.[4]

Yet if the image informing such evaluations is that of a modern politician or executive fleeing from the corrupt corridors of power to the higher realms of art and culture, we are on the wrong track. Such distinctions between "politics" and "art" would have been quite foreign to a tenth-century prelate, but even if they were not, it is important to note that most of the works associated with Egbert were completed in the *early* years of his pontificate, between 977 and 984. The extraordinary reliquary housing part of St. Peter's legendary staff can be firmly dated to the year 980, while the so-called "Egbert Shrine," containing many of the cathedral's most precious relics, can be dated on the basis of its metalwork to around the same period.[5] In turn, the most celebrated manuscripts associated with Egbert's scriptorium in Trier and the Reichenau bookpainters whom he patronized can be dated as well to around 980: the "Egbert Psalter" (Cividale del Friuli, Museo Archeologico MS 136), two single leaves depicting the emperor enthroned (Chantilly, Musée Condé MS 14b), and the Trier *Registrum Gregorii*, with its famous image of St. Gregory dictating to his scribe (Trier, Stadtsbibliothek, MS 171/1626).[6] The painter of this latter work, often called the greatest illuminator of the Ottonian period, also worked on the famous *Codex Egberti* (Trier, Stadtsbibliothek, MS 24), which includes a cycle of scenes from the New Testament and a dedication miniature showing Egbert receiving the manuscript from two Reichenau scribes. Finally, as I have argued elsewhere, there is good reason to believe that the brilliant gospelbook of Ste.-Chapelle (Paris, Biblio-

---

[4] Franz-Reiner Erkens, "*In tota cunctis gratissimus aula?* Egbert von Trier als Erzbischof," in *Egbert, Erzbishof von Trier*, ed. Ronig, 2: 40; Seibrich, "Egbert als Metropolit," 195.

[5] Hiltrud Westermann-Angerhausen, *Die Goldschmiedearbeiten der Trierer Egbertwerkstatt* (Trier: Spee-Verlag, 1973), 100.

[6] On book illumination at Trier, see Franz Ronig, "Erzbischof Egbert und die Entstehung seines Evangeliars," in *Codex Egberti: Teilfaksimile des Ms. 24 der Stadtbibliothek Trier*, ed. Gunther Franz and Franz Ronig (Wiesbaden: L. Reichert, 1983), 36-40.

thèque Nationale, MS lat. 8851) dates from the same time, although some scholars contend that it was written two decades later.[7]

Egbert also was active as a builder early in his episcopal tenure. The rebuilding of the abbey of St. Eucharius took place in conjunction with the installation of a new reform abbot from Ghent and the introduction of the Gorze observance around 980;[8] so too did the discovery of a grave containing a certain "Celsus", whom Egbert declared to be a saint. The chapel of St. Andrew on the north side of the cathedral, where Egbert's predecessor Dietrich was buried and where Egbert had a grave site prepared for himself, dates from the same period. Likewise, dendrochronological testing on wood fragments within masonry in the huge columns at the center of the episcopal church suggests that extensive construction work on the already ancient cathedral must have begun early in Egbert's reign.[9]

In fact, the only important piece produced in the Trier workshops after Egbert's assumed "retreat" from important political activity is a bookcover, dedicated to the monastery of St. Willibrord at Echternach, depicting Theophanu and Otto III (bearing the title *rex*) as donors (fig. 9). This item was made before the empress' death in 991, probably after her reconciliation with the archbishop of Trier in 985.[10] Incorporated into the bookcover is one of the most famous ivories of the period, a crucifixion which Wilhelm Vöge has shown to belong to a small but outstanding group of ivory carvings produced before 1000.[11] Another such

---

[7] Hiltrud Westermann-Angerhausen, "Blattmasken, Maskenkapitelle, Säulenhäupter: Variationen über ein vorgegebenes Thema," *Boreas: Münster'sche Studien zur Archäologie* 6 (1983): 208 and notes 4, 9, and 30; cf. Ulrich Kuder, "Die Ottonen in der ottonischen Buchmalerei: Identifikation und Ikonographie," in *Herrschaftsrepräsentation im ottonischen Sachsen*, ed. Gerd Althoff and Ernst Schubert (Sigmaringen: Thorbecke, 1998), 137-234.

[8] See Michel Margue and Jean Schroeder, "Zur geistigen Ausstrahlung Triers unter Erzbischof Egbert," in *Egbert, Erzbischof von Trier*, ed. Ronig, 2: 114.

[9] These fragments have been dated to 989/90; since the capitals are set over 18 meters high, however, construction would have been going on for some time before the wooden scaffolding and the masonry next to it reached the top of the building. On Egbert's work on the cathedral, see Jochen Zink, "Die Baugeschichte des Trierer Doms von den Anfängen im 4. Jahrhundert bis zur letzten Restaurierung," in *Der Trierer Dom*, ed. Gustav Bereths and Franz Ronig (Neuss: Verlag Gesellschaft für Buchdruckerei, 1980), and Franz Ronig, "Der Trierer Dom und sein Verhältnis zur Antike," *Zeitschrift des Deutschen Vereins für Kunstwissenschaft* 44 (1990): 112-23.

[10] Gunther Wolf has suggested that the bookcover was given on the 250th anniversary of Willibrord's death in November 989; see "Zur Datierung des Buchdeckels des Codex aureus epernacensis," *Hémecht* 42 (1990): 147-51.

[11] Wilhelm Vöge, "Ein deutscher Schnitzer des 10. Jahrhunderts," *Jahrbuch der Königlich-preussischen Kunstsammlungen* 20 (1899): 118-25.

group recently has been localized to Trier as well, including a plaque of St. Gregory (now in Vienna) with stylistic ties to the work of the "Master of the *Registrum Gregorii*."[12]

All of these major achievements in architecture, manuscript illumination, and plastic arts thus must be seen in the context of Egbert's political and pastoral activities as a bishop, as well as his interests as a patron of the arts. To explain them simply as aesthetic compensation for the loss of political influence is both inadequate and anachronistic. For Archbishop Egbert, art was not *otium* in the Ciceronian sense, cultivated leisure as opposed to serious business (*negotium*). Rather, art and its patronage were integral parts of the existence and duties of an Ottonian bishop, and art served as an important vehicle for the assertion and communication of status, identity, and intentions. In the remainder of this chapter, I will explore the ways in which these functions were performed by Egbert through the "art of representation"—in particular, the establishment of a representative model (Gregory the Great), the integration of representation and tradition, and the use of art for pastoral ends.[13]

At the outset, it should be noted that the art of representation, in its political and theological aspects, has nothing to do with luxury or simple ostentation. Rather, the art of representation is concerned with showing something, even something that cannot normally be seen. It is a way to demonstrate power, to impart propaganda, and to visualize invisible "things": facts, demands, and intentions. The art of representation played a central role in the many duties of an Ottonian bishop. As such, it was not only manifested in the way that an episcopal patron influenced the decoration of religious and secular buildings, the art applied to liturgical books and hardware, or painting and metalwork in general.

---

[12] Surmann, "Der Meister der Weiner Gregortafel," 207-29.

[13] The concept of "representative art" is one rarely applied in a systematic fashion to art produced under the patronage of high-ranking Ottonian ecclesiastics, despite the fact that many of the same characteristics are shared by portraits of episcopal patrons and contemporary depictions of rulers. See Hiltrud Westermann-Angerhausen, "Heinrich der Löwe: ein Mäzen?" in *Heinrich der Löwe: Herrschaft und Repräsentation*, ed. Johannes Fried and Otto-Gerhard Oexle (forthcoming). For "representative patronage" in the Ottonian and Salian period, see idem, "Die Stiftungen der Gräfin Gertrude: Anspruch und Rang," in *Der Welfenschatz und sein Umkreis*, ed. Johannes Ehlers and Dietrich Kötzsche (Mainz: Philipp von Zabern, 1998), 51-76. On depictions of rulers in Ottonian and Salian bookpainting, cf. Hagen Keller, "Herrscherbild und Herrschaftslegitimation. Zur Deutung der ottonischen Denkmäler," *FmS* 19 (1985): 290-311.

In a very direct way, the art of representation was concerned with the bishop himself, and the way in which he presented his own image to the world.

A good place to begin our analysis is with two famous miniatures of Otto II and Pope Gregory the Great, which together with a dedicatory poem stood at the beginning of an elaborate copy of Gregory the Great's collected letters, the *Registrum Sancti Gregorii* (figs. 10-11). Egbert of Trier had this manuscript produced for Otto II, and also commissioned for it the kind of precious bookcover normally reserved for liturgical books. Due to Otto II's premature death, however, the book never reached its intended recipient. In his analysis of these miniatures, Carl Nordenfalk has shown that the pope assumes the role of advisor vis-à-vis the emperor, but in a very specific fashion. Tracing the pictorial tradition of enthroned rulers back to antiquity, Nordenfalk points out that the ruler normally is approached by advisors who appear opposite him, while persons approaching in salutation or bearing tribute are relegated to a lower level. In the composition produced by the Master of the *Registrum Gregorii*, the emperor is seated in majesty within a ceremonial architectural frame, surrounded by four personifications of provinces subject to his rule. Opposite him, the traditional grouping of advisors addressing the ruler has been replaced by an image of Pope Gregory in a state of divine inspiration, dictating to his scribe. The representative image of the ruler thus is confronted not with courtiers ministering to him, but with a figure equivalent to his own, obviously meant to serve not only as his advisor but as his model as well. The message here is clear: if the emperor rules and enforces the law as God's representative on earth, then he should follow the guidance of a pope who was the model of Christian virtues.[14]

Henry Mayr-Harting recently has emphasized Gregory the Great's importance during the Ottonian period as the ideal figure of the spiritual ruler.[15] Within the reform movement which emanated from Gorze, Gregory's writings were widely known and copied throughout the tenth century; John of Gorze himself, the founder of the Lotharingian monastery whose rulers were to influence monastic reform throughout the Ottonian realm, was said to have known Gregory's *Mora-*

---

[14] Karl Nordenfalk, "Archbishop Egbert's 'Registrum Gregorii'," in *Studien zur Mittelalterlichen Kunst, 800-1200. Festschrift für Florentine Mütherich zum 70. Geburtstag*, ed. Katharina Bierbrauer, Peter Klein, and Willibald Sauerländer (Munich: Prestel-Verlag, 1985), 87-100.

[15] Mayr-Harting, *Ottonian Book Illumination*, 2: 118-23.

lia on Job by heart.[16] It is no coincidence that even before Egbert's time, when the scriptoria and ateliers of Trier became centers of Ottonian art, a monumental edition of this important work was written and lavishly illuminated at the monastery of St. Maximin (c. 970), for it was through this monastery that the Gorze reforms reached religious foundations in Regensburg, Magdeburg, and elsewhere under the direct patronage of Ottonian rulers. In his analysis of the Trier manuscript of the *Moralia*, Joachim Plotzek has traced the development of ornamental initials from straightforward copies of Turonian models to new variations and derivations, which lead us to the ornamental vocabulary of the Master of the *Registrum Gregorii*, who produced the minatures in question.[17]

There are, then, a number of connections between the writings of the sixth-century pope and the art of Egbert's Trier. More importantly, however, Egbert's intended gift to Otto II makes a more explicit connection between the archbishop and Gregory. In the dedicatory poem which accompanied the miniatures, Egbert describes himself as the emperor's friend, advisor, and companion, thus not only placing himself in the role of the author whose works he is giving to Otto, but in fact identifying himself with Gregory. In the words of Carl Nordenfalk, "if [the portrait of Gregory] does not give us an idea of what Egbert looked like in real life, it certainly shows how he would have liked to appear."[18]

Given the analogical and pictorial way of thinking that seems to have prevailed a thousand years ago, this identification is far from astonishing. If an emperor could be described as a new Constantine or Charlemagne, there was no reason why a bishop could not be likened to a great pope. Nevertheless, Egbert's identification with Gregory is notable since it is attested not only by verbal, but also pictorial evidence. In her recent study of the Trier group of ivories, Ulrike Surmann has drawn attention to Egbert's dedication portrait in the Egbert Psalter, where the bishop is depicted with curled locks of hair on either side of his forehead (fig. 12). This small detail, she suggests, was introduced in imitation of Gregory, whose portrait at the monastery of St. Andrew was said by Paul the Deacon to have shown the pope with two curls draped symmetrically on his

---

[16] See John of St.-Arnoul, *Vita Iohannis Gorzie coenobii abbatis*, c. 83, in *La Vie de Jean, abbé de Gorze*, ed. and trans. Michel Parisse (Paris: Picard, 1999), 110.

[17] Joachim Plotzek, "Zur Initialmalerei des 10. Jahrhunderts in Trier und Köln," *Aachener Kunstblätter* 44 (1973): 101-28.

[18] Nordenfalk, "Archbishop Egbert's 'Registrum Gregorii'," 96.

forehead.[19] It cannot be a coincidence, moreover, that Egbert's hairstyle in the dedication portrait from the Egbert Codex (fig. 13) is similar to that found in the Psalter. Thus, whereas the dedication poem in the *Registrum Gregorii* suggests that the bishop is hiding behind the image of a pope, in the Egbert Psalter and the Egbert Codex we are presented with an image of the bishop which echoes a now-lost image of the pope.

Even if Egbert did not know Paul the Deacon's description of Gregory's portrait in Rome, he may well have seen the portrait itself during his sojourn there while a member of the imperial court. This possibility is bolstered by the devotion to St. Andrew's cult in tenth-century Trier as well as Cologne, where Egbert had watched his mentor, Archbishop Brun, found a monastery dedicated to Andrew.[20] Both Trier and Cologne must have had direct ties with the Roman monastery of St. Andrew (founded, notably, by Gregory the Great), and it was likely Egbert himself who brought St. Andrew's sandal to Trier, a relic which is the foremost treasure in the reliquary altar now known as the Egbert Shrine. Francis Dvornik, in his study of the legend of St. Andrew in Byzantium, has demonstrated how important it was for Constantinople to be able to trace its ecclesiastical origins back to an apostle, as Rome was able to do.[21] In turn, towards the end of the tenth century, with the intensification of relations between the Ottonian court and Byzantium, Andrew became a figure of renewed interest—particularly in light of the rivalry between Cologne, Trier, and Mainz to establish their primacy within the German church, when diocesan status and power was linked to claims of apostolic succession and foundation.[22]

Andrew's presence in Trier was established most strikingly by the casket-reliquary which housed his sandal, the so-called "Egbert Shrine" (fig. 14). In the dedicatory inscription on the reliquary, we are told that "This holy receptacle for relics was made at the command of Archbishop Egbert; in it he commanded to

---

[19] Surmann, "Der Meister der Wiener Gregortafel," 219.

[20] On this foundation, see Barbara and Ulrich Kahle, "St. Andreas," in *Köln: Die romanischen Kirchen von den Anfängen bis zum zweiten Weltkrieg*, ed. Hiltrud Kier and Ulrich Krings (Cologne: J.P. Bachem, 1984), 154-82. On Brun's time in Cologne, see Margue and Schroeder, "Zur geistigen Ausstrahlung Triers," 113.

[21] Francis Dvornik, *The Idea of Apostolicity in Byzantium and the Legend of the Apostle Andrew* (Cambridge, MA: Harvard University Press, 1958).

[22] See Egon Boshof, "Köln, Mainz, Trier—Die Auseinandersetzungen um die Spitzenstellung im deutschen Episkopat in ottonisch-salischer Zeit," *Jahrbuch des Kölnischen Geschichtsvereins* 49 (1978): 19-48.

be kept the sacred testimonies [*pignora sancta*]." There then follows a list of the reliquary's contents in what should be the correct protocol—i.e., relics of Christ's passion (particles from the cross and a nail), relics of St. Peter (a hair from his beard and links from his chain), and finally the sandal of Peter's brother, Andrew. Nevertheless, it was this latter relic which was represented on the reliquary itself. There are several reasons to assume that Egbert began his career as a patron (at least of the treasury arts in Trier) with this object, not least because some of the relics mentioned in the inscription were already part of the cathedral treasury, in particular the nail, which is enclosed in its own, beautiful late-Carolingian case.[23] Egbert, whose reforming activities in his new diocese included the restitution of diocesan lands and the reestablishment of monastic and scholarly discipline, seems to have considered the augmentation of his cathedral's liturgical and ritual fittings as another of the duties of his office.

The contents of the Egbert Shrine suggest that it was intended to be the church of Trier's key reliquary. This impression is strengthened by its decoration. On four sides of the casket, we find four variations on the *Maiestas*-scene in reduced, almost pictographic form. The first of these, on the front of the shrine, is a linear composition decorated with pearls, gold, and red glass, of a kind familiar from illuminated Gospel-books—in particular, the *Codex Aureus* produced at St. Emmeram for Charles the Bald (figs. 15-16). There is a striking resemblance between the *Codex*'s incipit page to the Gospel of St. Matthew and the front panel of the shrine, which represents the manuscript's pictorial content in metal and precious stones. In both cases, we are presented with a modified *Maiestas*. Similar parallels can be drawn between this incipit page and the reverse side of the shrine. The former's lion, surrounded by a circular inscription likening the rising lion of Judah to Christ resurrected, is echoed by the latter's gold Justinian solidus, set in a beautiful cruciform garnet decoration, which functions as an image of Christ (fig. 17). This central image is surrounded, as in the *Codex*, by figures of the four evangelists; in turn, these evangelist symbols appear again on large enamels set into ivory on the two long sides of the shrine, flanking the figure of an animal cast in gold. Upon closer examination, this figure turns out to be a tetramorph, with bird's claws, the curly chest of a lion, a bovine tail, and a

---

[23] On this, see Hiltrud Westermann-Angerhausen, "Das Nagelreliqiar im Trierer Egbertschrein—Das 'künstlerisch edelste Werk der Egbertwerkstätte'?" in *Festschrift für Peter Bloch zum 11. Juli 1990*, ed. Hartmut Krohm and Christian Theuerkauff (Mainz: P. von Zabern, 1990), 9-23.

human head, the latter two elements similar to examples from insular manuscript illumination.

On each side of the shrine, therefore, we find versions of the *Maiestas*-motif, Christ accompanied by the four beings. As I have shown elsewhere, the textual idea behind this decoration likely was provided by St. Jerome's "Plures fuisse" prologue to the Gospels, included at the beginning of most Gospel-books in the early Middle Ages.[24] The message of this text, as well as of the four sides of the Egbert Shrine, was the fourfold propagation of the Good News through the four gospels of Matthew, Mark, Luke, and John. This also suggests, however, why a life-sized foot was placed on top of the shrine. The foot, that is, was not only a way to represent the whole person, reminiscent of the votive offerings of antiquity, but also a symbol of apostleship itself: as an early Christian source put it, the apostles' mission to spread the Gospel throughout the world made them the "feet of Christ."[25] By prominently including his name in the dedicatory inscription, Egbert thus integrated himself into a context appropriate to his episcopal calling. His presentation—and representation—of the invisible relic of St. Andrew as the dominant element of an extraordinary reliquary established his participation in the apostolic mission, i.e. the spreading of the Gospel.

A further example of Egbert's visual and conceptual self-representation is provided by the second reliquary produced under his patronage: the staff reliquary of St. Peter, dateable on the basis of its lengthy inscription to 980 (fig. 18).[26] During his time in Cologne, Egbert had witnessed Archbishop Brun's systematic creation of an apostolic, Roman tradition for his church through the use of relics of St. Peter, including a piece of St. Peter's staff obtained from the treasury at Metz for his newly-built cathedral. Ruotger's *Vita Brunonis* records the "love, passion, and joy" with which it was brought to Cologne, and reports that in honor of the event Brun began to enlarge and redecorate the new church.[27] Scholars continue to debate whether a number of documents recording the role

---

[24] Westermann-Angerhausen, "Spolie und Umfeld," 305-36.

[25] Clement of Alexandria, *Christ the Educator*, trans. Simon P. Wood (New York: Fathers of the Church, 1954), II.8 (146-47); cf. Westermann-Angerhausen, "Spolie und Umfeld," 318-20.

[26] For the text of the inscription, see Westermann-Angerhausen, *Goldschmiedearbeiten*, 36.

[27] Ruotger, *Vita sancti Brunonis*, c. 31 (224). Cf. Irmingard Achter, "Die Kölner Petrusreliquien und die Bautätigkeit Erzbischof Brunos am Kölner Dom," in *Das erste Jahrtausend: Kultur und Kunst im werdenden Abendland an Rhein und Ruhr*, 3 vols., ed. Kurt Böhner et al (Düsseldorf: L. Schwann, 1962), 2: 948-81.

of Peter's staff in the founding of the archbishopric of Trier (including a forged privilege of Pope Sylvester I and a *Vita* of St. Eucharius) were written before or after the staff reliquary was made.[28] Nevertheless, I would argue that the reliquary's inscription indicates that these written sources were available in Trier before 980, when the staff reliquary was produced. This inscription reports that the reliquary contains the staff of St. Peter, which was used to raise Trier's first bishop, St. Maternus, from the dead, and which was given to Maternus and his companions, Valerius and Eucharius, by St. Peter himself. After being kept for a long while in "this church" (i.e., the cathedral at Trier), it was taken to Metz to protect it from barbarian invaders. Here, the inscription continues, Archbishop Brun of Cologne found the staff, ordered it given to him by the people of Metz, and brought it back to his see. In the final two sentences, however, we are told that Archbishop Egbert convinced the church at Cologne of Trier's rightful claims to the relic, and reached an agreement with Archbishop Warinus to divide it between Cologne and Trier.

The staff reliquary, like the Egbert Shrine, thus presents us with a representation of something that is not (or not totally) there. While the reliquary gives the impression of completeness, it in fact contains only one half of the staff; the other half, topped by part of a late-antique consular staff, still remains in Cologne. With the Egbert Shrine, the archbishop of Trier demonstrated his church's apostolicity by stressing in enigmatic yet powerful images the Church's fundamental evangelical mission. With the staff of St. Peter, on the other hand, Egbert

---

[28] Earlier scholarship argued that the forged diploma as well as the *Vita* of Eucharius were written during the pontificate of Egbert's predecessor, Archbishop Dietrich (965-77), providing the foundation for a papal confirmation of Trier's primacy issued by John XIII in 969. More recently, however, Mogens Rathsack (*Fuldaforfalskningerne: en retahistorisk analyse af klostret Fuldas pavelige privilegier, 751- ca. 1158* (Copenhagen: Jurisforbundet, 1980)) has argued that the papal privileges of 969, 973, and 975 confirming Trier's primacy were in fact written in the early eleventh century, a position adopted by Harald Zimmerman in his edition of papal diplomata (*Papsturkunden 896-1046* (Vienna: Österreichische Akademie der Wissenschaften, 1988-89), nos. 237, 471-73). In turn, Thomas Head ("Art and Artifice in Ottonian Trier") has suggested that the staff reliquary's role in Trier's claims to apostolic tradition was artistic and ritual in nature, and that the Sylvester diploma, the *Vita* of Eucharius, and the papal privileges were later, written reactions to Egbert's artistic politics. Rathsack and Zimmerman's dating of the papal documents, however, has been criticized on a number of fronts; moreover, their arguments only provide evidence for half of Head's claim. See Hermann Jakobs, "Zu den neuen Thesen über die Fuldaer Papsturkunden," *DA* 37 (1981): 792-95; Ulrich Hussong, "Studien zur Geschichte der Reichsabtei Fulda bis zur Jahrtausendwende. Erster Teil," *Archiv für Diplomatik* 31 (1985): 204-212; and *Germania Pontificia*, vol. X/1, *Provincia Treverensis: Archidiocesis Treverensis*, ed. Egon Boshof (Göttingen: Vandenhoeck and Ruprecht, 1992), nos. 69, 71, and 73.

meant to link Trier's status, and that of its bishops, directly to Roman apostolic tradition. On the long shaft of the reliquary, clad in repoussé goldwork, a band containing the inscription separates two equally fashioned rows of medallion portraits. On one side, we find clipeated images of ten saintly popes; on the other, equivalent images of ten bishops of Trier including Egbert, who alone is depicted with the square halo reserved for living individuals. Notably, the series of bishops on the staff corresponds (albeit in different sequence) to that found at the beginning of the Egbert Psalter—an unusual choice of images for such a manuscript, which would normally feature a portrait of King David.[29] And, as we have seen earlier, Egbert's image in the Psalter is modelled on that of Pope Gregory at St. Andrew's, Rome.

Twice, then, we find Egbert heading a list of bishops of Trier. In the book, he has placed himself (in papal fashion) at the beginning of a succession-list; on the reliquary, he demonstrates the equality of all bishops by juxtaposing the portraits of each of his predecessors with a portrait of a Roman bishop. This is a spectacular pairing. What makes it more important from an art-historical as well as theological perspective, however, is the entire pictorial context in which these two rows are situated. Popes and bishops alike are standing directly "underneath" the heavily ornamented end of the shaft. Here the material changes, from gold to cloisonné enamel set in gold, depicting twelve apostles arranged in two rows, one above the other. Above them, the staff terminates in a spherical knob divided into eight fields by beautifully jeweled bands. At the tip of the reliquary is a large sapphire, likely meant as a Christological image given its cruciform setting and the evangelist symbols which surround it. On the lower half of the sphere, the four enameled fields contain images of the three legendary founders of the church at Trier (Eucharius, Valerius, and Maternus) as well as St. Peter. The founding fathers of the Christian community at Trier, followed by the apostles, followed in turn by popes together with bishops—this is the message of the staff reliquary.

Three years after the beginning of his episcopacy, therefore, Egbert is demonstrating through art the position of the church entrusted to him. Regardless of the written sources which lie behind this pictorial message, it is clear that the staff reliquary represents a tangible element of Ottonian ecclesiastical policy. Moreo-

---

[29] This correspondence is seen by Franz Ronig as evidence that the Egbert Psalter should be dated no later than the staff reliquary; see "Der Psalter Erzbischof Egberts von Trier in Cividale," in *Egbert, Erzbischof von Trier*, ed. Ronig, 2: 163-68.

ver, it is not simply an illustration of possibly earlier sources, such as the forged diploma of Sylvester I (which was copied in the early eleventh-century at the beginning of the Codex Egberti), but an artistic masterpiece illustrating a particular text. It is itself text and source. In turn, it is more than an insignia, designed to proclaim the dignity of the church of Trier. Like the Egbert Shrine, it is not illustration but representation. It portrays a reality beyond texts or images, because it represents a vision of the church itself as a living community within as well as beyond history. The overall form, materials, and sequence of images found in the reliquary speak a language that goes beyond written texts. Through this masterpiece of medieval art, Egbert uses the art of representation to convey his own opinion of the primatial status of his church, and of the church as a spiritual body.

In our examination of these two reliquaries, we have seen the close links which existed between representation and tradition, and more particularly how the representation of history was transformed into art. Egbert's concern was to bring traditional authorities to bear on contemporary concerns, a goal which he achieved through the textual and pictorial "quotation" of those authorities. This was not, however, the only way in which Egbert used tradition to establish a message of legitimation. In particular, more than any other Ottonian patron, Egbert employed spolia to convey his messages, and did so in a very distinctive way.[30] On all but one side of the Egbert Shrine, a spolium occupies the center of each pictorial or linear composition: the cast figures of tetramorphs, almost certainly of eighth-century Anglo-Saxon design; the *solidus* of Justinian on the reverse side of the shrine, in a sixth-century Merovingian garnet setting; and the now-empty hexagonal setting atop the foot, which contained a late-antique miniature cut stone with three small figures.[31] Even the altarstone of the Egbert Shrine is a spolium—an unusually large Roman millefiori plaque. Apart from the numerous cut stones set in the jewelled border of the shrine, therefore, these

---

[30] See Westermann-Angerhausen, "Spolie und Umfeld" and, on the use of spolia in Ottonian and Salian goldwork more generally, *idem*, "Spolie—Zitat—Tradition: Die vorgotischen Emails und der Vorgänger des Schreins," in *Schatz aus den Trümmern: Der Silberschrein von Nivelles und die europäische Hochgotik*, ed Hiltrud Westermann-Angerhausen and Gudrun Sporbeck (Cologne: Schnütgen-Museum, 1994), 117-34.

[31] We know this from a seventeeth-century engraving of the treasures at the cathedral of Trier; see Antje Krug, "Die Bekrönung des Egbertschreins," *Trierer Zeitschrift* 63 (2000): 353-63.

major spolia clearly are meant to emphasize the antiquity, legitimize the tradition, and enforce the authority of each message which is conveyed.

Spolia do not seem to be as prominent in the staff reliquary. Yet here too, their placement appears to have been significant. The double row of apostle portraits on the staff is awkwardly shaped, on account of the triangles of pearls and sapphires which are set between the rows. These are patently spolia, pieces from a Byzantine collar necklace of the fifth or sixth century. The Ottonian goldsmiths, or their patron, obviously thought it adviseable to keep these items together, resulting in the peculiar shape of the apostles' images. In turn, the sequence of images on the staff echoes that found in the decoration of a church building: a sequence of medallion portraits of popes, bishops, or abbots in the nave (standard in any late antique Roman basilica and in later edifices such as the church of St. George at Reichenau), apostles and patron saints in the sanctuary, and the *Maiestas* with evangelist symbols in the apse. When viewed in this way, the staff reliquary again presents us with a picture of the Church, but from a different angle: namely, the Church as community and the church as spiritual and tangible edifice. Within this edifice, moreover, we find the apostles and saints, known since the early Fathers as the "living stones" of the Church. Spolia thus represent another way to reveal the weight and authority—as well as the beauty—of God's word, for which the bishop is responsible and which, through the art of representation, can be transformed into tangible pictorial evidence for the faithful.

Here we are brought back to the figure of Gregory the Great, the authority *par excellence* in the Middle Ages for the use of pictorial representation to teach the illiterate faithful, and hence for the pastoral function of art.[32] Yet the themes which we have considered here are summed up best in a letter by one of Egbert's contemporaries, Gerbert of Aurillac, written in 987 for the archbishop of Reims and addressed to Egbert himself. Gerbert's superior had ordered a jewelled cross from the latter's workshops, and had sent gold and precious stones for its creation. "We are sending you designs for the item that we ordered," wrote Gerbert. "May you, as brother for brother and sister for sister, produce a pleasing form that might nourish the mind and the eyes."[33] As Franz Ronig has shown, Ger-

---

[32] See the discussion by Robert Suckale, *Rogier van der Weyden, die Johannestafel. Das Bild als stumme Predigt* (Frankfurt am Main: Fischer Taschenbuch Verlag, 1995), 52 ff. and note 70.

[33] "Destinato operi designatas mittimus species. Admirabilem formam, et quae mentem et oculos pascat, frater efficiet fratri, soror sorori . . .." Gerbert of Aurillac, *Ep.* 104 (1: 254).

bert's phrase *mentem et oculos pascare* is in fact taken from Cicero. I would, however, suggest that this rhetorical conceit can also be linked to Gregory the Great's pastoral aims in instructing the faithful through pictures. According to Gregory, images first stir the memory (*recordatio et memoria*), then lead to veneration and ultimately devotion (*veneratio* and *devotio*); thus images become the *scriptura vel litteratura laicorum*. When Gerbert writes to Egbert about a work of art that will nourish the eyes and the mind, therefore, he is not only quoting Cicero—he is providing us with an eloquent definition of an Ottonian patron of the arts. By nourishing the eyes and the mind, Egbert was acting as a teacher as well as a shepherd. He was, that is, doing exactly what a bishop should do.

Fig. 9. Front cover of the "Codex Aureus" of Echternach (c. 989). Nürnberg, Germanisches Nationalmuseum, inv. no. KG 1138. Photo courtesy of Hiltrud Westermann-Angerhausen.

Fig. 10. Portrait of Otto II, originally from the frontispiece to the *Registrum Gregorii* (c. 983/4). Chantilly, Musée Condée, MS 14b. Photo by R.G. Ojeda, © Réunion des Musées Nationaux/Art Resource, NY.

Fig. 11. Portrait of Pope Gregory the Great, frontispiece to the *Registrum Gregorii* (c. 983/4). Trier, Stadtbibliothek MS 171/1626. Photo © Stadtbibliothek Trier.

Fig. 12. Egbert of Trier, dedication portrait from the *Egbert Psalter* (977-80). Cividale del Friuli, Archivi e Biblioteca di Palazzo dei Provveditori Veneti, MS 136, f. 17r. Photo © Ministero per i Beni e le Attività Culturali, Soprintendenza per i beni architettonici ed il paesaggio e per il patrimonio storico artistico e demoetnoantropologico del Friuli Venezia Giulia. Reproduction or duplication prohibited without consent of the copyright holder.

Fig. 13. Egbert of Trier, dedication portrait from the *Egbert Codex* (*ante* 985). Trier, Stadtbibliothek, MS 24, f. 2r. Photo © Stadtbibliothek Trier.

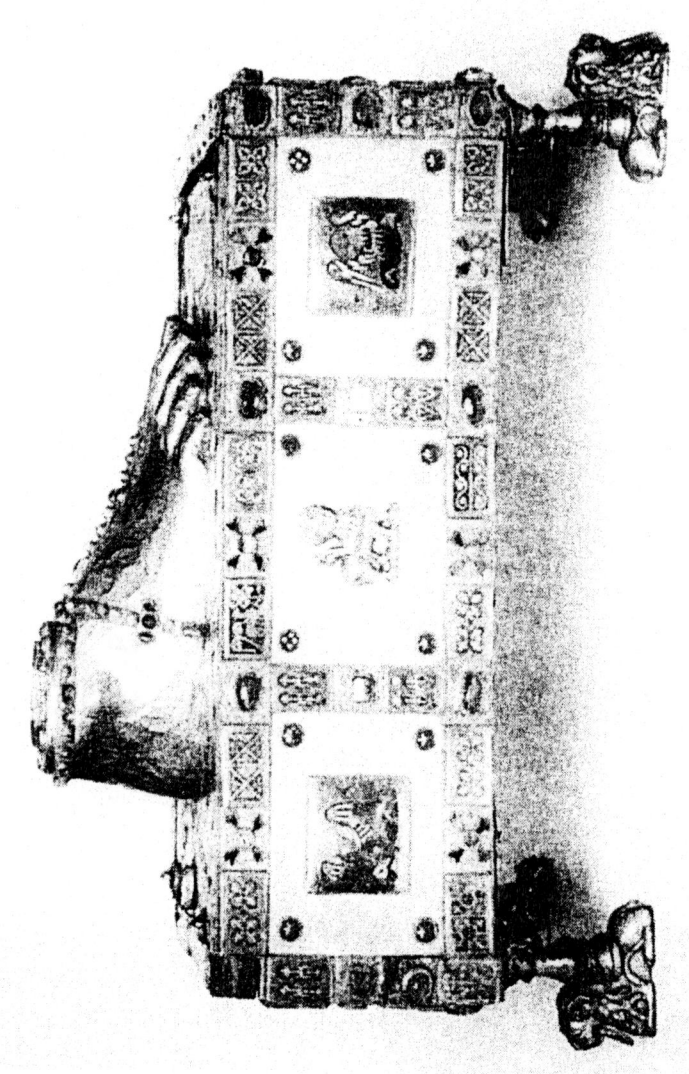

Fig. 14. Egbert Shrine (c. 980). Trier, Domschatz. Photo by D. Thomassin, © Amt für Kirchliche Denkmalpflege, Bistum Trier.

Fig. 15. Egbert Shrine (front view). Photo by D. Thomassin, © Amt für Kirchliche Denkmalpflege, Bistum Trier.

Fig. 16. Incipit page to Gospel of St. Matthew, from the Codex Aureus of St. Emmeram (c. 870). Munich, Bayerische Staatsbibliothek, MS Clm. 14000, f. 16v. Photo © Bayerische Staatsbibliothek.

Fig. 17. Egbert Shrine (rear view). Photo by D. Thomassin, © Amt für Kirch-liche Denkmalpflege, Bistum Trier.

Fig. 18. Staff reliquary of St. Peter (c. 980). Limburg, Domschatz. Photo by A. Luisa, © Diözesanmuseum Limburg.

Chapter Seven
The Bishop Makes an Impression:
Seals, Authority, and Episcopal Identity
Brigitte Miriam Bedos-Rezak

The previous chapter demonstrated the central role played by images and image-production in expressing the presence, authority, and even personality of an early medieval bishop. This chapter addresses another, equally important medium by which bishops—specifically, those of northern France—made themselves and their office visible: the episcopal seal.[1] While such documentary sealing, heretofore a prerogative of the royal chancery, constituted a radical departure from the previous non-royal diplomatic tradition, it also preceded a dramatic increase in episcopal charter production during the last quarter of the eleventh century. Sealing thus may have facilitated the increased production, rather than having been the result of it. The episcopal milieus responsible for initiating the novelty of non-royal documentary sealing were Northern European, and were largely centered around the cathedral schools, where teaching and doctrinal debate took place, and the writing bureaus or chanceries, where documents were produced. In fact, schools and chanceries shared not only the same locations but, more significantly, the same staff, whom I have come to term chancery-scholars. Characteristic of such prescholastic milieus was a heightened semiotic sensitivity which, stimulated primarily by renewed enquiry into the reality of the eucharist (at Liège, Rheims, Cambrai, and Laon), fostered debates over presence and representation, image and resemblance, authority and authenticity, and covenant

---

[1] For a panoramic treatment of the appearance of episcopal seals, see Robert-Henri Bautier, "Apparition, diffusion et évolution typologique du sceau épiscopal au Moyen Age," in *Die Diplomatik der Bischofsurkunde vor 1250 / La diplomatique épiscopale avant 1250. Referate zum VIII. Internationalen Kongress für Diplomatik, Innsbruck, 27. September-3. Oktober 1993*, ed. Christoph Haidacher and Werner Köfler (Innsbruck: Tiroler Landesarchiv, 1995), 225-41. On the appearance of seals on Northern French episcopal charters, see Ghislain Brunel, "Chartes et chancelleries épiscopales du Nord de la France au XIe siècle," in *A propos des actes d'évêques. Hommage à Lucie Fossier*, ed. Michel Parisse (Nancy: Presses universitaires de Nancy, 1991), 234-38. On the epistolary use of signet-rings by bishops throughout the early middle ages, see Bautier, "Apparition, diffusion et évolution," 225. Hartmut Atsma and Jean Vezin ("Remarques paléographiques et diplomatiques sur les actes originaux des évêques de France du VIIe siècle à l'an mil," in *Die Diplomatik der Bischofsurkunde vor 1250*, ed. Haidacher and Köfler, 210) note that no episcopal charters prior to the eleventh century were sealed, although episcopal signet-ring-impressions were sometimes affixed to *constitutiones* issued in synods (216). See also below, note 12.

and causality in the operations of sacramental and other signs.[2] I will argue that while the rise of the sealed episcopal charter in northern France was intimately linked to this general reevaluation of signs and images, it also marked a new intersection of visibility, authority, and representation in post-millennial Europe, one with important implications for the notion of the person and the formulation of medieval identity.

Throughout the eleventh century, bishops tended to resort to letters rather than to charters as means of communication.[3] Such letters were sealed, that is, closed with wax impressions from episcopal rings. Opening the letter therefore involved destruction of the seal impression, whose significance was confined to its integrity upon initial receipt.[4] By means of the skilled deployment of a carefully learned rhetoric, such letter-writing was experienced as instrumental both for self-representation and for ordering affairs. The principal and characteristic assumption in these letters was that two *personae* were speaking face to face. Since this effect could be achieved only by those who had mastered the craft of composition through training in rhetoric, rhetorical style was crucial for imprinting the identity of the letter-writer within the body of the letter. Thus, two assumptions informed the efficacy of letters as media: first, that there was a symbiotic relationship between human presence and representation, and second, that the written text was an embodiment of its author, articulating a notion of

---

[2] A fuller analysis of the semiotic culture of schools and chanceries appears in Bedos-Rezak, "Medieval Identity," 1489-1533.

[3] See for instance the case of Bishop Lambert of Arras (1093-1115), who had 23 acta issued in his name and gathered a corpus of 128 letters, 41 of which he sent and 73 of which he received (14 letters were neither sent by nor addressed to him). Lambert's epistolary corpus is unusual by contemporary standards, in that it contains a greater number of received rather than sent letters: Laurent Morelle, "La pratique épistolaire de Lambert, evêque d'Arras (1093-1115)," in *Regards sur la correspondance (de Cicéron à Armand Barbès)*, ed. Daniel Odon Hurel [= *Les Cahiers du GRHIS* 5(1996)], 37-57, and "Archives épiscopales et formulaire de chancellerie au XIIe siècle. Remarques sur les privilèges épiscopaux connus par le *Codex* de Lambert de Guines, évêque d'Arras (1093/94-1115)," in *Die Diplomatik der Bischofsurkunde vor 1250*, ed. Haidacher and Köfler, 255. Giles Constable, in *Letters and Letter-Collections* [Typologie des sources du Moyen Age occidental 17] (Turnhout: Brepols, 1976), stresses the variety of medieval epistolary styles and contents, notes the prodigious flowering of letter-writing in the eleventh and twelfth centuries, and reminds us that a wide variety of business could be cast in the form of a letter. Some diplomatists have argued that, unlike charters and diplomas, medieval letters served no legal or administrative purpose, but others have successfully shown that there is no clear distinction between official documents and private letters. See Constable, *Letters and Letter-Collections*, 21-23.

[4] See above, note 1. On letter sealing, see Constable, *Letters and Letter-Collections*, 47 and 53.

authenticity which revolved around author-ity and identity. The ultimate fluency and utility of this epistolary genre demonstrates the achievement of cathedral schools in the eleventh century, where the work of scholars in cathedral chapters overlapped considerably with that of chancellors and secretaries in the bishops' courts.[5]

The milieu just described, however, did not have the same degree of control over another aspect of episcopal writing, the charter. While bishops' letters emanated from the world of their schools and courts, episcopal charters were often designed and drafted in the writing bureaus of the charters' beneficiaries, usually monastic establishments.[6] Copies of epistolary texts remained in the archives of their senders, while episcopal charters were typically kept in the archives of the recipients. Thus, whereas letters derived their authority from the projection of authorial identity, charters invoked God's authority, and derived their import from a visible affinity with Holy Scripture. Such an affinity was suggested by graphic logic, which involved the inscription of a Chrismon, trinitarian invocations, biblical arenga, signing with the cross, divine maledictions, and threats of excommunication against whomever might challenge the action recorded in the charter.[7] So, while letters functioned in the place of their authors as their per-

---

[5] John Van Engen, "Letters, Schools, and Written Culture in the Eleventh and Twelfth Centuries," in *Dialektik und Rhetorik im früheren und hohen Mittelalter*, ed. Johannes Fried (Munich: Oldenbourg, 1997), 97-132. While cogently demonstrating the extent to which the postmillennial world of affairs drew upon the resources of epistolary rhetoric, Van Engen also notes that great prescholastic masters, several of whom were chancery-scholars (Anselm of Laon, Peter Comestor) or bishops (William of Champeaux, Peter Lombard), left virtually no letters. He ponders the possibility of a shift in intellectual emphasis from letter to commentary (see 130), and I would suggest that this shift also involved the passage from letter to sealed charter. In general, the immense corpus of letters exchanged throughout the eleventh and twelfth centuries shows a particular tendency toward a personalization of style and contents, and a reliance on authorial style as a proof of authenticity. Nevertheless, important information could be left out of letters and entrusted to their couriers for oral delivery; see Constable, *Letters and Letter-Collections*, 34, 48, and 53, and (for specific examples of letters referring explicitly to the messenger's knowledge of questions to be put orally to the recipient) Morelle, "La pratique épistolaire de Lambert," 45-46.

[6] Instances of episcopal acta drafted by beneficiaries can be found in *Actes des archevêques de Reims*, ed. Demouy; *Actes des évêques de Laon*, ed. Dufour-Malbezin; and *Les actes des évêques d'Amiens jusqu'au début du XIIIe siècle*, ed. Suzanne Lecoannet, Thèse de l'Ecole nationale des chartes, Paris, 1957. In Reims and Laon, the episcopal staff maintained a relatively strong control over the production of episcopal charters; in Amiens, the proportion of episcopal *acta* prepared by the beneficiaries seems higher.

[7] The best analysis, with current bibliography, of the textual, graphic, and linguistic components of diplomatic discourse is provided by Olivier Guyotjeannin, Jacques Pycke, and Benoît-Michel Tock, *Diplomatique médiévale* (Turnhout: Brepols, 1993), 71-102.

sonal rhetorical self-representations, charters, even though formulated in the first-person voice of the bishop, were fundamentally impersonal, and were not instruments for representing oneself to another. In using the first person form, the anonymous charter-scribe in fact maintained the referentiality of a third person, only semiotically entering the subjectivity of an episcopal author. Hence, the locus of subjectivity transcended the individual, and diplomatic discourse, that is, the discourse of the charter, incorporated a cultural "self" quite distinct from the nominal author.[8]

Notably, episcopal activities in northern France around the turn of the first millennium only rarely resulted in the writing of episcopal charters—a low rate of production which was maintained until the 1070s.[9] Writing around 1025, the author of the *Gesta Episcoporum* of Cambrai, a diocese within the northern French ecclesiastical province of Rheims, reassured his readers that he had reported only those facts described by trustworthy oral witnesses, read in earlier chronicles, or found in the charters still extant in the local episcopal archives.[10] He clearly expected such charters to be archaic documents which recorded past events, referring to them as *adhuc in archivio*, surviving remnants of a type no longer produced, in order to explain why he was obliged to depend upon oral testimonies for more recent events.

---

[8] Bedos-Rezak, "Medieval Identity," 1507-8.

[9] See in general Michel Parisse's remarks in chapter one, pages 5-8, and Michèle Courtois, "Remarques sur les chartes originales des évêques antérieures à 1121 et conservées dans les Bibliothèques et Archives de France," in *A propos des actes d'évêques. Hommage à Lucie Fossier*, ed. Michel Parisse (Nancy, 1991), 51. Brunel ("Chartes et chancelleries épiscopales," 227-244), who takes into consideration all episcopal acta extant for the eleventh century (that is, both originals and copies), comes up with larger numbers, but his tables make it clear that the bulk of documentary activity took place in the later years of the eleventh century. French episcopal charters prior to 1200 are currently receiving much attention on the part of a team of French medievalists (GR 0121 of the French C.N.R.S.) who are preparing a critical edition of all such texts. For an overview of the project, particularly as it relates to episcopal acts from the bishoprics of Amiens, Arras, Beauvais, Cambrai, Laon, Noyon, Reims, and Soissons, see Michel Parisse, "Importance et richesse des chartes épiscopales. Les exemples de Metz et de Toul, des origines à 1200," in *A propos des actes d'évêques*, ed. Parisse, 19-43, especially the appendix at 41-43 which lists available publications and work in progress on each bishopric. This report is updated in Parisse's "La recherche française sur les actes des évêques. Les travaux d'un groupe de recherche," in *Die Diplomatik der Bischofsurkunde vor 1250*, ed. Haidacher and Köfler, 203-8.

[10] Michel Sot, "Rhétorique et technique dans les préfaces des *gesta episcoporum* (IXe–XIIe s.)," *Cahiers de civilisation médiévale* 28 (1985): 195.

Nevertheless, by the late eleventh century the charter was emerging as the preferred means of episcopal representation. A key distinction between letter- and charter-operation is that the letter's performance centered on its legibility (as a rhetorical text exchanged between individuals of similar schooling) whereas the charter's performance hinged on its visibility (as a form of "Scripture"). Thus the charter ultimately achieved a wider circulation, particularly among lay elites who, seeing the manuscript charter as kindred to Scripture, could conceive of it as a space of sacred and secure inscription. At stake in this polarization between legibility and visibility was a profound change in the conception of the relationship between phenomenal appearances and the person or thing represented. The shift in favor of the visible was signalled around 1050 (and thus during the period of limited episcopal documentary output) with a significant change in the format of the episcopal charter—namely, its incorporation and display of an impressed image, the seal.

That the seal was initially conceived as an image when it was systematically affixed, from the late eleventh century onward, to the episcopal charters of Langres, Noyon, Laon, Reims, Cambrai, Beauvais, Soissons, and Therouanne, may be deduced from several observations. First, final textual clauses within the charters specifically refer to the seal as *imago*.[11] Second, seals were already part of the pre-existent episcopal panoply of signs; from the early medieval period, rings had been symbols of episcopal investiture, and bishops regularly used their signet rings to close letters, to accredit relics, and to seal vessels containing the chrism and other sacred oils.[12] Third, the seal used on eleventh-century episco-

---

[11] Patrick Demouy, "Les sceaux des archevêques de Reims des origines à la fin du XIIIe siècle," in *Actes du 109e Congrès national des Sociétés savantes, Dijon, 1984: section d'histoire médiévale et de philologie*, vol. 1 (Paris: C.T.H.S., 1985), 687; idem, *Actes des archevêques de Reims*, 183-84. Among the many charters that refer to the archepiscopal seal as *imago*, see *Actes des archevêques de Reims*, no. 103 (294-95: Archbishop Manasses confirms in 1096 the possession of the church of St Georges of Hesdin by the abbey of Anchin): ". . . ut autem hoc decretum nostrum posteris inconvulsum permaneat, auctoritate imaginis nostrae testimonioque fidelium corroboravi decrevimus;" no. 108 (305: Archbishop Manasses confirms in 1097 donations to the abbey of St-Acheul): ". . . nos auctoritate metropolitana et sigilli nostri ymagine, personarumque autenticarum signis et testimonio, in eternam quietem corroboramus."

[12] See above, note 1; Jean-Luc Chassel, "L'essor du sceau au XIe siècle," *Bibliothèque de l'Ecole des chartes* 155 (1997): 227- 230; P.C. Barraud, "Des bagues à toutes les époques et en particulier de l'anneau des évêques et des abbés," *Bulletin monumental* 30 (1864): 364-86 and 643-70; Maximin Deloche, *Etude historique et archéologique sur les anneaux sigillaires et autres des premiers siècles du moyen âge* (Paris, 1900), lviii and *passim*; and idem, "Le port

pal charters was no longer imprinted from the bishop's signet ring, but rather from a much enlarged seal matrix which could accommodate a full-fledged representation of the bishop in vestments (see fig. 19). Lastly, between the seventh and the eleventh century, systematic documentary sealing had, in France, been the prerogative of the royal chancery.[13] By the time bishops undertook to seal their charters, royal seals themselves already had undergone a major transformation; much increased in size, by c. 1031 they displayed the full figure of the ruler in majesty (fig. 20).[14] Despite the long precedence of royal sealing, however, it is noteworthy that at the same period royal seal usage had in fact become quite sporadic.[15] Thus one must consider the possibility that the king's majestic new seal was simply a part of, rather than the model for, the new significance of sealing and its subsequent spread to non-royal elites. In any case, at the heart of this newly expanding sealing practice stood an object—the seal—whose operative format—the image—implied likeness as a signifying mode. By introducing this mimetic economy into the signifying process, the seal as sign marked a radical departure from the semiotic system that previously had governed the rapport between sign and thing.

The same departure also is noticeable in those fields of eucharistic and sacramental theology which were simultaneously preoccupying the very same episcopal milieus responsible for launching the production of episcopal charters. Reflection on the nature of the eucharistic sign had begun in the nine century when a monk of Corbie, Paschasius Radbertus († c. 860), in the first theological treatise ever written on the eucharist (*De corpore et sanguine Domini*), asserted that

---

des anneaux dans l'antiquité romaine et dans les premiers siècles du Moyen Age," *Mémoires de l'Académie des Inscriptions et Belles-Lettres* 35/2 (1896): 64-70.

[13] Bedos-Rezak, "Ritual in the Royal Chancery: Text, Image, and the Representation of Kingship in Medieval French Diplomas (700-1200)," in *European Monarchy. Its Evolution and Practice from Roman Antiquity to Modern Times*, ed. Heinz Duchhardt, Richard A. Jackson, and David Sturdy (Stuttgart: F. Steiner, 1992), 27-40.

[14] *Corpus des sceaux français du Moyen Age*, vol. II: *Les sceaux des rois et de régence*, ed. Martine Dalas (Paris: Archives nationales, 1991). The size of French royal seals began to grow with Charles the Bald († 877; see nos. 24-26 (103-4)), but the image remained that of an antique profile. A crowned bust with regalia appeared at the very end of the tenth century on the seal of King Rudolph III of Burgundy († 1018; no. 59 (135)) and remained on the seals of the two first Capetians, Hugh († 997; no. 60 (139)) and Robert the Pious († 1031; no. 61 (140)), but it was replaced by an effigy in majesty when Henry I († 1060) had a new seal cut upon his accession to the throne (no. 62, 141).

[15] Bedos-Rezak, "Ritual in the Royal Chancery," 34-37.

the consecrated bread and wine were the true body and blood of Christ. The eucharist was truth (*veritas*) because it was, in reality, what it affirmed to be. This position was opposed by Ratramnus († 868), a fellow monk at Corbie who, in his own *De corpore et sanguine Domini*, allegorized the physical element in the eucharist as the figuration (*figura*) of a truth which resided elsewhere. This debate continued into the next century, taken up by scholars from the bishopric of Liège who tended to support the eucharistic physicalism of Radbertus. Heriger of Lobbes († 1007), in his *De corpore et sanguine Domini*, was fundamentally a physicalist in his conception of the eucharist. He nevertheless tried to reconcile the two positions by de-emphasizing the relevance for eucharistic doctrine of any distinction between *veritas* and *figura*. He argued that whatever interpretation might attach to the eucharist (which then was treated as *figura*), its meaning was rooted in the fundamental fact that the bread and wine were the actual body and blood of Christ. Interpretation could neither detract from nor alter the *veritas* of the eucharist.[16] Significantly, Heriger of Lobbes was responsible for the production of the earliest sealed episcopal document in Liège, issued on 19 June 980 in the name of Bishop Notker (972-1008) (fig. 21).[17] This seal, actually the earliest extant non-royal medieval seal, precedes episcopal French seals by three quarters of a century, a gap which corresponds to a pause in the eucharistic debate.

The debate resumed in the mid-eleventh century when bishops and their chancery-scholars faced new challenges from dissenting voices, particularly those of Berengar of Tours († 1088) and his followers, whose forceful ideas prompted

---

[16] For a lucid summary of these earlier debates, see Miri Rubin, *Corpus Christi: The Eucharist in Late Medieval Culture* (Cambridge and New York: Cambridge University Press, 1991), 14-16; Gary Macy, *The Theologies of the Eucharist in the Early Scholastic Age* (New York: Oxford University Press, 1984), 21-25; Brian Stock, *The Implications of Literacy: Written Language and Models of Interpretation in the Eleventh and Twelfth Centuries* (Princeton: Princeton University Press, 1983), 259-72; and Celia Chazelle, *The Crucified God in the Carolingian Era: Theology and Art of God's Passion* (Cambridge and New York: Cambridge University Press, 2001), 209-38.

[17] This document (a letter to Abbot Womar of St. Bavo, Ghent, accompanying a copy of *Vita Sancti Landoaldi*) has been published, with facsimile, French translation, diplomatic and historical commentaries, and bibliography, by Jean-Louis Kupper in *Autour de Gerbert d'Aurillac, le pape de l'an mil. Album de documents commentés*, ed. Olivier Guyotjeannin and Emmanuel Poulle (Paris, 1996), no. 44 (300-305). The seal is also discussed and illustrated in René Laurent, *Sigillographie* (Brussels: Archives Générales du Royaume, 1985), 39, no. 210 (69-70), and plate XVII. 50 millimeters in diameter, the seal displays the bust of a figure holding a book, surrounded by the legend NOTKERUS EP(ISCOPU)S.

the Northern French schools and chanceries to re-consider the nature of the eucharistic sign. Berengar rejected physicalism. Refusing to admit something that was denied by the evidence of the senses or by simple logic, Berengar insisted that it was bread and wine that remained on the altar even after consecration. Thus, it was interpretation, a process deeper than surface senses, which gave the eucharist its true meaning.[18]

This rejection of physical symbolism was opposed by Hugh, bishop of Langres, in his *De corpore et sanguine Christi*, written just before the reforming council held at Reims in 1049, the approximate date at which sealing commenced in Langres.[19] At the council of Reims, its convener, Pope Leo IX, complained of many heresies and illicit practices.[20] The archbishop of Reims, Guy († 1055), himself stood accused of simony, although he was able to clear himself of the charge.[21] Guy, the first archbishop of Reims to use a seal, refused to endorse the pro-Berengar letter he received from Eusebius Bruno, bishop of Angers, around 1050,[22] and it was also under Guy's tenure that the school of Reims re-emerged from the obscurity into which it had been plunged after the departure of Gerbert of Aurillac. Associated with this resurgence of the school's fame was Master Herimann († c. 1075), lauded by his contemporaries as one of the distin-

---

[18] Bedos-Rezak, "Medieval Identity," 1501-2. Good analyses of Berengar's position may be found in A.J. MacDonald, *Berengar and the Reform of Sacramental Doctrine* (London: Longmans, Green, 1930; repr. Merrick, NY: Richwood, 1977); Stock, *Implications of Literacy*, 273-87; and Macy, *Theologies of the Eucharist*, 35-43.

[19] Hugh of Langres, *Tractatus de corpore et sanguine Christi*, PL 142: 1325-1334; Stock, *Implications of Literacy*, 282, 287-89; McDonald, *Berengar and the Reform of Sacramental Doctrine*, 51-53, 273-77. Jean-Luc Chassel, "L'apparition du sceau dans les actes de la chancellerie de Langres au XIe siècle," *Cahiers Hauts-Marnais* 167 (1986): 77-95, dismisses the documents sealed by Hugh of Langres, but Bautier ("Apparition, diffusion et évolution," 228) dates the appearance of the episcopal seal at Langres around 1050. The difficulty in dating the earliest use of seals comes from the fact that seals were initially not textually announced, and since most documents no longer exist as originals but as copies, it is difficult to assess whether they were originally sealed. Additionally, some of the extant originals bear dubious traces of sealing that may point to a later sealing.

[20] Leo IX knew of Berengar's teachings, but politics precluded his taking a stance against them at Reims, where he issued only veiled threats; he took action against Berengar only later at the council of Rome (1050). MacDonald, *Berengar and the Reform of Sacramental Doctrine*, 55-58.

[21] *Ibid.*, 60.

[22] For the unsuccessful attempt by Eusebius Bruno, bishop of Angers, to secure the support of Archbishop Guy in favor of Berengar, and on the letter sent by Eusebius to Guy, see *ibid.*, 65, 84, 90.

guished scholars and men of authority who repudiated the thesis of Berengar of Tours.[23] Herimann's contemporary and successor at Reims was a second famous schoolmaster, Bruno († 1101), who also served as archepiscopal chancellor and whose scriptural exegesis and theories on the eucharist greatly influenced yet another episcopal chancellor, Anselm of Laon († 1117).[24] Throughout the eleventh century, then, the school and the chancery at Reims remained a bastion of orthodoxy supporting the doctrine of the real presence.

At Cambrai, the anti-Berengar position of Bishop Gerard († 1051) was recorded in the mid-eleventh century *Acta Synodi Atrebatensis*, a much-revised and expanded version of his confrontation with a group of dissenters at the synod of Arras of 1025. The chapter of the *Acta* devoted to *De corpore et sanguine Domini* is a virtual textbook of eucharistic orthodoxy; indeed, underlying the entire text of the *Acta* is the idea of sacramental realism, based on the principle that an invisible reality can be meted out in palpable form. It is noteworthy, therefore, that the seal of the bishop of Cambrai appeared in 1057, contemporaneously with the redaction of the *Acta*.[25] Similarly, Guy, bishop of Amiens († 1075), presided on 13 July 1058 over the translation of the relics of Paschasius Radbertus, abbot of Corbie, whose earlier views on the eucharist were directly opposed to those espoused by Berengar. In turn, the first episcopal seal of Amiens, belonging to Bishop Guy, appeared in 1058.[26]

---

[23] John R. Williams, "The Cathedral School of Rheims in the Eleventh Century," *Speculum* 29 (1954): 663-64.

[24] *Ibid.*, 669. Williams has suggested (note 61) that Anselm may have been one of Bruno's disciples at Reims. Cf. John R. Williams, "The Cathedral School of Rheims in the time of Master Alberic, 1118-1136," *Traditio* 20 (1964): 93-114.

[25] I follow here Stock's analysis of Gerard's positions in *The Implications of Literacy*, 120-22, 132-33. On the episcopal seal of Cambrai, see Brunel, "Chartes et chancelleries épiscopales," 234-36.

[26] On the translation of Radbertus's relics, see *Les actes des évêques de Cambrai antérieurs à 1167*, ed. Suzanne Lecoannet, 2 vols., Thèse de l'Ecole nationale des chartes, Paris, 1957, 1: 13. The appearance of the episcopal seal is discussed in Bautier, "Apparition, diffusion et évolution," 228. As with the episcopal seal of Langres, the early evidence for episcopal sealing at Amiens is rendered complicated by the absence of extant original charters (see above, note 19). The chronological correlation I have attempted to establish between the appearance of episcopal sealing and episcopal support for the doctrine of real presence must be seen as fragile, given the incomplete nature of the charter evidence. It is clear, however, that sealing practices emerged from the very episcopal milieus involved in elaborating the semiotics that would underlay the eucharist doctrine of real presence. On the implications of such semiotics for strategies of representation, see below.

Northern French bishops and their chancery-scholars thus were strong promoters of the notion of real presence in the eucharist; indeed, it was in defense of this concept that they engaged in broader debates about sign theory, involving themselves in a renewed study of the fundamental corpus of semio-linguistic theory developed earlier by St. Augustine. Early Church doctrine had followed the lead of Augustine, who espoused the Platonic notion that sign and thing were joined by a relationship based upon difference, in which only the thing, though ideal and not of this world, had reality. In this dualistic mode, Augustine's main concern was whether signs could adequately represent the ultimate reality, God. Since signs operated through dissimilarity from their e(x)ternal referent, they were unable to express God's essence as pure presence, or God's identity as the perfection of self-reference.

Augustine, however, also elaborated an alternative semiotic system in order to come to grips with the metaphysical concept of truth as presence. The Augustinian solution for connecting sign and thing is Christ, God incarnate, the word-become-flesh, the image consubstantial with God. "The word of God [the Logos] suffered no change although it became flesh in order to live in us."[27] In Augustine's doctrine of the incarnation and the eucharist, Christ bridges the gap between sign and thing, since substance (God) and its representation (Logos) are one and the same. The incarnate divinity, that is, has unmediated meaning and instantaneously reveals its presence.[28] Therefore, although Augustine reiterated the Platonic dichotomy between sign and thing, he also presented an alternative to the mere referentiality of signs through his theory of ontological immanence and participation. On the one hand, transcendental things were said to inhere in and thus guide the properties of signs; on the other, the participation of signs in the transcendental produced resemblance—congruence—between sign and thing. Although he relied on the tools of linguistic philosophy, Berengar argued from and for the dualistic Augustinian distinction between the sensible and the spiritual, between symbol and reality, and between sign and thing. Bishops and chancery-scholars in the anti-Berengar camp also explored this dualism in the

---

[27] Augustine, *De Doctrina Christiana*, ed. and trans. R.P.H. Green (Oxford: Clarendon, 1995), 24-25.

[28] Bedos-Rezak, "Medieval Identity," 1498-99; Margaret W. Ferguson, "Saint Augustine's Region of Unlikeness: The Crossing of Exile and Language," *The Georgia Review* 29 (1975): 842-63; Susan A. Handelman, *The Slayers of Moses: The Emergence of Rabbinic Interpretation in Modern Literary Theory* (Albany: State University of New York Press, 1982), 89-90, 113-20.

course of developing their own eucharistic theology. Redirecting attention toward Augustine's appreciation of a sign's tangible aspect, they not only scrutinized the economy by which an iconic sign might resemble that which it denotes, but also the extent to which—indeed, the mode *by* which—the sign itself might actually partake of the object represented. In the course of this analysis, the cultural content of the analogy, that is, the relationship between the object and its image, was altered so that an iconic representation might be seen as more real than the empirical experience. This was the claim of the doctrine of transubstantiation. The eucharistic debate produced the idea that reality was capable of being perceived through an iconic convention; as a result, the eucharistic motif now became the foundation of a representational model articulated around the theme of real presence.

In such a cultural crucible, the sign became representative less because of its relationship to a conceptual ideal than because of its capacity to embody the referent's ontological characteristics. Scholars have tended to attribute the rise of this notion—that a symbol partakes of the reality it expresses—to the growing acceptance of Aristotelian thought within prescholastic culture. Eleventh-century debates, however, show that the Augustinian semiotic corpus was itself perfectly capable of inspiring the belief that immanence was central to the operation of symbolism. The newly elaborated semiotic doctrine, although it maintained distinctions between objects, the signifying functions of iconic signs, and their representative capacity, in fact sanctioned a conflation of sign and object, so that immanence rather than transcendence came to govern the rapport between signifier and signified. Such semiotics, enabling and empowering new forms for the representation of reality, countenanced strategies of personal representation in which the individual acquired definition and was constituted as a category of referential authority.[29]

The extent to which seals became effective at representing their owners owed much to this eucharistic debate. Bishops, in the grip of a strident yet stimulating semiotic crisis which called forth substantial affirmations of authority, launched a new experiment in the signature and significance of both person and personal identity. They abandoned the personal letter for charters, now personified and substantiated by their seals. The projection of episcopal authority henceforth centered on visibility, and was re-organized around iconic signs (seals) con-

---

[29] Bedos-Rezak, "Medieval Identity," 1499, 1502-3, 1521.

ceived and created to produce a presence which while not actual was nonetheless real.

Though the signs inaugurated by the bishops manipulate the effect of presence, they seem to do so, paradoxically, by showing rather abstract images. Episcopal seals display a figure in liturgical vestments without any attempt at individualization (see fig. 19).[30] The images on such seals seem limited to a prototype, imitating a standardized model. Actually, one could even say that the central motif on these seal images is not so much a *subject*, that is, a specific bishop, but a *mode*, that is, resemblance or duplication. In the first place, seal imprints reproduce and resemble the seal matrix from which they were issued. In turn, seal imprints from any given matrix duplicate one another. Episcopal seal images, furthermore, resemble each other irrespective of their particular owners. Finally, the point is insistently made that such reduplicated seal impressions are the "images" of their owners.

In the midst of so much reproduction, what signifying process, what notion of personal identity, emerges, or what conception of the subject himself? Even though the operative mode of seals emphasized likeness, the seals themselves obviously were not expected to reflect their owners, that is, to act as mirror images; rather, the signifying process at work was the imprint. The imprinting process conveyed a specific meaning, as evidenced by scholars in episcopal schools who now seized upon the metaphor of sealing to interpret the scriptural teaching from Genesis (1:26) that man was created in the image and likeness of God. By doing so, they abandoned the metaphor of the mirror, which until then had been the favored explanatory trope for this passage. This is not the place for a lengthy discussion of the implications of this metaphorical shift for ontological understanding. It is relevant, however, to ponder the possible reasons why, in the eleventh-century concept of image, impressions became more meaningful than reflections.[31]

---

[30] Thus seal images are surrounded by an inscription, the legend, which bears the baptismal name and title of a specific bishop.

[31] See the analysis of the seal metaphor in Bedos-Rezak, "Medieval Identity," 1522-26. On the metaphor of the mirror, see Gerhart B. Ladner, *Ad Imaginem Dei: The Image of Man in Mediaeval Art* (Latrobe, PA: Archabbey Press, 1965), 13-15; as he notes, the mirror metaphor, when used to account for man's likeness to God, tended to dematerialize the human image. This spiritualization of the image of man in Western art, however, gave way around 1100 to more concrete renderings (41). For an interpretation of the metaphorical shift from mirror to seal, see Brigitte Miriam Bedos-Rezak, "Replica: Images of Identity and the Identity

The mirror displays a cause as a result. When a mirror projects the image of an individual, it shows that same individual, that is, the origin of the image, as an outcome of the mirroring process.[32] In transforming a cause into a consequence, in constraining the original individual to apprehend himself as an effect, the mirror could be understood as canceling the origin of its reflection, as creating an effect of presence when there in fact was not only absence but nothingness. Such a conclusion stands in contradiction to the essentialist notion, developed by eucharistic thinking, of the image as the bearer of the inner presence of that which it represents. The imprint, unlike the mirror, contains and preserves the traces of its origin within its very matter. The imprint also is an immediate effect of a cause which it reproduces, and whose presence it materializes.[33] As imprint, the seal image is self-referential, at one with its cause, and thus produces itself as authentic and authoritative.

There was, however, an interesting slippage: authority now became vested not in the subject, the bishop, but in its representative object, the seal.[34] While proclaimed as the image of its owner, the seal eschewed portraiture. Both the bishop and the charter's recipients recognize the person of the bishop in this image, but not the individual himself. The bishop's *ego*, his self, which is the point of reference for his own presence in the world (and in the seal), receives an image on seals not of himself but of another, that functional *persona* which he shares with all bishops. Thus, the seal as image establishes the notion that for human identity to be signified, *identitas* must shade its theological meaning of self-sameness and presume a differentiation, and thus a relationship, between *ego* and an

---

of Images in Prescholastic France," in *The Mind's Eye: Art and Theological Argument in the Medieval West*, ed. Jeffrey Hamburger and Anne-Marie Bouché (forthcoming).

[32] Pierre Legendre, *Dieu au miroir. Etude sur l'institution des images* (Paris: Fayard, 1994), 51.

[33] Louis Marin, *Portrait of the King* (Minneapolis: The University of Minnesota Press, 1988), 126-27.

[34] The vocabulary used in the final clauses of charters to announce the affixation of the seal is most revealing. Throughout the eleventh and twelfth century, the preferred term for the seal is *imago* (image) (see above, note 11), and the preferred expression for the affixation of the seal is *impressio* (imprint). In the eleventh century, the episcopal charter speaks of the bishop's seal as the *sigillum episcopalis auctoritatis* (the seal of episcopal authority). By the twelfth century, however, the order of words is significantly reversed to *auctoritas sigilli* (the authority of the seal). See Brigitte Miriam Bedos-Rezak, "Une image ontologique: sceau et ressemblance en France préscolastique (1000-1200)," in *Etudes d'histoire de l'art offertes à Jacques Thirion, des premiers temps chrétiens au XXe siècle*, ed. Alain Erlande-Brandenburg and Jean-Michel Leniaud (Paris: Ecole des chartes, 2001), 46-47.

"other," an *alter ego*, that is, *imago* and *persona*. Only the eucharist was perceived as having a pure *identitas*, that is, an identity with itself. The eleventh-century formulation of mundane identity required a distinction between *ego* and *persona*. On episcopal seals the focus was upon *persona*, upon the bishop's function, not upon his individuality. The seal, therefore, presents a principle of alterity (between *ego* and *persona*), while representing by means of a principle of resemblance (between *imago* and *persona*, and between persons sharing a similar function). The mimetic operation at work in the articulation of identity emphasized those elements of resemblance which link diverse members of a single functional cohort, and those that identify an official with the emblems of his office (the crozier, miter, and pallium).

In manipulating the economy of resemblance as a representational mode, episcopal seals also employed a reproductive technique that assured the multiplication of identical seal images. Such a technique of replication ultimately deflected attention away from human agency and toward the mechanical aspects of the process itself. The personal contact between a seal owner and his seal matrix, and the unique contact between that matrix and its seal impression, came to be displaced conceptually toward the notion that successive impressions were identical, that what really mattered was the relationship between one imprinted image and another. For such a relationship to guarantee, retrospectively, the surety of the seal's origin and authority, seal impressions had to be true replicas of one other. The representativeness of seals *qua* replicas was not tested by reference to an "original" (the bishop or the matrix); rather, the seal was accepted as being itself a reproduced original, generating its own accuracy. In other words, actual reference to the seal's owner was de-emphasized as the imprint metamorphosed into the replica.

Who and what guaranteed this rapport of resemblance which so effectively channeled identity? In addressing this issue, episcopal sealing practice probed the limits of eucharistic theology as applied to human systems of signification.[35] The seal as imprint *was* presence. The seal as image was representation. The seal as replica required no immediate generator, and thus brought directly to its con-

---

[35] No prescriptive text is available on seals and seal usage before the end of the twelfth century, when canon lawyers began to address issues of diplomatic forgery. Significantly, their methods for establishing authenticity turned exclusively on the material aspects of the seal and on the extent to which these features resembled traditional traits known from other impressions: Michael Clanchy, *From Memory to Written Record: England 1066-1307*, 2nd ed. (Oxford: Blackwell, 1993), 323-25.

text that authority, that precedent, which organized those multiple relationships of resemblance enacted by the seal. Even more importantly, that authority served as the very principle constituting the rapport between individual subjects and replicating objects. The seal may have been conceived as operating like, but never as, a sacrament, a God-given sign. So when the seal produced itself as replica, it in fact performed as a transparent icon of social templates. In generating personal identity as replicated resemblance, seals enacted a principle whereby such identity could be conceived only by reference to an instance, itself responsible for deflecting the individual from his self- image.

The signs of identity that emerged among eleventh-century French northern bishops were conceived and enabled by a culture that derived its values from charismatic and real presence.[36] Actualization through seals did not result in individualization *on* seals. These, once imprinted, focused rather on the official *persona*, short-circuiting reference to the particular seal owner in favor of the *persona*'s image, and invoking the framework of society as the validating template. The seals' signifying modes thus rerouted referentiality away from the subject and toward the object, the seal itself. In the course of producing presence, seals ultimately empowered not the individual but signs. The emergence of episcopal seals thus charted a voyage during which the authority of the subject passed on to the authenticity of the object, the sealed document.

---

[36] C. Stephen Jaeger argues powerfully for the charismatic nature of the eleventh century in *The Envy of Angels: Cathedral Schools and Social Ideals in Medieval Europe, 950-1200* (Philadelphia: University of Pennsylvania Press, 1994).

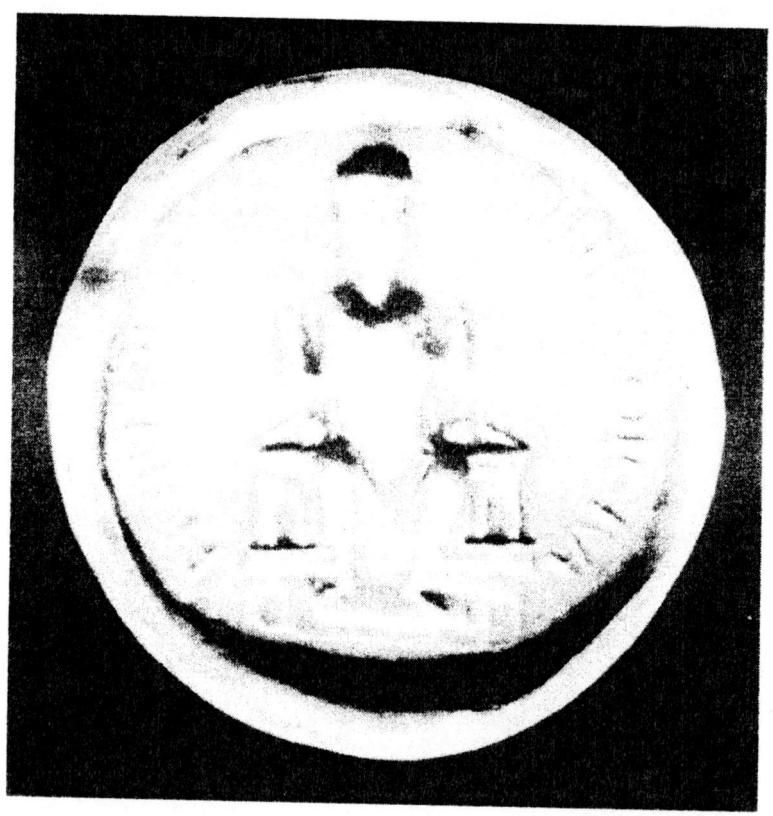

Fig. 19. Seal of Bishop Peter Lombard of Paris, 1159. Photo courtesy of Brigitte Miriam Bedos-Rezak.

Fig. 20. Seal of Henry I of France, c. 1031. Photo courtesy of Brigitte Miriam Bedos-Rezak.

Fig. 21. Seal of Bishop Notker of Liège, 980. Brussels, Algemeen Rijksarchief. Photo © Algemeen Rijksarchief.

Chapter Eight
The Bishop as Artist?
The Eucharist and Image Theory Around the Millennium[†]
Pierre-Alain Mariaux

Once, relates Paul the Deacon, Gregory the Great refused to give the body of Christ to a Roman woman.[1] When the moment came to receive Holy Communion, she began to laugh and could not stop. After mass was over, Gregory summoned the woman and asked her why she had behaved in this way while he was offering the host. She replied that when she had recognized the piece of bread she made as that which Gregory claimed to be the body of Christ, she could not help but laugh. Paul's story, which reveals the blurry distinction between "sacred" and "profane" in the early Middle Ages, also expresses in quite blunt terms the contentious nature of the doctrine of the Real Presence—a doctrine that, as we have just seen, was the focus of debates in the eleventh century which provoked new notions of identity and representation among the contemporary episcopacy. In this chapter, however, I argue that these debates contributed to another set of reflections in which the act of confection, and the notions of image-making and image-maker which it entailed, led not only to new modes of episcopal representation and projection, but to a new identity for the *sacerdos*: that of the artist. In turn, episcopal attempts to claim unique sacerdotal status as "vessels of the elect" and receptacles of the Holy Spirit—a status they would eventually have to share with the priesthood in general—would pave the way for a new set of spiritual claims by visual artists at the beginning of the twelfth century—in particular, the claim that the artist was himself a *sacerdos*.

This aspiration is clearly recognizable in the numerous signatures left by twelfth-century artists. At Saint-Pierre in Chauvigny, for instance, the sculptor Gofridus signed one of the capitals in the choir with the usual *me fecit* (fig. 22).

[†] I am grateful to Arnold Angenendt, Sean Gilsdorf, Jean Wirth, and the late Michael Camille for their valuable comments.

[1] Paul the Deacon, *S. Gregorii magni vita*, 1.23 (*PL* 75: 52-53); John the Deacon, *S. Gregorii magni vita*, II.41 (*PL* 75: 103). According to Joseph Jungmann, this episode is a ninth-century legend; the text later would be reformulated to fit the theory of the transsubstantiation. Joseph A. Jungmann, *The Mass of the Roman Rite: Its Origins and Development*, 2 vols., trans. Francis A. Brunner (New York: Benziger Brothers, 1951-55), 2: 390 n. 118, and Marta Cristiani, "La controversia eucaristica nella cultura del secolo IX," *Studi Medievali* 9 (1968): 167-233.

The scene to which he chose to apply his name depicted the Adoration of the Magi. In it, Christ raises his hand for the benediction, a gesture which also denoted an act of speech. The sculptor's own gesture is rendered equally ambiguous: did his "fecit" refer to the capital itself, or did he mean that, in one way or another, he participates in the Incarnation of Christ? In fact, the signature "Gofridus made me" can indeed refer to both the *imago* and the model it represents, linking incarnation, that is the creation of Christ's body, with what we will call artistic creation (echoes of which can still be heard today in the use of expressions like "giving birth" to describe the process of art-making).[2] This association, in fact, was grounded in the increasingly hieratic nature of the eucharistic rite in the early Middle Ages. Indeed, Paul the Deacon's story would probably have made little sense in the ninth century, since the faithful no longer brought to the altar the offerings which the priest would then consecrate. From the Carolingian period on, attention came to be focused on the performance at the altar, and the progressive dramatization of the mass displaced the idea of communion as a common sacrifice in favor of consecration by the priest alone. The central part of the mass, the canon, was whispered by the priest, who now became the sole agent of sanctification. The recitation of prayers in a low voice, away from the congregation, indicated the progressive separation of the priest from the rest of the flock.[3] This separation often led to abuses, which were regularly condemned from the tenth century on.[4] Furthermore, since the sacrifice of the mass was now concentrated in the hands of the priest, a literal creator of sacred matter, accidents committed during the eucharistic celebration (summarized in a few passages of the *libri penitentiales*) tended to highlight the prob-

---

[2] Among other examples, see for instance the porch of Santa Maria la Real in Sangüesa, where the Virgin holds a book containing Leodegarius' signature (MARIA MATER XPI LEODEGARIUS ME FECIT). or a capital at Notre-Dame-du-Port in Clermont-Ferrand depicting an angel holding a scroll with the artist's signature (ROTBERTUS ME FECIT). Jean Wirth has demonstrated the highly self-referential character of donation scenes and the staging of good works and works of art during that same period, leading to the wider diffusion of both portraits and signatures of artists; see his *L'image à l'époque romane* (Paris: Editions du Cerf, 1999), 303 ff..

[3] On the history of the Mass see, in addition to the work of Jungmann, Marius Lepin, *L'idée du sacrifice de la messe d'après les théologiens depuis les origines jusqu'à nos jours* (Paris: Gabriel Beauchesne, 1926).

[4] See in particular Rather of Verona, *De contemptu canonum*, II.2 and II.4, and *Synodica*, c. 5, in *Complete Works*, 375, 378, 447-48.

lematic relationship between the sacred and the profane.[5] At any time, the priest might stumble; he might bite the chalice or spill its contents; the *sacrificium* might fall on the ground; or, worst of all, the priest might trip over the words he was speaking and thus mispronounce the consecratory prayer.[6]

These theological and practical problems surrounding the Eucharist were addressed by a number of tenth century writers, most of whom worked within the boundaries established by the earlier Carolingian controversy over the mass, and tried to reconcile Paschasius and Ratramnus' views on the nature of the Eucharist. In doing so, however, they were forced to consider the validity of priestly consecration and the conditions for creating Christ's body. All of their texts thus share a common concern—namely, the position of the *sacerdos*, whose role is presented as crucial, even fundamental, for the conversion of the species. In turn, these discussions about the performance of the sacrament led their authors to reflect upon the prerogatives of the bishop as well, because bishops considered themselves to be *supersacerdotes*.[7] This is illustrated well by Berno of Reichenau's *De officio missae*, composed slightly after 1024. In his second chapter, he distinguishes what properly derives from the power of the bishop and what is a gift of the Holy Spirit. Particular to the bishop, he claims, is the capacity to ordain clerics, to dedicate churches, and to prepare the holy chrism, while the sacred imposition of hands, a gift of the Holy Spirit, is common to both bishops and priests. Likewise, Christ's body is no more or less holy according to who actually consecrates it, since it is neither the priest nor the bishop who acts, but the Holy Spirit through them. For Berno, quoting Jerome, priests and bishops are *consortes*, associates, in the benediction. And, contrary to what some

---

[5] Hubertus Lutterbach, "The Mass and Holy Communion in the Medieval Penitentials (600-1200): Liturgical and Religio-Historical Perspectives," in *Bread of Heaven. Customs and Practices Surrounding Holy Communion*, ed. Charles Caspers, Gerard Lukken, and G.A.M. Rouwhorst (Kampen: Kok Pharos, 1995), 61-81.

[6] Raymund Kottje, "Oratio periculosa—Eine frühmittelalterliche Bezeichnung des Kanons?" *Archiv für Liturgiewissenschaft* 10/1 (1967): 165-68.

[7] Canon 7 of the Second Council of Seville in 619 forbade the priests "eo [episcopo] praesente sacramentum corporis et sanguinis Christi conficere" (quoted in Jungmann, *Mass of the Roman Rite*, 1: 195 n. 4), a prohibition that also can be found in Theodulph of Orléans, *Capitulare*, 1.45 (*PL* 105: 208). Around the millennium, bishops were trying to defend their old prerogatives, and it seems that Berno's discourse should be read against the background of the progressive elaboration of the *missa sollemnis*, at a time when more and more priests celebrated mass like bishops.

bishops believe, there do not exist *two* bodies of Christ, a major one consecrated by the bishop, and a minor one consecrated by the priest.[8]

Berno of Reichenau's argument leads us in two directions. First, we have to understand that around the beginning of the eleventh century, some bishops intended to arrogate to themselves something common to all priests, the grace of the Holy Spirit, and thus tried to put themselves above the priesthood. Berno's claim that episcopal and priestly consecration are equivalent provides a useful indication of the opinion bishops had of themselves, and can be compared with more or less contemporary texts written by Rather of Verona, Atto of Vercelli, or the author (now thought to be Ademar of Chabannes) of the anonymous *Sermo de informatione episcoporum*. It is not necessary to analyze these particular texts in detail; their authors concur that, on the one hand, the sacerdotal body occupies the highest position in the scale of beings, and that, on the other hand, within the sacerdotal *ordo* itself a further hierarchy applies in which the bishop occupies the first place. The author of the *Sermo de informatione episcoporum* thus says that while there is nothing more excellent than priests, there also is nothing more sublime than bishops, because bishops are the favored receptacle of Divine Grace.[9] For Atto of Vercelli, bishops are the guarantors of the world order established by God and the main instrument of His love, which regulates interaction within Christian society. The bishop is thus seen as a *superinspector*.[10] Finally, Rather of Verona elevates the bishop to the highest level, and makes him literally touch the sky: "Bishops are gods, lords, christs, heavens, angels, patriarchs . . . [they] are the foundations on which the whole

---

[8] Berno of Reichenau, *De officio missae*, c. 2 (*PL* 142: 1061): "Et mirum valde videtur cum certa sit ratione discretum, quid soli liceat episcopo, non autem presbytero: videlicet, ut ad episcopum pertineant ordinationes clericorum, dedicationes aecclesiarum, sacris chrismatis confectio, ad dandum Spiritum paracletum, sacra impositio manuum, quid aliud esse possit in sacramentis divinis quod non sit presbyteris commune cum episcopis, praecipue cum id quod excellentissimum est in omnibus sacramentis, sanctum videlicet corpus et sanguinem Domini, quotidie sicut episcopi, ita et consecrent presbyteri, nec sanctius sit illorum quam istorum . . . Hi [sc. presbyteri] namque in benedictione cum episcopis consortes sunt mysteriorum ac nulla in conficiendo corpore Christi ac sanguine inter vos et episcopos credenda distantia est . . . credens Deum duo corpora habuisse, unum majus, aliud minus; quod episcopus conficit majus, quod presbyteri minus; qui Christum ita divisit, Deo injuriam fecit."

[9] *Sermo de informatione episcoporum*, 17. I have used the edition of Flavio Nuvolone in "Il *Sermo pastoralis* Pseudoambrosiano," 524.

[10] Atto of Vercelli, *Sermo* 13 (*PL* 134: 853).

building of God's Temple stands."[11] Likewise, these authors agree that the figure of Christ can be seen implicitly in the figure of the *sacerdos* (and for Rather, more specifically in the figure of the bishop). This position, of course, was not a novel one at the turn of the millennium; Carolingian authors like Amalarius of Metz and Florus of Lyons already had made such a comparison, pointing out that while we need a human priest who represents us, it is Christ who accomplishes what has to be done at the altar. This "double vision" constitutes the first point of contact between Eucharist and image theory, a point to which I will return.

Second, Berno assumes a semantic equivalence between *consecrare* and *conficere corpus Christi*. As Bernard Botte has shown, this latter expression appears in three different forms during the Middle Ages. [12] The first and oldest of these is *conficere sacramentum*; used by Ambrose and Augustine, it simply means that the bread and wine effectively become Christ's flesh and blood. The second, *conficere corpus*, appeared with Isidore of Seville. Although this phrase is similar to its predecessor, it is more direct and hence provocative, insofar as it gives the impression that the priest conceives or produces Christ Himself. Finally, in the thirteenth century *conficere* appears alone and simply means *consecrare*; any implications about the explicit creation of Christ have thus been put aside.

There is something in this expression, however, that Botte did not analyze: the verb "conficere" itself, which means "to succeed", "to realize entirely", "to achieve", or "to perfect". The word was used for different things, from the successful conclusion of a transaction to the performance of sacrifices, and applied to all kinds of activities involving the preparation and transformation of one thing into another—most notably in the kitchen, with the meaning of reducing, elaborating or shaping, a meaning that we find in the modern French words *confit* and *confiture*. When the verb is applied to the sacrament of the Eucharist, it is used in this sense of transformation and achievement. Eleventh-century authors

---

[11] Rather of Verona, *Praeloquia*, III.6.12, in *Complete Works*, 102-3. It is worth quoting the entire passage (*PL* 136: 227): "Dii sunt, Domini sunt, Christi sunt, celi sunt, angeli sunt, patriarchae sunt, prophetae sunt, apostoli sunt, evangelistae sunt, martyres sunt, uncti sunt, reges sunt, principes sunt, iudices sunt, non tantum hominum, sed et angelorum, arietes gregis Domini sunt, pastores ovium —non quarumcunque, sed Christi sanguine lotarum —sunt, pupilla oculi Dei sunt, amici Dei viventis sunt, filii Dei sunt, patres sunt, luminaria mundi sunt, stellae celi sunt, columnae Ecclesiae sunt, medici animarum sunt, ianitores paradysi sunt, claves celi portant, reserare et claudere celum valent, nubes quas Dominus ascensum suum posuit, bases super quas tota iacet structura templi Dei."

[12] Bernard Botte, "Conficere Corpus Christi," *Année théologique* 8 (1947): 309-15.

were not embarrassed to use the same verb for activities particular to cooking and for the sacramental conversion of the species. Gregory VII, for instance, uses *conficere* to describe the production of a compound with butter as well as the confection of Christ's body.[13]

What happens during the Eucharistic sacrifice, then, is the mixing or confection of Christ's body by the *sacerdos*. When he describes the conversion of the species as a *confectio*, Berno implies that the priest is working with matter, that he is transforming the bread and the wine in order to achieve or create Christ's flesh and blood.[14] We are now confronted with a very important problem: *who creates what?* Is it the priest, the priest as Christ *in aenigmate* or *in persona Christi*, or the Holy Spirit animating or working through him? In turn, what is the nature of the created body: is it the sacramental body, the historical body of Christ, or both at the same time? This latter question was central to the Eucharistic controversies, in which we confront once more the problem of vision and the image. According to Gregory the Great, as the liturgical ceremony progresses, the eucharistic conversion opens the heavens and signals the unity of the visible realm with the invisible one.[15] The author of the *Confessio fidei* (probably John of Fécamp) clarified this notion, distinguishing two modes of vision at the altar: while the believer sees with his carnal eyes (*oculis corporeis*) a priest offering bread and wine, with the eyes of his heart—that is, with the gaze of faith (*intuitu fidei*)—he sees Christ offering himself.[16] Moreover, according to

---

[13] Gregory VII, *Das Register Gregors VII*, ed. Erich Caspar [MGH ES 2] (Berlin: Weidmann, 1920), VIII.1: "Audivimus etiam quod contra morem sanctae Ecclesiae vestrae non ex balsamo sanctum chrisma sed ex butyro conficiat," and VIII.21: "quod maximum est in christiana religione, quis eorum valet proprio ore corpus et sanguinem Domini conficere?"

[14] I would suggest that the prohibition against confecting the body of Christ in wooden chalices may have been meant precisely to avoid the confusing collusion between mortar and chalice, between the art of cooking and liturgical performance.

[15] Gregory I, *Dialogues*, IV.58 (*PL* 77: 425): "Quis enim fidelium habere dubium possit, in ipsa immolationis hora ad sacerdotis vocem coelos aperiri, in illo Jesu Christi mysterio angelorum choros adesse, sumaris ima sociari, terrena coelestibus jungi, unumque ex visibilibus atque invisibilibus fieri?"

[16] *Confessio fidei*, IV, 1 (*PL* 101: 1087): "Ideo quamvis corporeis oculis ibi ad altare Domini videam sacerdotem, panem et vinum offerentem, tamen intuitu fidei, et puro lumine cordis inspicio illum summum sacerdotem, verumque pontificem Dominum Jesum Christum, offerentem seipsum . . . ."

Faustus of Riez (cited by Paschasius), Christ as an invisible priest (*invisibilis sacerdos*) converts the visible creatures into His own substance.[17]

Two modes of vision, each with a different object, thus must be distinguished in the context of the sacrament. We need a human priest who represents us, but it is Christ who accomplishes what has to be made at the altar. In order to better understand the implications of this double vision for the priest's function at the altar, it is useful to review the Carolingian eucharistic debates between Paschasius Radbertus and Ratramnus regarding the nature and role of *figura* and *res*.[18] Following Ambrose, Paschasius had contended that the sacramental body was identical with Christ's historical body. Since it is difficult to deny the Eucharist's figurative quality, he had to explain how it could nevertheless contain the truth. His solution was to argue that since every figure is a figure of another thing, and always refers to it, there must be a true thing of which it is the figure. More precisely, the Eucharist is the figure of what it contains, though what is contained is concealed from sight. Since Christ is the figure—Paschasius here adds "or the imprint (*character*)"—of the Father's substance (cf. Heb. 1:3), the Eucharist may properly be called both figure and truth: truth, because it contains the true, real body of Christ, and figure, since it is the "imprint" of the truth. In summary, then, "[the Eucharist] is the figure or imprint of the truth insofar as it is outwardly perceived, but whatever is correctly understood or believed inwardly from this mystery is the truth."[19]

Although Paschasius does not explicitly cite Ambrose, it is clear that the latter's concept of the progression from *umbra* to *veritas* through *imago* influenced his views. According to Ambrose, we must seek realities, in which perfection and truth will be found. To do so, however, we must first learn *how to look*, because "here is shadow and image, there the truth; the shadow is in the Law, the image in the Gospels, the truth in the heavenly realities." "Here," he adds, "we

---

[17] Faustus of Riez, *Sermones*, IV.3 (*PL* 83: 1225): "Nam invisibilis sacerdos, visibiles creaturas in substantiam corporis et sanguinis sui, verbo suo secreta potestate convertit."

[18] See the brilliant study by Celia Chazelle, "Figure, Character, and the Glorified Body in the Carolingian Eucharistic Controversy," *Traditio* 47 (1992): 1-36.

[19] Paschasius Radbertus, *De corpore et sanguine Domini*, ed. Beda Paulus [*CCCM* 16] (Turnhout: Brepols, 1969), c. IV (28-29): "Omnis enim figura alicuius rei figura est . . . Hoc mysterium aut veritas est aut figura ac per hoc umbra est . . . Sed si veraciter inspicimus, iure simul veritas et figura dicitur, ut sit figura vel caracter veritatis quod exterius sensitur, veritas vero quicquid de hoc mysterio interius recte intellegitur aut creditur. Non enim omnis figura umbra vel falsitas."

walk in image, we see in image; there, we will see face to face."[20] *Umbra* thus is equated to the historical and carnal aspect of things, prefiguring an expected spiritual reality; *imago* is the point at which that spiritual reality "co-adheres" to the flesh; and *veritas* points to the zone of preexistence and eschatology. The image seems to be at the same time accomplishment and anticipation, just as Christ both fulfills the prophecies and announces the kingdom of God. As well, the image is a vision *in aenigmate*: what is perceived is reality as it appears physically, not reality in itself. The truth, in contrast, is the complete spiritual reality, a manifest vision *facie ad faciem* of that which was presented in visible and historical form with Christ's Incarnation. According to Ambrose, this means that after Christ's Incarnation the truth is made visible or present in the eucharist, because Christ is *imago Dei* and not *vacua imago*.[21]

The minister of the eucharist, according to Paschasius, thus does not create anything at the altar. He is a mediator between divine grace and the consecrated species, which will be brought up to the celestial altar by the angels. It is no surprise, therefore, that Paschasius does not use the verb *conficere* to describe the priest's role; indeed, in his *Epistola de corpore et sanguine domini ad Frudegardum* he explicitly states that the only artist is the Holy Spirit. It would be absurd, he concludes, to suppose that the priest creates Christ's body at the altar, since this would mean that the creature is creating its creator. God, and only God, is the *opifex*.[22]

---

[20] Ambrose, *De officiis*, 2 vols., ed. Maurice Testard (Paris: Les Belles Lettres, 1984-1992), I.48.239 (1: 210-11): "Hic umbra, hic imago, illic veritas. Umbra in lege, imago in Evangelio, veritas in coelestibus . . . Hic ergo in imagine ambulamus, in imagine videmus: illic facie ad faciem."

[21] Ambrose, *De excessu fratris*, II.109, in *Sancti Ambrosii opera*, vol. 7, ed. Otto Faller [*CSEL* 73] (Vienna: Tempsky, 1896), 311-12: "Christus non umbra, sed imago Dei, non vacua imago, sed veritas."

[22] See Paschasius, *Epistola ad Fredugardum*, in idem, *De corpore et sanguine Domini*, 160: "Ac per hoc apostolo teste sicut nemo dicit Dominum Iesum nisi in Spiritu Sancto [1 Cor 12:3], ita nemo credit hoc ita esse nisi per Spiritum Sanctum, per quem haec fides data est et per quem hoc efficitur sacramentum, ut vera caro atque ipsa et non alia quam ipsa caro. Alias autem sine Spiritu Sancto sicut nec caro Christi prodest quicquam [John 6:63], ita nec hoc sacramentum carnis et sanguinis prodesse potest. Quia in his omnibus unus est opifex Spiritus Sanctus, unus et Christus qui conceptus de Spiritu Sancto ex Maria virgine, unus et creator atque sanctificator corporis ac sanguinis ipse Spiritus." Cf. idem, *De corpore et sanguine Domini*, XII.53-55 (78): "Unde sacerdos non ex se dicit, quod ipse creator corporis et sanguinis esse possit, quia si hoc posset quod absurdum est, creator creatoris fieret . . . ."

A quite contrary position on this issue was taken by Ratramnus of Corbie. At the beginning of his *De corpore et sanguine Domini*, he offers his own analysis of the relationship between truth and figure.[23] A figure, he argues, is a kind of overshadowing: it says one thing but signifies another, and cannot make its referent clear or obvious to the senses. Truth, on the other hand, is the demonstration of something manifest, something that is not veiled.[24] The Eucharist presents a spiritual or intangible content. Since it has nothing to do with something visible or tangible, therefore, the sacramental body is not identical with the real body of Christ. Although Ratramnus claims that Christ is not really, materially, or sensibly present in the species, however, this does not mean that he questions the truth of Christ's spiritual presence. The sacramental body offers a pledge, the image, the likeness and appearance of Christ's body, which itself will be revealed to the faithful on the last day. For Ratramnus, as Celia Chazelle has shown, "a proper historical presence requires a belief either that the body and blood in the Eucharist are separate *material* entities lying beneath an outer, material covering of bread and wine, perhaps hidden by that covering but still potentially visible; or the bread and wine must be totally replaced by perceptible flesh and blood, as though consecration has produced a sensible, material presence."[25]

These arguments were repeated in the tenth century, when Gezo of Tortona and Heriger of Lobbes propounded a realist, even sensual, conception of the eucharist. Everyone agreed that the eucharist involves some kind of creation of Christ, with the help of the Spirit. Two principles are involved in this creation: the first is material and visible, specific to the priest (*conficere*), while the second is spiritual or intellectual and invisible, specific to the Spirit (*creare*). It was this very same Spirit at work when the Virgin came to be with child; thus, the ineffable *operatio* of the Spirit produces the same result in the Incarnation and in the eucharist, i.e., the body of Christ. There still is a danger, however, that the faithful may confuse what pertains to the Spirit's action with what pertains to the priest's. Berengar of Tours clearly understood the risks of such a sensual ap-

---

[23] Chazelle, "Figure, Character, and the Glorified Body," 20.

[24] Ratramnus of Corbie, *De corpore et sanguine Domini*, 7-8 (*PL* 121: 130): "Figura est obumbratio quaedam quibusdam velaminibus quod intendit ostendens . . . Veritas vero est rei manifesta demonstratio, nullis umbrarum imaginibus obvelatae, sed puris et apertis, utque plenius eloquamur, naturalibus significationibus insinuatae . . . ."

[25] Chazelle, "Figure, Character, and the Glorified Body," 25.

proach to the Eucharist, and denounced the notion that the priest could materially create Christ's body. One even wonders whether Berengar accused his opponents of worshipping (if not making) images, since he protested against the idea that the *sacerdos* could create Christ's body *de novo*. Peter the Deacon's exclamation at the Council of Vercelli in 1050, which condemned Berengar's theses for the first time, is a telling one: "If we still are in the image, when will we be able to grasp the reality?"[26]

Peter's *cri du cœur* reflects the degree to which Berengar had gone beyond even Ratramnus, his major intellectual and doctrinal influence. While Ratramnus had argued that the sacramental body is an "image" of Christ's historical body, Berengar radically separated the figure from the truth. For Berengar, Christ's presence in the eucharist is one *in figura*, not *in veritate*. The sacrament is its sign, its pledge, its image, its similitude. Employing the familiar Augustinian formula, he concludes that since the sacrament is a sacred and visible sign of invisible Grace, similar to but not identical with that which it signifies, then the bread and wine are visible signs, offered to the senses and perceived with corporeal eyes, of Christ's body, which is truly perceived only with the intellect or spiritually. For Berengar, Christ is now sitting at the right hand of the Father, and is no longer visible in this world of images. He cannot be created *de novo* each day at the altar, much less be divided into parts. The consecration thus does not imply a sensible change: the conversion happens *intellectualiter*, with the bread and wine remaining in their essential nature. As a result, the priest does not in fact create anything.

At the Council of Rome in 1059, Berengar was forced to renounce this eucharistic theory, and to profess his belief in the sensible conversion of the species. Twenty years later, however, he was made to accede to a second confession, one in which the eucharistic body was identified so completely with the body born from the Virgin that the priest now replaces Mary, giving birth to Christ anew in the sacrament. It seems that the warnings of Ratramnus, and even Paschasius, had been forgotten. As René Laurentin has shown, Peter Damian was familiar with the parallel between the priest's role and that of the Virgin;[27] indeed, the

---

[26] Berengar of Tours, *Rescriptum contra Lanfrancum* , ed. R.B.C. Huygens [*CCCM* 84] (Turnhout: Brepols, 1988), I.439-40 (48): "Si adhuc in figura sumus, quando rem tenebimus?" On the dispute surrounding Berengarius' views, see Jean de Montclos, *Lanfranc et Bérenger: La controverse eucharistique du XIe siècle* (Louvain: Spicilegium sacrum Lovaniense, 1971).

[27] René Laurentin, *Marie, l'Eglise et le Sacerdoce*, 2 vols. (Paris: Nouvelles Editions Latines, 1952-1953), 1: 114.

priest's daily creation of Christ's body was a main reason why the priesthood became such a central element of religious life in the eleventh century.[28]

This model of the priest as creator of Christ, I would argue, was deeply influential for later medieval artists. The reasons for this appeal can be found in a fantastic story told by Thietmar of Merseburg in his *Chronicon*.[29] Archbishop Gero of Cologne had commissioned a wooden crucifix for his church, one which still stood above his tomb in Thietmar's day. When Gero noticed a crack in the crucifix's head, he decided to "heal it" (*curare*). Taking a bit of the consecrated host (*Dominici corporis portio*) and a piece of the True Cross (*pars salutifere crucis*), he tied them together and set them in the crack. Then, crying and prostrate, he invoked God's name and thus completely repaired the damage.

When Gero repairs his wooden crucifix, he is presenting himself as an artist of a particular kind, working with an extraordinary material. Gero succeeds in fixing the crucifix when he fills the crack with a mixture of Christ's body and the True Cross, and then recites a blessing. There is no doubt about the story's miraculous and eucharist-related nature. But there is more than that: the episode binds in the simplest and even bluntest way the body of Christ, which is produced at the altar by the priest, and the crucifix made by the artist. The text thus leads the reader to the heart of the Eucharistic controversy, and more particularly to the central distinction between figure and truth. It is noteworthy that Thietmar makes no claim about, and thus does not allow us to distinguish between, what is said *in figura* and what is said *in veritate* about Christ's body. First, he stresses the identity of the body created at the altar with the crucified one, i.e., he proclaims the identity of the sacramental with the historical body. Second, he states that Christ's image *is* Christ. Once the blessing has been performed, the mixture used for repair disappears into the wood and conceals the fissure; the fragment of the True Cross apparently serves here as a binding agent. Third, by directly associating priestly creation with artistic creation, the text affirms the superiority of the former over the latter: the priest not only uses a sacred and miraculous material, but he also creates through the power of blessing, that is, with his speech. Gero of Cologne thus makes the body of Christ with his hands and

---

[28] See in particular Laudage, *Priesterbild und Reformpapsttum*.

[29] Thietmar, *Chronicon*, III.2-4 (86-88). Cf. Reiner Haussherr, *Der tote Christus am Kreuz. Zur Ikonographie des Gerokreuzes*, Ph.D. dissertation, Friedrich-Wilhelms-Universität zu Bonn, 1963, 35-41, and Annika Fisher's paper "Making the Body of Christ: The Crucifix of Archbishop Gero of Cologne," read at the conference "*Genus Regale et Sacerdotale*: The Image of the Bishop Around the Millennium," Chicago, October 1999.

through the invocation of the divine name—a striking reflection of the formula found in the *Libri Carolini*, "per manum sacerdotis et invocationem divini nominis conficiatur."[30] Yet while in the ninth century those words were used to separate the eucharist *from* the image, around the first millennium they served to define the creation of the true body of Christ *as* an image, if not the image of Christ *as* Christ.

Was the *sacerdos*, then, an artist? The answer is yes—when he was performing the sacrament at the altar. With the help of the Holy Spirit, he creates Christ's body; more precisely, it is the Holy Spirit that creates what the priest confects. As Peter Lombard would later say in his *Sentences*, it is only God who creates something; man can just make, that is compose, things.[31] It is possible, however, to speak of creation as long as the Spirit intervenes during the process. Thanks to bishops and priests, therefore, medieval artists little by little became aware that they too worked in conjunction with that same Spirit, and some of them even came to consider themselves as a kind of priesthood (or better, as theodidacts).[32] This belief was an understandable one, since priests before them had considered themselves to be not only ministers, but artists as well.

---

[30] *Opus Caroli regis contra synodum (Libri Carolini)*. ed. Ann Freeman (MGH *Conc* II, Suppl. 1) (Hannover: Hahn, 1998), II.27.

[31] Peter Lombard, *Sententiae*, II, Dist. I.1 (*PL* 192: 651): "Creator enim est qui de nihilo aliquid facit. Et creare proprie est de nihilo aliquid facere; facere vero non modo de nihilo aliquid operari, sed etiam de materia. Unde et homo et angelus dicitur aliqua facere, sed non creare; vocatur factor sive artifex, sed non creator. Hoc enim nomen soli Deo proprie congruit, qui de nihilo quaedam, et de aliquo aliquid facit. Ipse est ergo creator et opifex et factor, sed creationis nomen sibi proprie retinuit, alia vero etiam creaturis communicavit."

[32] Cf. 1 Thess. 4:9. On this issue, see Pierre-Alain Mariaux, "La Vierge dans l'atelier de Tuotilo. De l'artiste médiéval considéré comme un 'théodidacte'," *Revue de l'Histoire des religions* 218/2 (2001): 171-93.

Fig. 22. Choir capital with Adoration of the Magi. Church of St.-Pierre, Chauvigny. Photo courtesy of the Institute d'Histoire de l'Art, Université de Neuchâtel.

Chapter Nine
Elusive Bishops:
Remembering, Forgetting, and Remaking
the History of the Early Danish Church
Michael H. Gelting

The conversion of the major realms of northern and eastern Europe in the tenth and eleventh centuries resulted in the creation of numerous new dioceses. Setting up these basic ecclesiastical structures was not just a question of seeing to the spiritual needs of the new Christian communities. The episcopal office as it was introduced to the freshly converted kingdoms came to be invested with the same combination of spiritual and secular powers as its counterparts in the old Christian monarchies of western and central Europe. Appointments to the new bishoprics and their ecclesiastical allegiance were therefore matters of the highest political concern. In the case of Denmark, however, such political considerations ultimately led to the deliberate obfuscation of the history of the Danish church during the first century of its existence.[1]

The evidence which we possess for the history of the Danish church in its early years, following the creation of the first Danish bishoprics in 948 and the conversion of King Harald Bluetooth c. 958/65, is fragmentary at best. Since indigenous written evidence in Denmark, apart from runic inscriptions, does not occur until the end of the eleventh century, the later Danish chroniclers' information about the tenth and eleventh centuries poses a familiar problem: to what extent were their accounts derived from written texts or from oral traditions? It does not take much research, however, to discover that a surprisingly large part of what medieval Danish clerics knew about the earliest century or so of their church's existence was derived from the *Gesta Hammaburgensis ecclesiae pontificum*, completed in the 1070's by Master Adam of Bremen as a statement of the greatness of the archbishops of Hamburg-Bremen and of their unique achievements in the evangelization of Scandinavia.[2] Part of the reason for this situation certainly was that the Danish episcopal sees lacked the full institutional

---

[1] I owe special thanks to professor Peter Sawyer, who long ago made the suggestion from which the present chapter has ultimately sprung; to my colleague Anders Leegaard Knudsen for incisive and fruitful comments upon an earlier version of this article; and to research fellow Helle Sørensen for valuable help in bringing it down to a reasonable length.

[2] Adam of Bremen, *Hamburgische Kirchengeschichte*, 3rd ed., ed. Bernhard Schmeidler [MGH *SSRG*] (Hannover: Hahnsche Buchhandlung, 1917).

framework for preserving their historical traditions until they were provided with cathedral chapters. The earliest such chapters were founded at the cathedrals of Roskilde towards the middle of the 1070s and of Lund in 1085 or slightly earlier.[3] Yet even granted that, the extreme paucity of local historical tradition about the early bishops is puzzling.

This chapter, therefore, focuses not upon the light which medieval historiography sheds on early medieval bishops and their communities, but on the shadows cast by the chronicler of the missionary see of Hamburg-Bremen—shadows which not only obscured the history of the early Danish church, but even came to replace it for later generations. As I intend to show, a substantial part of the early 'Danish' bishops that we know of were no more than titular bishops in exile, while we ignore the identity of some of those bishops who actually held office in Denmark during the century in question. I also will argue that this peculiar situation was due in large part to the fact that the authority of the archbishops of Hamburg-Bremen over the Danish church, and hence the canonical legitimacy of their metropolitan status, was even more insecure than has hitherto been admitted. What follows, in short, is a partial demolition of the consensus version of eleventh-century Danish ecclesiastical history elaborated by Scandinavian and international medieval historians over the last century, and an attempt to replace it by an alternative reconstruction of the course of events. Much of it is hypothetical, but so is the consensus version, and I believe my reconstruction has the advantage of greater coherence.[4]

---

[3] Ludvig Helveg, *De Danske Domkapitler: deres Oprindelse, Indretning og Virksomhed, før Reformationen* (Copenhagen: C. G. Iversen, 1855), 6-21.

[4] Space does not permit a full discussion of the historiography. Among recent general works in English may be cited: Richard Fletcher, *The Conversion of Europe: From Paganism to Christianity, 371-1386 A.D.* (London: Fontana Press, 1998), 403-10; Else Roesdahl, *Viking Age Denmark* (London: British Museum Publications, 1982), 176-83; Peter Sawyer, "The process of Scandinavian Christianization in the tenth and eleventh centuries," in *The Christianization of Scandinavia: Report of a Symposium held at Kungälv, Sweden, 4-9 August 1985*, ed. Birgit Sawyer, Peter Sawyer, and Ian Wood (Alingsås: Viktoria Bokförlag, 1987), 68-87; and Birgit and Peter Sawyer, *Medieval Scandinavia: From Conversion to Reformation, circa 800-1500* (Minneapolis: University of Minnesota Press, 1993), 100-108. The early history of the Danish bishoprics is discussed thoroughly in *Series episcoporum ecclesiae catholicae occidentalis ab initio usque ad annum MCXCVIII*, vol. VI/2, *Archiepiscopatus Lundensis*, ed. Helmuth Kluger (Stuttgart: Anton Hiersemann, 1992). All subsequent references to this volume will use the shortened form *Ser. ep.*, 6:2.

Table 2
Kings of Denmark, c. 948-1134

The Jelling Dynasty

Gorm the Old	† c. 958
Harald Bluetooth (son)	c. 958–c. 986/7
Baptized c. 958-65	
Sven Forkbeard (son)	c. 986/7–1014
Harald II (son)	1014–1018
Cnut the Great (brother)	1018/19–1035
King of England	*1015/16-1035*
Harthecnut (son)	1035–1042
King of England	*1040-1042*

Conquered by Norway

Magnus the Good	1042–1047
King of Norway	*1035-1047*

The Knytling Dynasty

Sven Estrithson	1047–1074/76
(sister's son of Cnut the Great)	
Harald Hein (son)	1074/76–1080
St. Canute (Cnut IV) (brother)	1080–1086
Olav Hunger (brother)	1086–1095
Eric the Evergood (brother)	1095–1103
Nicholas (brother)	1103/4–1134

Shadow bishops: Schleswig and Ribe

In 831/34, Saint Ansgar was elevated to the archiepiscopal dignity, with Hamburg as his see, in anticipation of the future success of the evangelization of the Nordic and Slavic lands.[5] Instead, however, Hamburg was devastated by the Danes in 845; in 847 the see of Bremen was detached from the ecclesiastical province of Cologne and given to Ansgar for his living, and shortly afterwards it was united with the see of Hamburg. Itinerant missionary bishops were sent out from Bremen, but it remained impossible to establish permanent dioceses. Thus the archiepiscopal see of Hamburg-Bremen had an Achilles' heel: its lack of proper suffragans, which was the normal prerequisite for the existence of an archdiocese. The appointment of bishops to the three new Danish sees of Schleswig, Ribe, and Århus in 948 was not necessarily a sign of success for the mission as much as the fulfillment of an urgent need on the part of the archbishop of Hamburg-Bremen.[6] It is doubtful whether they gained immediate access to their putative dioceses. The conversion of the Danish king Harald Bluetooth c. 958/65 probably enabled the bishops to take up residence in their sees, and the success was followed up with the creation of a fourth Danish bishopric in Odense.[7] However, the new ecclesiastical province was vulnerable to political change, because the suffragans were subject to the Danish king, while the archbishop belonged to the German *Reich*. By 988, Harald's son and successor Sven Forkbeard (c. 986/87—1014) had expelled the four bishops, and the last thing we hear of them is that Otto III provided for their maintenance during their exile by a privilege of 18 March 988.[8] One further suffragan bishopric had been created at about the same time, that of Aldenburg/Starigard in Wagria (now the

---

[5] For this and the following, where nothing else is indicated, see *Ser. ep.*, 6:2. and *Series episcoporum ecclesiae catholicae occidentalis ab initio usque ad annum MCXCVIII*, vol. V/2, *Archiepiscopatus Hammaburgensis sive Bremensis*, ed. Stefan Weinfurter and Odilo Engels (Stuttgart: Anton Hiersemann, 1984) (hereinafter *Ser. ep.*, 5:2).

[6] Horst Fuhrmann, "Die Synoden von Ingelheim," in *Ingelheim am Rhein*, ed. Johanne Autenrieth (Stuttgart: Ernst Klett, 1964), 163-64.

[7] Tore S. Nyberg, *Die Kirche in Skandinavien: Mitteleuropäischer und englischer Einfluß im 11. und 12. Jahrhundert. Anfänge der Domkapitel Børglum und Odense in Dänemark* [Beiträge zur Geschichte und Quellenkunde des Mittelalters 10] (Sigmaringen: Thorbecke, 1986), 114.

[8] DO III no. 41. Tore Nyberg mistakenly has claimed that the bishopric of Odense was erected on this occasion; see *Monasticism in North-Western Europe, 800-1200* (Aldershot: Ashgate, 2000), 52.

eastern part of Holstein), which was created by Emperor Otto I shortly after 968. Upon the great Slavic revolt of 983, however, the bishop of Aldenburg suffered exile; although the see continued to be provided at least until the time of Archbishop Bescelin Alebrand (1035—1043), its titular bishops mostly lived in exile as auxiliary bishops in various German dioceses. By the end of the 980s, the archbishop of Hamburg-Bremen was for all practical purposes back to square one.

According to Adam of Bremen, however, the breakdown of the diocesan structure in Denmark was only partial. Adam ignores the very existence of the ephemeral see of Odense, and fails to mention the expulsion of the bishops, but he tells that King Sven organized a great persecution of the Christians in Denmark (this likely refers to Sven's repudiation of the Danish church's allegiance to Hamburg-Bremen, rather than to a full-fledged pagan reaction).[9] Adam also admits that the see of Århus was discontinued after the death of Archbishop Adaldag in 988.[10] Thus, he says, the only bishops left in Denmark in the days of Archbishop Unwan (1013—1029) were the "theologian" Poppo and Odinkar;[11] they were the only bishops in Jutland before Cnut the Great came to the throne (i.e. before c. 1018). Odinkar was the only one to visit the lands beyond the sea, while Esico stayed at home, and persecution hindered the rest.[12] Bishop Odinkar is said to have had his see in Ribe,[13] while a previous chapter informs us that Esico was Poppo's successor as bishop of Schleswig.[14]

Yet the imperial diploma of 988 leaves no doubt that the bishops of Schleswig and Ribe, too, were in exile at that time. Upon closer inspection, both Poppo and Odinkar look rather dubious. Whether or not Bishop Poppo of Schleswig was the same as the missionary Poppo who converted Harald Bluetooth by success-

---

[9] Adam of Bremen, II.29 (90-91); cf. Niels Refskou, "Det retslige indhold af de ottonske diplomer til de danske bispedømmer," *Scandia* 52 (1986): 197-99.

[10] Adam of Bremen, II.46 (106-7).

[11] All translations from Adam of Bremen are based upon those in *Adam of Bremen: History of the Archbishops of Hamburg-Bremen*, trans. Francis J. Tschan (New York: Columbia University Press, 1959); here page 89.

[12] Adam of Bremen, II.49 (110).

[13] *Ibid.*, schol. 35 (110); cf. xli-xlii.

[14] *Ibid.*, II.46 (106).

fully passing an ordeal,[15] his episcopate must be dated to sometime in the 990s, and it is unlikely that he ever resided in his see.[16] His successor Ekkihard/Esico remained as an auxiliary bishop in the diocese of Hildesheim from his first appearance in the year 1000, and there he was buried in 1026 after unsuccessfully attempting to take possession of his titular see.[17] This confirms Adam's statement that Esico "stayed at home", but belies his claim that Poppo was still active in the days of Archbishop Unwan.

Something also seems to be wrong with Adam's picture of Bishop Odinkar. We are told that there were two bishops of that name. Odinkar the Elder was a Danish noble who was ordained as a missionary bishop to the Swedes by Archbishop Adaldag (937—988).[18] In addition to Sweden, he also proselytized in the eastern parts of Denmark (Funen, Sealand and Scania). Odinkar the Younger, his disciple and nephew, was baptized by Archbishop Adaldag and consecrated as a missionary bishop by Archbishop Libentius I (988/89—1013), taking up his see in Ribe.[19] The elder Odinkar was buried in St. Peter's cathedral in Bremen.[20] On the face of it, there is nothing suspicious about the careers and chronology of the two Odinkars as they are presented by Adam, and it generally has been assumed that the Bishop Odinkar who participated in the synod of Dortmund on 7 July 1005 was the bishop of Ribe.[21] Yet, unlike the other bishops present, including Ekkihard of Schleswig, no see is indicated for Odinkar. This detail makes it likely that he was in fact Odinkar the Elder, who was a missionary bishop without a fixed see.

---

[15] The complicated evidence is surveyed by Lene Demidoff, "The Poppo Legend," *Mediaeval Scandinavia* 6 (1973): 39-67. See also Sture Bolin, *Om Nordens äldsta historieforskning: Studier över dess metodik och källvärde* [Lunds Universitets årsskrift, n.s., 1/27 no. 3] (Lund: H. Olsson, 1931), 63-112.

[16] Cf. Christian Radtke, "Anfänge und erste Entwicklung des Bistums Schleswig im 10. und 11. Jahrhundert," in *850 Jahre St.-Petri-Dom zu Schleswig*, ed. Horst Appuhn, Christian Radtke, and Walter Körber (Schleswig: Schleswiger Druck- und Verlagshaus, 1984), 133-60, 145.

[17] *Ser. ep.*, 6:2, 103-105; cf. Radtke, "Anfänge," 145. For his death, see note 39 below.

[18] Adam of Bremen, II.26 (85).

[19] *Ibid.*, II.36 (96-97).

[20] *Ibid.*, II.64 (124).

[21] Thietmar, *Chronicon*, VI.18 (262) (= *MGH Const.* I.28 (58) and *Diplomatarium Danicum*, vol. I/1, ed. C.A. Christensen and Herluf Nielsen (Copenhagen: Munksgaard, 1957), no. 362, 141 (cited hereinafter as *DD*)). Cf. *Ser. ep.*, 6:2, 68 and Nyberg, *Monasticism*, 31-32.

On the other hand, according to Adam's scholion 25 (one of those that Schmeidler assumed to be Adam's own work), the younger Odinkar had a peculiar professional career: after being educated in Bremen before 988 and consecrated as a bishop between 988 and 1013, he was nonetheless sent to England and France for further education by King Cnut the Great, i.e. after c. 1018.[22] Writing several generations after the events, Adam may easily have confused the two homonymous bishops. It makes better sense to assume that Odinkar the Younger received his foreign education before his episcopal consecration, which then would have been performed at the hands not of Archbishop Libentius I, but of Libentius II (1029—1032).[23] In turn, the Odinkar who was baptized and educated in Bremen in the days of Archbishop Adaldag, and who appeared in Dortmund in 1005, would have been the elder Odinkar who also received his episcopal consecration from Adaldag. Of course, Adam's confusion may have been involuntary; but it does look suspiciously as if he wanted to gloss over the fact that all of the first Danish episcopal sees were discontinued from c. 987 until the time of Cnut the Great.

King Cnut's church

During Sven Forkbeard's reign, the Danish magnate Odinkar the Elder seems to have been the only missionary bishop in Hamburg-Bremen's obedience who was tolerated in Denmark. Adam all but admits this, although he feebly adds that the other surviving missionary bishops from Archbishop Adaldag's time were "not idle."[24] When King Sven around the year 1000 began recruiting bishops, he fetched them from England, which he invaded regularly in those years, even though he had not yet made himself master of that kingdom. Adam tells that at this time Sven placed a certain Gotebald from England as "teacher" (*doctor*) in Scania.[25] Because he was later commemorated in the necrology of Lund cathe-

---

[22] Adam of Bremen, schol. 25 (97); cf. xli-xlii.

[23] I owe this hypothesis to professor Peter Sawyer. Cf. *Ser. ep.*, 6:2, 68, n. 53, where I did not yet dare to follow his suggestion. The present article springs from the doubts which have been nagging me since then. Sawyer's point seems to have been misunderstood by Nyberg, *Monasticism*, 33.

[24] Adam of Bremen, II.36 (97).

[25] *Ibid.*, II.41=schol. 26 (101).

dral, Gotebald is usually considered to have been the first bishop of Lund.[26] He was commemorated, however, under 21 August in a consolidated obituary of three early bishops, Gotebald, Bernard and Henry; the former two are simply called "bishops", while Henry is said to have been "the first bishop of our church."[27] Adam also states that Gotebald evangelized sometimes in Sweden and frequently in Norway,[28] so he would seem rather to have been another itinerant missionary bishop, albeit with Scania as his base.

Gotebald was not the only bishop recruited from England. Adam says of Archbishop Unwan that "because of his friendship with the kings he also left it to other [learned men], who had been consecrated in England, to build up the Church, as long as they were satisfactory. Many of them he kept with him, but all he loaded with gifts when they left, making them willing to acknowledge subjection to the Church at Hamburg."[29] While the kings in question may be all of the contemporary Scandinavian rulers, the Danish kings—Sven Forkbeard, Harald II (1014—1018) and Cnut the Great —likely are meant as well. The reality of the submission of their English bishops to Hamburg-Bremen may well be doubted. After Cnut's final conquest of England, Adam says, he brought many bishops to Denmark from England. Among these he chose Bernard for Scania, Gerbrand for Sealand, and Reginbert for Funen. This incensed Archbishop Unwan—not exactly in keeping with Adam's previous picture of a harmonious compromise between the archbishop and the Scandinavian kings. Yet, Adam continues, as Gerbrand was on his way to Denmark from England after having been ordained by Archbishop Æthelnoth of Canterbury, he was captured by Unwan and forced to recognize Hamburg-Bremen's authority. From then on he was "very intimate" (*familiarissimus*) with Unwan. The archbishop of Hamburg-Bremen sent emissaries to Cnut to congratulate him upon his conquest of England, but also to upbraid him for having presumed to transfer bishops from England. The Danish king stood corrected, and he too became a loyal friend of the German archbishop.[30]

---

[26] *Ser. ep.*, 6:2 (13).

[27] *Necrologium Lundense: Lunds domkyrkas nekrologium*, ed. Lauritz Weibull (Lund: Berlingska, 1923), 88. For the latter claim, cf. below at 197 – 198 and note 61.

[28] Adam of Bremen, II.41=schol. 26 (101).

[29] *Ibid.*, II.49 (110-11).

[30] *Ibid.*, II.55 (116).

Gerbrand's story allows a fairly close dating, since he appears in an English charter of Cnut in 1022, while Æthelnoth, who ordained him, became archbishop of Canterbury in 1020.[31] Bernard of Scania and Reginbert of Funen were probably installed at the same time. Cnut thus sought to organize a Danish church, dependent on the archbishopric of Canterbury, as soon as possible after his accession to the Danish throne. The organization of that church was to follow a simple plan, with one bishop for each of the main provinces: Scania, Sealand, Funen, and Jutland. Adam, of course, could not mention the appointment of a bishop of Jutland by Cnut, since he assumed that Odinkar was in charge already. According to our revision of Odinkar's chronology, however, there would have been no bishop in Jutland at the beginning of Cnut's reign. On the other hand, Odinkar the Younger's educational tour of England and France could hardly have been completed by 1020/22, and if our hypothesis is correct, he was not consecrated until the pontificate of Archbishop Libentius II (1029—1032). Cnut's plan is likely to have included a bishop for Jutland from the outset, so Odinkar must have been preceded by an unknown 'Anglo-Danish' bishop. Cnut's episcopal church, in other words, was constituted without the slightest reference to the diocesan structure that had been introduced in the previous century under the auspices of Hamburg-Bremen.

There is another catch to Adam's story. The whole tale of Gerbrand's submission to Archbishop Unwan and Cnut's ensuing docility was not taken by Adam from the archives and traditions of his own diocese; it was told to him by his illustrious Danish informant King Sven Estrithson, and Adam is unable to suppress his astonishment that Sven did not try to conceal the ignominious capture of Bishop Gerbrand.[32] If Gerbrand's capture was not remembered in Bremen, the reason might be that Sven had made up the whole story; Cnut's utter docility—"thenceforth he gladly would do everything to Unwan's satisfaction"—certainly looks too good to be true, from Bremen's point of view. We shall see later on why Sven might have desired to distort his predecessor's history in such an apparently unfavorable way.

---

[31] Peter Sawyer, *Anglo-Saxon Charters: An annotated list and bibliography* (London: Royal Historical Society, 1968), no. 958 (288) (= *Ser. ep.*, 6:2, 79.).

[32] Adam of Bremen, II.55 (116): "Haec nobis de avunculo suo rex Danorum innotuit et de captione Gerbrandi non tacuit."

More shadow bishops: Schleswig and Ribe

An improvement in the relations between the Danish king and the archbishop is more likely some years later, as a consequence of direct negotiations between the kings of Denmark and Germany. Adam says that it was the archbishop of Hamburg-Bremen who mediated a peace treaty between Cnut and the new German king, Conrad II (1024—1039), to be sealed by a marriage between Cnut's daughter and Conrad's son.[33] This agreement is usually dated to c. 1025—a date, however, which is dependent upon the assumption that Gerbrand's capture and King Cnut's subsequent acceptance of Hamburg-Bremen's authority around 1022 made Unwan the obvious mediator between the two kings.[34] If this part of Adam's story is fictitious, the grounds for both the dating and Unwan's pivotal role disappear. Adam's account of the peace agreement between Cnut and Conrad is part of a general presentation of major events in the latter's reign, associated with Conrad's accession to the throne. It follows immediately upon events that occurred in 1033, and it is only because this passage is inserted into the portion of Adam's chronicle that deals with Unwan's pontificate that historians have assumed that he was the unnamed archbishop who negotiated the peace according to Adam.[35] It has been argued cogently that the first contact between Cnut and Conrad occurred while Cnut attended the German king's imperial coronation in Rome in 1027, and that it is definitely unlikely that a Danish marriage could have been considered seriously until the hopes for a Byzantine bride for Conrad's son had been shattered by the death of Emperor Constantine VIII in 1028.[36] The only secure dates in the sequence of events are those of the betrothal of Cnut's daughter Gunhild to Conrad's son Henry in 1035 and their marriage in 1036.[37]

---

[33] *Ibid.*, II.56 (116-17).

[34] Harry Bresslau, *Jahrbücher des Deutschen Reichs unter Konrad II.*, vol. 1 (Berlin: Duncker and Humblot, 1879), 101-104.

[35] Adam of Bremen, II.56 (116); cf. Bresslau, *Jahrbücher des Deutschen Reichs unter Konrad II.*, vol. 2 (Berlin: Duncker and Humblot, 1884), 79-81, 84, 89-98.

[36] M.K. Lawson, *Cnut: The Danes in England in the Early Eleventh Century* (New York: Longman, 1993), 108-109. Cf. Bresslau's doubts about Adam's attribution of a crucial role to Archbishop Unwan; Bresslau, *Jahrbücher*, 2: 145, n. 1.

[37] Bresslau, *Jahrbücher*, 2: 145-47, 169-70.

The bone of contention between the German and the Danish king was possession of the important emporium of Haithabu, close to Schleswig and the fortified line of the Dannevirke at the base of the Jutish peninsula. The German kings' claim to dominion over this 'march of Schleswig' likely was the legal pretext that enabled the archbishops of Hamburg-Bremen to maintain the illusion of having a suffragan bishop of Schleswig.[38] The last episode in this conflict seems to have been connected with the titular bishop of Schleswig, Ekkihard/Esico. He tried to take possession by force of the diocese whose title he had carried for more than a quarter-century, but lost his life in the attempt, on 2 August 1026.[39]

A main point in the Dano-German marriage agreement was that Conrad II dropped his claim to Schleswig. If serious negotiations were going on between the German and the Danish king around 1030, it would make sense if Cnut and the archbishop of Hamburg-Bremen had approached each other at the same time in order to remove another point of contention between Germany and Denmark. The first steps may have been taken before Unwan's death, if Adam is right that he invited Cnut as well as the Slavic princes Uto and Sederic to a meeting in Hamburg.[40] Cnut, his wife Queen Emma, and their son (Hartha-) Cnut were inscribed in the fraternity book of Bremen cathedral,[41] and it seems likely that this happened under Archbishop Libentius II, since it was during his pontificate that Hamburg-Bremen's authority was at least nominally recognized by the Danish church. Adam says that "first of all," which may mean shortly after his accession, Libentius ordained Avoco as Gerbrand's successor to the see of Sealand, but that he did this in order to win over the Danish king, implying that the appointment was actually made by Cnut.[42] As we have seen, Odinkar the Younger

---

[38] Cf. Erich Hoffmann, "Beiträge zur Geschichte der Beziehungen zwischen dem deutschen und dem dänischen Reich für die Zeit von 934 bis 1035," in *850 Jahre St.-Petri-Dom zu Schleswig*, ed. Appuhn *et al*, 126.

[39] While an early scholion to Adam's history reports that he fell ill and died upon reaching the boundary river Eider, his epitaph in Hildesheim alludes to an armed confrontation. See Adam of Bremen, schol. 44 (124); *Ser. ep.*, 6:2, 105 n. 101. Cf. Walter Schlesinger, "Unkonventionelle Gedanken zur Geschichte von Schleswig/Haithabu," in *Aus Reichsgeschichte und Nordischer Geschichte*, ed. Horst Fuhrmann, Hans Eberhard Mayer, and Klaus Wriedt (Stuttgart: Ernst Klett, 1972), 84 n. 86, who takes this to refer to events at the beginning of Ekkihard/Esico's episcopate.

[40] Adam of Bremen, II.60 (119).

[41] *Ibid.*, schol. 37 (112), explicitly citing the fraternity book.

[42] *Ibid.*, II.64 (123): "concilians sibi Chnud regem Danorum"; cf. *Ser. ep.*, 6:2, 80 n. 76.

was probably consecrated to the see of Ribe by Libentius II under similar circumstances, and it may have been in connection with his own consecration that Odinkar attended the funeral of Bishop Thurgot of Skara in Bremen.[43] Adam states that this 'normalization' of the ecclesiastical organization in Denmark was accompanied by close co-operation on the military front against the Wends between Cnut the Great and Duke Bernard II of Saxony.[44]

The détente between the Danish king and Hamburg-Bremen barely outlived King Cnut, who died in 1035, and the implementation of the Dano-German marriage agreement in 1036. Henry III's Danish marriage ended with Gunhild's death in Italy in 1038,[45] and shortly afterwards, probably as commander of his cousin King Harthacnut's fleet, the Danish prince and later king Sven Estrithson attacked the archiepiscopal territory of Hadeln. He was captured by the pontiff's knights and brought to Archbishop Bescelin Alebrand who, according to what Sven later told Adam, received him honourably, concluded friendship with him, and let him leave after a few days, laden with sumptuous gifts.[46] Once again, King Sven seems to have wanted to give Master Adam a picture of events that minimized the conflicts between Denmark and the archbishops of Hamburg-Bremen. It is much more likely that the attack upon Hadeln stemmed from a rejection by the Danish king and his church of their earlier acknowledgement of Hamburg-Bremen's supremacy.

If this was the case, Hamburg-Bremen was not simply back to square one, but in an even worse position than before the short-lived Dano-German alliance. The agreement between Conrad II and Cnut had removed the legal fiction enabling the archbishop to continue appointing shadow bishops of Schleswig, leaving him destitute of suffragans except for the almost equally shadowy bishopric of Aldenburg.[47] Upon Ekkihard/Esico's death in 1026, he was still able to appoint a new bishop of Schleswig, Rodulf, a cleric from Cologne. But Rodulf was just as much of a titulary bishop in exile as his predecessors, staying as an auxiliary bishop in his native diocese of Cologne, where he was buried in St. Kunibert's

---

[43] Adam of Bremen, II.64 (124-25).

[44] *Ibid.*, II.65 (125-26).

[45] Lawson, *Cnut*, 109.

[46] Adam of Bremen, II.75 (135); cf. II.77 (135).

[47] *Ser. ep.*, 5:2, 54 and 60-62.

church upon his death in 1047.[48] If Rodulf was a prominent ecclesiastic, he was so in the diocese of Cologne, not in the archdiocese of Hamburg-Bremen.

Upon Harthacnut's death in 1042, a war of succession broke out between Sven Estrithson and the Norwegian king Magnus the Good. Magnus got the upper hand, and Bescelin Alebrand seems to have hoped to profit from the change of dynasty in order to reaffirm his authority over the Danish church. He started negotiations with the new master of Denmark, and a meeting was arranged in Schleswig in 1042. Yet while Bishop Rodulf was present at the meeting, Adam explicitly states that he went to Schleswig in his archbishop's retinue.[49] If Rodulf had nourished any hopes of remaining in his titular see after the negotiations, they were obviously thwarted.[50] The Norwegian church was also largely staffed from the British isles,[51] and the Dano-Norwegian king would have had no more reason than his predecessors to submit his church to Hamburg-Bremen. The only result of the talks mentioned by Adam was a marriage alliance between King Magnus and Duke Ordulf of Saxony, and while Ordulf obligingly killed off a potential claimant to the Danish throne, the archbishop does not seem to have gained anything for himself.[52]

Bescelin Alebrand's archiepiscopal dignity thus was in a sorry state in the last year of his pontificate. In Denmark, the bishops of Jutland and Sealand had been consecrated by his predecessor, but like their colleagues in Funen and Scania they no longer obeyed him. The attempt to obtain the new Danish king's recognition of the shadow bishop of Schleswig had failed, and the legal justification

---

[48] *Ser. ep.*, 6:2, 105-106 and n. 116. Cf. Sven Seiler and Marianne Gechter, "Das Grab des Bischofs Rudolf von Schleswig in St. Kunibert zu Köln," in *Ein Land macht Geschichte: Archäologie in Nordrhein-Westfalen*, ed. Heinz Günter Horn, Hansgerd Hellenkemper, Harald Koschik, and Bendix Trier (Cologne: Römisch-Germanisches Museum der Stadt Köln, 1995), 300-03; Sven Schütte, "Zur frühen Baugeschichte von St. Kunibert in Köln und zur Grablege des Bischofs Rudolf von Schleswig," *Colonia Romanica: Jahrbuch des Fördervereins Romanische Kirchen Köln e.V.* 12 (1997): 13-15; and Marianne Gechter, "Die Grablege des Bischofs Rudolf von Schleswig in St. Kunibert," in *ibid.*, 17-20.

[49] Adam of Bremen, II.79 (136).

[50] Cf. Radtke, "Anfänge," 146; Andrea Boockmann, *Geistliche und weltliche Gerichtsbarkeit im mittelalterlichen Bistum Schleswig* (Neumünster: Karl Wachholtz, 1967), 19, against Schlesinger, "Unkonventionelle Gedanken," 72 and 88.

[51] Oluf Kolsrud, *Noregs kyrkjesoga*, vol. 1, *Millomalderen* (Oslo: Aschehoug, 1958), 151, 175-78.

[52] Adam of Bremen, II.79 (136-37).

for appointing a successor to Bishop Rodulf of Schleswig had vanished.[53] Hamburg-Bremen's shaky suffragan see in the Slavic territories, Aldenburg, seems to have been slipping from the archbishop's hands in the same years.[54] And the archbishop of Cologne, from whose province the see of Bremen had been detached in the ninth century, revived his claim to Bremen around 1040, although Bescelin Alebrand was able to ward off his pretensions.[55]

In these circumstances, the death of Bishop Odinkar of Ribe (in early 1043 at the latest) must have seemed a welcome windfall for the archbishop,[56] since it provided the justification for appointing a successor to a bishop who had been consecrated by an archbishop of Hamburg-Bremen. If King Magnus had refused to recognize the archbishop's authority in 1042, however, it is far from obvious that he would have accepted Hamburg-Bremen's candidate for the see of Ribe in 1043. To be sure, there is no doubt that Odinkar's ostensible successor, Bishop Wal, was the archbishop's choice and not the king's, since Adam says explicitly that he was taken from among the canons of Bremen.[57] Nevertheless, in his only appearance outside Adam's chronicle (a papal act from the council of Mainz in October 1049), Wal looks very much like yet another titular bishop in exile.[58] Indeed, both in that act and in Adam's mention of Wal's death, there is something puzzling about his title: in the former he appears as *Walo Iburgensis Danorum episcopus*, while Adam also calls him *Wal Danorum episcopus*, probably repeating the corresponding entry in Bremen's necrology.[59] Both sources, then, give him the title "bishop of the Danes". At this time, however, Denmark is supposed to have had several bishops. The existence of Bishop Avoco of Sealand is not in doubt, and he seems to have lived until the late 1050s. Adam contradicts his previous statement that Cnut the Great had instated Bernard as bishop in Scania when he later says that the province did not have bishops of its own, but

---

[53] Cf. below, 195, for Rodulf's successor, Ratolf, who is not mentioned until 1071.

[54] *Ser. ep.*, 5:2, 62; cf. Eduard Hlawitschka, "Zur Erschließung der Memorialüberlieferung aus dem Kloster Fulda," *DA* 38 (1982): 178.

[55] Adam of Bremen, schol. 55 (133); cf. Georg Dehio, *Geschichte des Erzbistums Hamburg-Bremen bis zum Ausgang der Mission*, vol. 1 (Berlin: W. Hertz, 1877), 173-74.

[56] Adam of Bremen, schol. 59 (141). For the problems in determing the exact date of his death, cf. *Ser. ep.*, 6:2, 68-69 n. 56.

[57] Adam of Bremen, II.72 (133): "Wal a Bremensi choro consecravit in Ripam."

[58] *MGH Const.* I no. 51 (100) (= *DD* I/1, no. 494 (196-97)).

[59] Adam of Bremen, III.25 (167).

that the Sealandian bishops Gerbrand and Avoco also took care of Scania.⁶⁰ The chronicler of Bremen seems simply to have wanted to ignore all bishops who had not entertained direct relations with the metropolitan. There is no reason to doubt that the Scanian see was continuously provided.⁶¹ Similarly, there would have been a bishop of Funen, although Adam is silent as to his identity. Wal ought to have been titled "bishop of Jutland" or "bishop of Ribe", not "bishop of the Danes"—that is, if the archbishop of Hamburg-Bremen actually acknowledged the rest of the Danish bishops at that time.

Wal's epithet in the 1049 document, *Iburgensis*, is sometimes supposed to be a scribal error for *Wiburgensis*, implying that Wal had transferred his residence to the town of Viborg in northern Jutland.⁶² But the explanation may be much more straightforward. His designation as *Wal Iburgensis Danorum episcopus* may indicate that he was but a titular bishop in exile, residing not in Viborg, but in the place indicated by the word as it stands, the castle of Iburg close to Osnabrück; and that he was the only 'bishop of the Danes' to be recognized by the archbishop of Hamburg-Bremen. Adam's use of the title *Danorum episcopus* when mentioning Wal's death makes it likely that this was still the case when he died in the late 1050s.⁶³ Just like the shadow bishops of Schleswig, Wal would have had to be provided for, and not necessarily in the diocese of Hamburg-Bremen: the last two titular bishops of Schleswig were auxiliary bishops in the dioceses of Hildesheim and Cologne, respectively. Iburg was an important position in a neighbouring diocese; a few years later a great Benedictine abbey was founded there. Wal may have been a native of the region; at the same time, a lay aristocrat named Wal, who may have been the bishop's kinsman, was *advocatus* of Bishop Alberic of Osnabrück (c. 1037—1052).⁶⁴ Indeed, the witness list to the act of 1049 discloses the archbishop's predicament. Adalbert of Hamburg-Bremen participated in the synod with only one exiled suffragan in his wake—a paltry indication of his archiepiscopal status.

If the archbishop's candidate was not admitted to his see after Bishop Odinkar's death in 1043, then who carried out the episcopal functions in Jutland?

---

⁶⁰ *Ibid.*, IV.8 (235).

⁶¹ Cf. the discussion below, at notes 81-83, of the date of accession of Bishop Henry of Lund.

⁶² Cf. *Ser. ep.*, 6:2, 117-18.

⁶³ For the date of Wal's death, see *Ser. ep.*, 6:2, 65 with n. 16.

⁶⁴ *Ser. ep.*, 6:2, 69 n. 60.

The answer is probably to be found in the small, early thirteenth-century *Chronicle* of the church of Ribe, which is remarkable among Danish chronicles and annals of the time for being independent of Adam of Bremen.[65] The Ribe chronicle claims that Odinkar was succeeded by his son Christian, and though it knows of Wal's existence, he is dismissed as an unsuccessful pretender to the see after Christian's death.[66] The details here are aberrant: Odinkar is said to have secured a papal privilege making the episcopal title hereditary in his descendance, because he had disinherited his offspring by donating all of his possessions to his church, and Wal is made into Christian's son. Yet the essential substance of the account is likely to be true.[67] Odinkar's donation would have given the church of Ribe a direct interest in remembering how the lands came to stay with the cathedral; and already in the middle of the twelfth century Odinkar seems to have been considered the founder of his see, since his remains were transferred to the new cathedral that was then being erected.[68] Hereditary bishops were not unknown in early eleventh-century Europe; in Brittany, which was at the time outside royal Frankish control, they were the rule rather than the exception in the first half of the eleventh century.[69] It would not be incongruous to imagine a hereditary line of bishops in Denmark, especially if such an episcopal line was also a branch of the royal kin—and Adam and the Ribe chronicle agree that Odinkar had royal blood in his veins.

---

[65] "Ribe Bispekrønike," ed. Ellen Jørgensen, in *Kirkehistoriske Samlinger*, ser. 6, vol. 1 (Copenhagen: G.E.C. Gad, 1933-35), 23-33; for the history of the text, see Michael H. Gelting, "Cronica ecclesiæ Ripensis (Chronicle of the Church of Ribe)," in *Medieval Nordic Literature in Latin*, ed. Lars Boje Mortensen *et al* (forthcoming).

[66] "Ribe Bispekrønike," 27.

[67] Nyberg, *Monasticism*, 89-90 is inclined to accept the filiation from Odinkar to Wal given in the Ribe chronicle, but does not discuss its incompatibility with Adam of Bremen's account.

[68] *Danmarks Kirker*, ed. Victor Hermansen *et al*, vol. 19: *Ribe Amt*, vol. 1 (Copenhagen, G.E.C. Gad, 1979), 114-15 and 526-27; his bones were identified by an almond-shaped plaque inscribed with his name in the manner of an ecclesiastical seal. Similar plaques were used for the reburials of bishops Nothulf (1134-*post* 1139) and Ascer (*post* 1139-1141/42). Nyberg (*Die Kirche in Skandinavien*, 84) assumes that part of Odinkar's landed wealth was located north of the Limfjord and thus passed to the bishopric of Wendel (Børglum) upon its erection c. 1059 (cf. below). This hypothesis, however, depends upon Schmeidler's tentative identification of Odinkar's father's ducal title (*Winlandensis*) with the island of Wendel (Vendsyssel), which is far from assured. See Adam of Bremen, schol. 35 (110) with n. 8.

[69] André Chédeville and Noël-Yves Tonnerre, *La Bretagne féodale, XIe-XIIIe siècle* (Rennes: Ouest-France, 1987), 240-42.

Table 3
Bishops of Ribe (Jutland), 948-1134

Consensus Version

Liafdag	948– ?
NN (Fulbert?)	?
Odinkar the Younger	988/1005–1043
Wal	1043–c. 1057/60
Oddo	1057/60–*post* 1072
?	?
Gerald	–1113–
Thore	*pre*-1131–1134

Alternative Hypothesis

Liafdag	948– ?
NN (Fulbert?)	?
Itinerant missionaries from	*c.* 983/88
Re-erection of the sea	1020/22
NN	1020/22–1029/32
Odinkar the Younger	1029/32–*pre*-1043
Christian (son)	*pre*-1043–1059

Not recognized by Hamburg-Bremen; deposed 1059. Bishop of Århus, 1059 – post-*1072*

Wal of Iburg	1043 (or earlier)–c. 1059

Not recognized in Denmark

Oddo	1059–*post*-1072
?	?
Gerald	*post*-1080–*pre*-1113
In exile 1113[70]	
Thore	*pre*-1131–1134

---

[70] *Urkundenbuch zur Geschichte der mittelrheinischen Territorien*, vol. 1, ed. Heinrich Beyer (Coblenz: J. Hölscher, 1860), 488 (= *DD* 1/2, no. 40 (85-86); "Ribe Bispekrønike," 27. Cf. Niels Skyum-Nielsen, *Kvinde og Slave* (Copenhagen: Munksgaard, 1971), 31.

Table 4
Bishops of Schleswig, 948-1134

Consensus Version

Hored	948– ?
Marco	?
Adaldag	?
Folcbert	c. 988?
Poppo	988/95–995/1000
Non-resident	
Ekkehard (Esico)	995/1000–1026
Non-resident	
Rodulf	1026–1047
Ratolf	*post*-1047–1072
Siward	–1085–
Gunner	*post*-1103–1121/25
Adalbero	1121/25–1134/35

Alternative Hypothesis[71]

Hored	948–972
Adaldag	972–984
Folcbert	984–991
In exile 988	
Itinerant missionaries until 1020/22	
Part of the diocese of Jutland 1020/22	

Non-resident titular bishops:

Poppo	991–996
Ekkehard (Esico)	996–1026
Rodulf	1026–1047
Re-erection of the see 1059	
Ratolf	1059–1072
In exile 1071?[72]	
Siward	–1085–
Gunner	*post*-1103–1121/25
Adalbero	1121/25–1134/35

---

[71] Mainly based upon Bolin, *Om Nordens äldsta historieforskning*, 9-28.

[72] Hermann von Lerbeck, "Catalogus episcoporum Mindensium," ed. K. Löffler in *Mindener Geschichtsquellen* (Münster: Aschendorff, 1917), 47.

It is likely, in fact, that both chroniclers were right: Archbishop Bescelin Alebrand did indeed appoint his canon, Wal, to be Odinkar's successor in Ribe, but Wal never resided in his see, which was occupied by Odinkar's son Christian. Instead, Wal served as an auxiliary bishop in the diocese of Osnabrück, whence he followed Archbishop Adalbert to the council of Mainz in 1049. The Danish church remained independent of Hamburg-Bremen throughout the 1040s and well into Sven Estrithson's reign.

King Sven's church

Upon King Magnus's death in 1047, his unlucky rival Sven Estrithson seized the reins of the kingdom. Upon his accession, the ecclesiastical structure of the kingdom remained as Cnut left it, with four dioceses, one for each of the main provinces. Sven had an obvious problem in that, unlike his predecessors, he did not have direct access either to the archbishopric of Canterbury or to the pool of English missionary bishops in the Norwegian kingdom. In the long run this would compromise his ability to maintain the independence of the Danish church in the face of Hamburg-Bremen's claims, while any acknowledgement of Hamburg-Bremen's authority might easily entail some degree of political subjection to the German *Reich*. This danger became acute when Pope Leo IX in 1053 not only confirmed Hamburg-Bremen's previous status as the metropolitan of Sweden and Denmark, but extended its rights to the whole of Scandinavia and conferred the status of apostolic legate and papal vicar upon the highly ambitious Archbishop Adalbert.[73] Under these circumstances, Sven was forced to seek an alliance with Archbishop Adalbert and Emperor Henry III. The Danish king bowed to the archbishop's demand for the dissolution of his incestuous marriage, and a solemn conference between Adalbert and Sven was held in Schleswig, probably in 1052, implying the acknowledgement of Hamburg-Bremen's supremacy by the Danish king and his church. The following year, Sven met with the emperor in Merseburg.[74]

---

[73] *DD* 1/2, no. 1 (1-5); for the interpretation of this privilege, see Carsten Breengaard, *Muren om Israels hus: Regnum og sacerdotium i Danmark 1050-1170* (Copenhagen: G. E. C. Gad, 1982), 85-86.

[74] Adam of Bremen, III.18 (161-62); Hermann of Reichenau, *Chronicon* [*MGH SS* V] (Hannover: Hahn, 1844), 132. Cf. Wolfgang Seegrün, *Das Papsttum und Skandinavien bis zur Vollendung der nordischen Kirchenorganisation (1164)* (Neumünster: Karl Wachholtz, 1967), 67-70; Breengaard, *Muren*, 83-84.

As his military position vis-à-vis Norway improved, no doubt partly as a result of his German alliance, King Sven seems to have sought ways to preserve his independence from Germany in the long run. The solution which he desired was the creation of an independent Danish ecclesiastical province, facilitated by augmenting the number of Danish dioceses. In itself, the creation of new suffragan dioceses would have appealed to Archbishop Adalbert, not only because of Hamburg-Bremen's former lack of proper suffragans, but also in view of Adalbert's own designs for a Nordic patriarchate. According to Adam, this latter plan was formed in response to Sven's wish for a Danish archdiocese, while Adalbert at the same time envisaged the creation of twelve diminutive dioceses within the boundaries of his own see and in the neighbouring Slavic lands, obviously to eliminate the risk of being left once again without direct suffragans if Sven's plans should succeed. Adalbert's patriarchal plans thus were an audacious response to a very real threat to the archiepiscopal status of his see.[75]

The first step towards realizing the designs of these two uneasy allies was the erection of new Danish dioceses. According to Adam, the occasion for this was the death of the two bishops who had been consecrated by archbishops of Hamburg-Bremen, Wal of Ribe and Avoco of Sealand. After Wal's death, King Sven, with the approval of Archbishop Adalbert, partitioned his diocese in four parts: Ribe, Århus, Viborg, and 'Wendila', i.e. the islands north of the Limfjord.[76] Avoco's death likewise was the occasion for dividing his diocese, in this case into three: Roskilde in Sealand, and Lund and Dalby in Scania. This division as well is ascribed to King Sven, while Archbishop Adalbert contributed by ordaining two of the three new bishops. The third bishop, Henry of Lund, did not need to be ordained, as he had previously been bishop of Orkney.[77] Adam further tells us that Adalbert consecrated "from among his own clerics" Ratolf as bishop of Schleswig, William as bishop of Sealand, and Eilbert as bishop of Funen.[78] The implication seems to be that this was done at about the same time as

---

[75] Adam of Bremen, III.33 (175); cf. III.59 (205-06); Horst Furhmann, "Studien zur Geschichte mittelalterlicher Patriarchate, III. Teil (Schluss)," *ZSfR* 41 (1955): 120-70; Breengaard, *Muren*, 84-88.

[76] Adam of Bremen, III.25 (167), IV.2 (230-31).

[77] *Ibid.*, IV.8 (235-36); cf. IV.3 (231).

[78] *Ibid.*, IV.3 (231).

the partition of the Jutish diocese, and Ratolf is not mentioned otherwise until 1071.[79]

Now, according to our hypothesis, Wal the 'bishop of the Danes' was not officiating as bishop of Ribe at all, but was living at Iburg in the diocese of Osnabrück. There is no reason to assume that Bishop Christian, whom we assume exercised the Jutish episcopal office, should have died at the same time as Wal. Christian's episcopal consecration, however, could hardly have failed to be canonically irregular: if he was not consecrated by the archbishop of Hamburg-Bremen, which other archbishop could have done so at a time when the Danish king could no longer use the archbishop of Canterbury? Moreover, he held a see to which the archbishop of Hamburg-Bremen had ordained another bishop, and no see could have two bishops at the same time. The fact that he succeded his father as bishop may also have been considered suspect, although he would have been born long before Odinkar's episcopal ordination.

A possible explanation might be that King Sven, as part of the reorganization of his church, admitted that his episcopal kinsman Christian had to be deposed, but that Archbishop Adalbert in return gave Christian a canonically regular episcopal ordination to Århus, one of the new sees carved out of his former diocese. It is at least curious that the bishop of Århus appointed upon the re-erection of the see was called Christian, a rare name at the time.[80] Adam says nothing about the origins of Christian of Århus. If he had been a foreign cleric, however, it would have been unusual to find him at the head of the fleet which King Sven sent against England in 1069/70, and which occupied the Isle of Ely for some time.[81] This would seem a rather more likely role if Bishop Christian was in fact Odinkar's son, as this would make him a scion of the highest Danish aristocracy with family links to the royal house.

If this hypothesis is correct, the partition of the Jutish diocese looks suspiciously like part of a package deal. Could all the Danish dioceses have been provided in one clean sweep? In fact, there is much to recommend such an idea. Most historians have seen the creation of the new diocesan structure as the realization of an overall plan, but with an approximate dating to c. 1057/60 that

---

[79] *Ser. ep.*, 6:2, 106.

[80] See *Danmarks gamle Personnavne*, vol. 1/1, ed. Gunnar Knudsen, Marius Kristensen, and Rikard Hornby (Copenhagen: G. E. C. Gad, 1936), col. 786-87.

[81] *The Peterborough Chronicle, 1070-1154*, 2nd ed., ed. Cecily Clark (Oxford: Clarendon Press, 1970), 2.

would not necessarily imply that the entire project was carried out simultaneously.[82] Actually, the circumstantial evidence we do have clusters in the year 1059.[83] Probably all of the new Danish bishops were appointed during that year, as the previous incumbents had either died or been deposed because of their uncanonical consecration.

There was one exception, however: Bishop Henry of Lund. The erection of two episcopal sees 11 kilometers apart, even in a rich province like Scania, seems incongruous—even more so since the see of Dalby was suppressed as soon as Bishop Henry died. Egino of Dalby simply moved to Lund, and the church of Dalby was converted into a college of canons.[84] Historians have speculated about the reasons for this ephemeral partition of the Scanian diocese, but without reaching any convincing conclusion.[85] The reason may be very simple: there never was, nor was intended to be, any diocese of Dalby. There was, however, one problem with making a clean sweep of the existing Danish bishoprics in order to effect the reorganization of 1059: unlike the heads of the three other old sees, Bishop Henry of Lund not only was alive, but was also canonically unimpeachable, for as former bishop of Orkney he had a proper ordination, probably from the Anglo-Saxon church.[86] It would be rather puzzling if either King Sven or Archbishop Adalbert had thought fit to recruit a bishop from Orkney to Scania in 1059.[87]

---

[82] E.g. Dehio, *Geschichte*, vol. 1, 192 (implicitly c. 1053/60); Schmeidler, n. 6 to Adam of Bremen, III.25 (167) (c. 1057/60), followed by Otto Heinrich May, *Regesten der Erzbsschöfe von Bremen*, vol. 1 (787-1306) [Veröffentlichungen der Historischen Kommission für Hannover, Oldenburg, Braunschweig, Schaumburg-Lippe und Bremen 11] (Hannover: Historische Kommission, 1937), no. 260 (62), and *Ser. ep.* 6:2, 2; Seegrün, *Das Papsttum*, 74 (c. 1060); Radtke, "Anfänge," 141 (c. 1060); and Breengaard, *Muren*, 88 (c. 1060). Nyberg, in *Die Kirche in Skandinavien*, 13-14, adopted the date 1065/66, based upon a strained reading of Adam of Bremen, III.24-25 (166-68) by Aage Trommer, "Komposition und Tendenz in der Hamburgischen Kirchengeschichte Adam von Bremens," *Classica et mediaevalia* 18 (1957): 209, 234-35. In *Monasticism*, 64, Nyberg reverts to the traditional date of c. 1060.

[83] *Ser. ep.*, 6:2, 36 (Egino of Dalby), 49 (Magnus and Albricus of Wendila), 58-59 (Eilbert of Funen), and 81 (William of Sealand). Adam states that Oddo of Ribe, Christian of Århus and Heribert of Viborg were consecrated at the same time as Magnus of Wendila: Adam of Bremen, IV.2 (230-31).

[84] Adam of Bremen, IV.8-9 (235-37).

[85] Most recently Nyberg, *Monasticism*, 44; cf. 10. See also *Ser. ep.*, 6:2, 7-8 with n. 17.

[86] Adam of Bremen, IV.8 (236).

[87] It is not clear why Nyberg (*Monasticism*, 44) believes that Henry was King Sven's uncle.

Moreover, it has been argued that Bishop Thorolf of Orkney was consecrated by Archbishop Adalbert of Hamburg-Bremen between 1049 and 1053. The argument presupposes that Thorolf's consecration was performed in close cooperation with the earl of Orkney. Since Adam states that Archbishop Adalbert subsequently sent further two bishops to Orkney, Henry's Orcadian episcopacy must be dated to some time before 1053.[88] The most likely time for the transfer of a bishop from Orkney to Lund would be during the reign of King Magnus the Good of Norway and Denmark. Orkney had been settled from Norway in the ninth century, and though the Norwegian kings' overlordship over the earls of Orkney was shaky at best in the eleventh century, King Magnus made a serious attempt to strengthen his influence in the islands, supporting one of the parties in a conflict over succession to the comital office. Magnus's candidate was ultimately killed towards the end of the king's reign,[89] an event which might have led the Norwegian-Danish king to find a safer see for a loyal Orcadian bishop.

If this was so, the ordination of Egino to Dalby in 1059 looks like an interim solution, one that did not imply the erection of a separate diocese. Dalby was a royal residence in the eleventh century,[90] and Egino may have been placed at the palace chapel as an auxiliary bishop with expectancy to the see of Lund upon the death of the ageing Bishop Henry; or he may have been consecrated as a missionary bishop without any specific diocese, but with Dalby as his base and expectancy to the see of Lund. Indeed, Adam extols Egino's missionary activities, which led to the conversion of the outlying provinces of Blekinge and Bornholm, and also tells us that he participated aggressively in the evangelization of Sweden.[91]

It seems, then, that the reorganization of the Danish church in 1059 implied the appointment of new bishops loyal to Hamburg-Bremen for every Danish

---

[88] C.A. Ralegh Radford, "St. Magnus Cathedral, Kirkwall, and the Development of the Cathedral in Northwest Europe," in *St Magnus Cathedral and Orkney's Twelfth-Century Renaissance*, ed. Barbara E. Crawford (Aberdeen: Aberdeen University Press, 1988), 17-18.

[89] Ebbe Hertzberg and Alexander Bugge, *Norges historie*, vol. 2/1, *Tidsrummet 1030-1103* (Kristiania: Aschehoug, 1915), 55-58 and 283-84.

[90] Erik Cinthio, "Dalby kungsgård: Medeltidsarkeologien som historisk vetenskap," *Kungl. Vitterhets, Historie och Antikvitets Akademiens Årsbok* (1983): 99; cf. *idem*, "Kungapalatset i Dalby," *Ale: Historisk tidskrift för Skåneland* (1966, no. 3): 16-19.

[91] Adam of Bremen, IV.8 (236), IV.30 (262). It is true that Archbishop Adalbert, in a letter to Bishop William of Roskilde in the late 1060s, speaks of the bishop of Dalby, but the context was precisely problems within the missionary church in Sweden, which Egino was to investigate. See *ibid.*, III.76 (222) (= *DD* 1/2, no. 8 (15-18)).

diocese, old or new, and that in Lund, the one diocese where the existing bishop could not be ousted, a bishop obedient to Archbishop Adalbert was given an expectancy while being entrusted with the evangelization of the neighbouring regions in the meantime.

King Sven, Master Adam, and beyond

Sven Estrithson was obliged to rely upon Archbishop Adalbert in order to establish his case for a Danish archbishopric, based upon a sufficient number of dioceses provided with canonically impeccable bishops. Having reached that goal, however, it was definitely not in his interest to allow the German archbishop too much direction over the affairs of the Danish church. It is difficult to imagine that the new Danish bishops could have abstained systematically from participating in Adalbert's provincial synod, unless they had the king's connivance.[92] Sven's choice of replacements when the bishops appointed in 1059 fell away, in so far as it is known, was hardly designed to please the archbishops of Hamburg-Bremen. Ricwal, who succeeded to Egino in Lund between 1072 and 1074/76, was a fugitive canon from Paderborn who had been excommunicated by Archbishop Adalbert;[93] Sven, who followed William in Roskilde some time between 1067 and 1074/76, was a Norwegian, and it is doubtful whether he received his ordination at the hands of the archbishop of Hamburg-Bremen.[94] In the same years, during the pontificate of Alexander II (1061—1073), King Sven opened up direct negotiations with the papal curia, and although the pope could hardly refuse to support Archbishop Adalbert's demand for obedience from his Danish suffragans, Sven was able to secure support for his cause from the powerful Cardinal Hildebrand.[95]

Adalbert died in 1072, and on 25 January 1075, after having acceded to the pontifical throne as Gregory VII, Hildebrand assured Sven of his continued in-

---

[92] *Ibid.*, III.74-76 (221-22).

[93] *Ser. ep.*, 6:2, 15-16.

[94] *Ibid.*, 82-83.

[95] Adam of Bremen, III.75 (221-22) (= *DD* 1/2, no. 5 (11-13)); Paul Ewald, "Die Papstbriefe der Brittischen Sammlung," *Neues Archiv der Gesellschaft für ältere deutsche Geschichtskunde* 5 (1880): 328-29 (= *DD* 1/2, no. 6 (13-14));

Das Register Gregors VII., II.51 (192-94) (= *DD* 1/2, no. 11 (21-24)).

terest in the latter's plans for a Danish archdiocese.[96] Relations between Gregory and the new German king, Henry IV, were rapidly deteriorating, however. This not only hindered the execution of Sven's plans, but may also have prompted the king to secure the good will of Liemar (1072—1101), the new archbishop of Hamburg-Bremen, who (depending on the outcome of the conflict between Henry IV and Gregory VII) might well have been able to obstruct the creation of a Danish archdiocese.

In the same years, Master Adam of Bremen was finishing his history of the archbishops of Hamburg-Bremen. As part of this project, the learned master interviewed King Sven, who supplied him with ample information about the history of Denmark in general and of the kingdom's relations with the archiepiscopal see in particular.[97] As we have seen, the version of the latter story which Sven gave to Adam seems consciously to have minimized the conflicts between the two parties. Cnut's organization of an independent Danish church which relied upon the church of his English kingdom was reduced to a short-lived aberrance, just as Sven Estrithson's attack, while still a prince, upon the possessions of the archbishopric of Hamburg-Bremen was transformed into an occasion for initiating lasting friendship. Sven, in other words, wanted to present a picture of an obedient and canonically correct Danish church, one ready to be made into a separate ecclesiastical province.[98] For his part, Adam wanted to glorify the pontiffs of his see, so he did not question the king's assertions, although he could not refrain from wondering at Sven's apparent frankness.

These political considerations retained all of their relevance, even after the Danish kings realized the dream of their own ecclesiastical province with the elevation of the see of Lund to metropolitan status in 1103/04. As late as 1133, Archbishop Adalbero of Hamburg-Bremen obtained a privilege from Pope Innocent II abolishing the archdiocese of Lund and reaffirming the subjection of the

---

[96] *Ibid.*

[97] Recent scholarship frequently has relied upon Erik Arup's erroneous assertion that Adam of Bremen explicitly records a journey to King Sven's Danish court c. 1068; see Erik Arup, "Kong Svend 2.s Biografi," *Scandia* 4 (1931): 57-59. In fact, despite his numerous references to conversations with the king, Adam never actually describes the circumstances under which they met. The archbishop (either Adalbert or his successor Liemar) may have used his eloquent schoolmaster as an envoy to Denmark, but the encounter might equally well have occurred in northern Germany, in connection with a meeting at Lüneburg between Sven Estrithson and the German king Henry IV in 1071. See Adam of Bremen, III.60 (206).

[98] Cf. Arup, "Kong Svend 2.s Biografi," 97-98.

Table 5
Bishops of Odense (Funen), c. 988–c. 1134/39

Consensus Version
NN   –988–
  In exile 988
Itinerant missionary bishops
Reginbert   c. 1020– ?
Eilbert   1043/60–1072
?
Hubald   *pre*-1100–1117/22
Herman   (1117/22–1134/37)

Alternative Hypothesis
NN   –988–
  In exile 988
Itinerant missionary bishops
Reginbert   1020/22–*pre*-1059
Eilbert   1059–1072
?
Hubald   *pre*-1100–1117/22
Herman   (1117/22–1134/37)

Table 6
Bishops of Lund (Scania), c. 1000-1137 (or 1020/22-1137)

Consensus Version
Gotebald   999/1014– ?
Bernard   1018/32

Vacancy 1029/32–1059/60; administered from Roskilde

Henry   1059/60–1067/71
  Former bishop of Orkney
Egino   1067/71–1072
  Bishop of Dalby   *1059/60–1067/71*
Ricwal   1072/74–1089
Asser   1089–1137
  Archbishop   *1103/4*

Alternative Hypothesis
Bernard   1020/22– pre-1029/32
?
Henry   1042/47–1067/71
  Former bishop of Orkney
Egino   1059–1072
  In Dalby   *1059–1067/71*
Ricwal   1072/74–1089
Asser   1089–1137
  Archbishop   *1103/4*

Table 7
Bishops of Roskilde (Sealand), 1020/22-1134

Consensus Version
Gerbrand	1020/22–1029/32
Avoco	1029/32–1043/59
William	1043/59–1067/73
Sven	1067/74–1088
Arnold	1088/89–1124/25
Peter	1124/25–1134

Alternative Hypothesis
Gerbrand	1020/22–1029/32
Avoco	1029/32–*pre*-1059
William	1059–1067/73
Sven	1067/74–1088
Arnold	1088/89–1124/25
Peter	1124/25–1134

Danish church to Hamburg-Bremen.[99] The change in the balance of power between the German kingdom and the papacy upon the death of Lothar III in 1137 ensured that this finally remained a dead letter,[100] but the threat to the autonomy of the Danish church probably remained a matter of deep concern for the archbishops of Lund well into the second half of the twelfth century.[101] This situation would explain why the memory of King Cnut's autonomous Danish church was obliterated after 1059 and replaced by Adam's version of the story, one based upon the evidence obligingly furnished him by Sven Estrithson. It remained of paramount importance to portray Christian Denmark as a dutiful daughter of the church, even while playing down Hamburg-Bremen's role in the mission. It seems to have been the aim of the *Roskilde Chronicle*, written c. 1138, to strike this difficult balance.[102]

Oblivion of the condition of the Danish church in the mid-eleventh century was made easier by the fact that no cathedral chapter existed at any of the Danish sees before c. 1075.[103] On the other hand, the cult of German bishops as missionary saints would have been encouraged. Poppo, the man who converted Harald Bluetooth, does seem to have had a cult at the Jutish church of Tamdrup at least until around 1200, when a reliquary with scenes from the conversion story was produced for the church.[104] Poppo, however, was unknown to the calendar of saints in Denmark as well as to the universal church.[105] The cult

---

[99] *DD* 1/2, no. 57 (109-12); cf. nos. 58-61 (112-17).

[100] *Roskildekrøniken*, trans. Michael H. Gelting, 2nd ed. (Højbjerg: Wormianum, 2002), 81-86; Michael H. Gelting, "Da Eskil ville være ærkebiskop af Roskilde: Roskildekrøniken, *Liber daticus Lundensis* og det danske aerkesaedes ophaevelse 1133-1138" (forthcoming in the proceedings of the symposium "Individ, kollektiv och kulturella mönster: Nya perspektiv på 1100-talets Danmark," Stiftsgården Åkersberg, 12-13 April 2002, ed. Lars Hermanson and Hanne Sanders); idem, "Chronicon Roskildense," in *Medieval Nordic Literature in Latin*, ed. Lars Boje Mortensen et al (forthcoming).

[101] This is one of the main theses of Breengaard, *Muren*.

[102] *Chronicon Roskildense*, in *Scriptores minores historiae Danicae medii aevi*, vol. 1, ed. M.Cl. Gertz (Copenhagen: Selskabet for Udgivelse af Kilder til dansk Historie, 1917-18), 1-33; cf. above, note 97.

[103] Cf. above, note 3.

[104] Tage E. Christiansen, "De gyldne Altre, I. Tamdrup-Pladerne," *Aarbøger for Nordisk Oldkyndighed og Historie* (1968): 174-96; Demidoff, "The Poppo Legend," 49-50; Ebbe Nyborg and Niels Jørgen Poulsen, *Tamdrup* [Danmarks Kirker, Århus amt, 52] (Heming: Nationalmuseet/Poul Kristensen, 2002), 5123-29.

[105] Demidoff, "The Poppo Legend," 65-66.

of Liafdag of Ribe was a similarly local phenomenon, and the fact that Bishop Ralph (1162—1171) attempted formally to canonize his first predecessor without the authorization of his metropolitan might indicate that the cult was not approved by the see of Lund. Even the great "apostle of the North", Saint Ansgar, archbishop of Hamburg-Bremen, was conspicuously absent from the Danish calendar of saints.[106]

In the end, Denmark only remembered one missionary saint, the politically inoffensive Saint Theodgar (*Thøger*). According to his legend, he was a German by origin, having been born in Thuringia, but he received his religious formation in England before serving as a chaplain to the Norwegian king St. Olaf. After the king's death in 1030, Theodgar went to Denmark to evangelize the region of Thy in north-western Jutland. He was canonized in the days of Sven Estrithson by Albric, bishop of 'Wendila', but remained essentially a local saint.[107] In any case, he too represented the English connection, and in general English saints enjoyed quite some favor in the early Danish church.[108] The only bishop of Cnut's church who was remembered independently of Adam of Bremen's chronicle was Odinkar of Ribe, because his see had a vital interest in remembering its title to the possessions with which Odinkar had endowed it.

Conclusion

The basic presupposition of this chapter has been that, throughout the period in question, the Danish kings enjoyed the undisputed allegiance of their bishops. This appears to be a reasonable proposition, for the establishment and maintenance of an ecclesiastical hierarchy must from the outset have been wholly dependent upon royal protection. Not until the second half of the twelfth century do we have evidence of serious conflict between the Danish king and members of the episcopacy.[109] The history of the Danish church in the eleventh century,

---

[106] Ellen Jørgensen, *Helgendyrkelse i Danmark: Studier over Kirkekultur og kirkeligt Liv fra det 11te Aarhundredes Midte til Reformationen* (Copenhagen: Hagerup, 1909), 9. On Liefdag, see "Ribe Bispekrønike," 29.

[107] His *vita* has only been preserved in liturgical fragments: see *Vitae sanctorum Danorum*, ed. M. Cl. Gertz (Copenhagen: G. E. C. Gad, 1908-12), 1-26; cf. Jørgensen, *Helgendyrkelse*, 53-54.

[108] Jørgensen, *Helgendyrkelse*, 17-19.

[109] Breengaard, *Muren*.

therefore, was largely conditioned by the relations of the successive Danish kings with their powerful German neighbor. This problem was of course not limited to the field of ecclesiastical politics, but the close ties between the kings and their episcopacy ensured that the question of ecclesiastical supremacy was an integral part of the political problem. As long as the dynastic union between Denmark and England lasted, the Danish kings had no major difficulties in warding off Hamburg-Bremen's pretensions. Nevertheless, it is interesting that even afterwards, Denmark's rulers seem to have been able to play the English card. From c. 1022 to 1059, Denmark had an episcopal church on the Anglo-Saxon pattern. The towering figures of the mighty bishops of the German imperial church should not obscure the fact that before the age of papal centralization heralded by the reforming popes of the mid-eleventh century, there were several regionally specific patterns of diocesan organization in catholic Europe.

In fact, Hamburg-Bremen seems only for short intervals to have enjoyed illusory victories, first pending the negotiations between Cnut the Great and Conrad II in the early 1030s, and a second time when Sven Estrithson needed Archbishop Adalbert's support for his reorganization and canonical regularization of the Danish church. In turn, the ultimate purpose of that operation was to ensure the autonomy of the Danish church as a separate ecclesiastical province, and after 1059, Hamburg-Bremen's supremacy over Denmark seems to have reverted to the realm of theory. Adalbert by now was able to bolster his metropolitan status by founding new dioceses in the nearby Slavic lands, and the threat that the autonomy of the Danish church would represent to Hamburg-Bremen was less acute. These new foundations, however, soon failed due to Slavic resistance, and the metropolitan see remained ready to press its claims to supremacy over the Danish bishoprics until its Slavic suffragan sees finally had been established on a permanent basis in the mid-twelfth century.[110]

The German kings do not seem to have been particularly eager to assist the archbishops of Hamburg-Bremen in pressing their claims. The marriage alliance between Conrad II and Cnut the Great was actually concluded to the detriment of the archbishop's rights, stripping him of his legal pretext for maintaining a titular bishop of Schleswig as his suffragan, and freeing Cnut to sever the links

---

[110] Aldenburg (Lübeck), 1149/54 (*Ser. ep.*, 5:2, 55), Ratzeburg, 1154 (*ibid.*, 71). Mecklenburg (Schwerin), 1149/60 (*ibid.*, 77; cf. 80-81). The last appearance of Hamburg-Bremen's claims to supremacy over the Nordic churches is in a privilege of Emperor Frederick I for Archbishop Hartwig (16 March 1158; *DD* 1/2, no. 125 (234-36)). Cf. Gelting, "Da Eskil ville vaere aerkebiskop af Roskilde" (above, note 100).

between his church and Hamburg-Bremen that he had only recently accepted. This forced the archbishop to create a new shadow bishop in the person of Wal, "bishop of the Danes". In the end, then, the central problem of the archbishops of Hamburg-Bremen in the first two-thirds of the eleventh century was not supporting and extending the nascent Scandinavian churches, but struggling to establish a proper canonical legitimation for their own metropolitan status.

This makes the ambitions of the flamboyant Archbishop Adalbert even more daring, and may help to explain his ultimate discomfiture. It was Adam of Bremen's task to transform this unedifying narrative into a triumphant tale of missionary success, one whose lustre was only temporarily tarnished by Archbishop Adalbert's failings. It is a tribute to his narrative skill that his chronicle was able to shape all successive interpretations of the early history of the Danish church for more than nine centuries.[111]

---

[111] In a wide-ranging and provocative book, the Swedish historian Henrik Janson recently has proposed a similar deconstruction of Adam of Bremen's account of the beginning of the Swedish church. See Henrik Janson, *Templum nobilissimum. Adam av Bremen: Uppsalatemplet och konfliktlinjerna i Europa kring år 1075* [Avhandlingar från Historiska institutionen i Göteborg 21] (Göteborg: Historiska institutionen, 1998).

Bibliography

Actes des archevêques de Reims d'Arnoul à Renaud II, 957-1139. Ed. PatrickDemouy. Thèse du doctorat, Université de Nancy II, 1982.

Les actes des évêques d'Amiens jusqu'au début du XIIIe siècle. Ed. Suzanne Lecoannet. Thèse de l'Ecole nationale des chartes, Paris, 1957.

Les actes des évêques de Cambrai antérieurs à 1167. Ed. Suzanne Lecoannet. 2 vols.. Thèse de l'Ecole des chartes, 1957.

Actes des évêques de Laon des origines a 1151. Ed. Annie Dufour-Malbezin. Paris: CNRS, 2001.

Actes des évêques de Limoges des origines à 1197. Ed. Jean Becquet. Paris: CNRS, 1999.

Les actes des évêques de Toul des origines à 1069. Ed. Andreas Schoellen. Thèse du doctorat, Université de Nancy, 1985.

Adam of Bremen, *Hamburgische Kirchengeschichte*. 3rd ed. Ed. Bernhard Schmeidler. Hannover: Hahnsche Buchhandlung, 1917.

_____. *Adam of Bremen: History of the Archbishops of Hamburg-Bremen*. Trans. Francis J. Tschan. New York: Columbia University Press, 1959.

Adalbold of Utrecht. *De rebus gestis S. Henrici imperatoris*. *PL* 140: 89-108.

Ademar of Chabannes. *Ademari Cabannensis Chronicon*. Ed. Pierre Bourgain, Richard Landes and Georges Pon. *CCCM* 129/1. Turnhout: Brepols, 1999.

Ambrose. *De excessu fratris*. In *Sancti Ambrosii opera*, vol. 7, ed. Otto Faller. *CSEL* 73. Vienna: Tempsky, 1896: 207-325.

_____. *De officiis*. 2 vols. Ed. Maurice Testard. Paris: Les Belles Lettres, 1984-1992.

_____. *Explanatio psalmorum xii*. Ed. Michael Petschenig. *CSEL* 64. Vienna: Tempsky, 1919.

The Annals of Fulda. Trans. Timothy Reuter. Manchester and New York: Manchester University Press, 1992.

Atto of Vercelli. *Sermones*. *PL* 134: 833-60.

Augustine. *De Doctrina Christiana*. Ed. and trans. R.P.H. Green. Oxford: Clarendon, 1995.

_____. *Epistulae*. Ed. Alois Goldbacher. *CSEL* 44. Vienna: Tempsky, 1904.

Autour de Gerbert d'Aurillac, le pape de l'an mil. Album de documents commentés. Ed. Olivier Guyotjeannin and Emmanuel Poulle. Paris: Ecole des Chartes, 1996.

Berengar of Tours. *Rescriptum contra Lanfrancum*. Ed. R.B.C. Huygens. CCCM 84. Turnhout: Brepols, 1988.

Berno of Reichenau. *De officio missae. PL* 142: 1055-80.

Bernold of Constance. *De officio presbyterum. PL* 148: 1243-50.

Cartulaire du prieuré de La Charité-sur-Loire (Nièvre), ordre de Cluny. Ed. René de Lespinasse. Nevers: Morin-Boutillier, 1887.

Cartulaire de prieuré de Paray-le-Monial. Ed. Ulysse Chevalier. Paris: A. Picard, 1890.

Cartulaire général de l'Yonne. 2 vols.. Ed. Maximilien Quantin. Auxerre: Perriquet, 1854-60.

The Cartulary of Flavigny, 717-1113. Ed. Constance Brittain Bouchard. Medieval Academy Books 99. Cambridge, MA: Medieval Academy of America, 1991.

The Cartulary of St.-Marcel-lès-Chalon, 779-1126. Ed. Constance Brittain Bouchard. Medieval Academy Books 102. Cambridge, MA: Medieval Academy of America, 1998.

Les chartes des évêques d'Arras (1093-1203). Ed. Benoît-Michel Tock. Paris: CTHS, 1991.

Chartes et documents de Saint-Bénigne de Dijon (990-1124). Ed. Georges Chevrier and Maurice Chaume. Dijon: Bernigaud et Privat, 1943.

Chronicon Mediani monasterii, alias Liber de successoribus S. Hildulfi in Mediano monasterio. Ed. Georg Waitz in MGH *SS* IV. Hannover: Hahn, 1841: 86-92.

Chronicon Roskildense. In *Scriptores minores historiae Danicae medii aevi*, vol. 1, ed. M.Cl. Gertz. Copenhagen: Selskabet for Udgivelse af Kilder til dansk Historie, 1917-18: 1-33.

Chronique de l'abbaye de Saint-Bénigne de Dijon, suivie de la chronique de Saint-Pierre de Bèze. Ed. E. Bougaud and Joseph Garnier. Analecta Divionensis 9. Dijon: Darantière, 1875.

Clement of Alexandria. *Christ the Educator*. Trans. Simon P. Wood. New York: Fathers of the Church, 1954.

Constantine of St. Symphorian. *Vita Adalberonis II Episcopi Mettensis* Ed. Georg Pertz in MGH *SS* IV. Hannover: Hahn, 1841: 658-72.

Constitutions of the Holy Apostles. In *The Ante-Nicene Fathers*, vol. VII, ed. Alexander Roberts and James Donaldson. New York: Scribner, 1926.

Corpus des sceaux français du Moyen Age, vol. 2, *Les sceaux des rois et de régence.* Ed. Martine Dalas. Paris: Archives nationales, 1991.

Dhuoda. *Liber Manualis.* 2nd ed.. Ed. Pierre Riché. Sources Chrétiennes 225 bis. Paris: Editions du Cerf, 1991.

Diplomatarium Danicum, vol. 1/1. Ed. C.A. Christensen and Herluf Nielsen. Copenhagen: Munksgaard, 1957.

(Ebbo of Worms). *Vita Burchardi episcopi.* Ed. Georg Waitz in MGH *SS* IV. Hannover: Hahn, 1841: 830-46.

Faustus of Riez. *Opera.* Ed. August Engelbrecht. *CSEL* 21. Vienna: Tempsky, 1891.

Gallia Christiana. Ed. Denis de Ste.-Marthe *et al.* 16 vols. Paris: Imprimerie royale and Firmin-Didot, 1715-1865.

Gerbert of Aurillac. *Correspondance.* 2 vols. Ed. Pierre Riché and J.P. Callu. Paris: Les Belles Lettres, 1993.

Gerhard of Augsburg. *Vita Sancti Oudalrici.* In *Lebensbeschreibungen einiger Bischöfe des 10.-12. Jahrhunderts*, ed. Kallfelz, 46-167.

_____. *Vita Sancti Uodalrici. Die älteste Lebensbeschreibung des Heiligen Ulrich.* Ed. and trans. Walter Berschin and Angelika Häse. Heidelberg: Universitätsverlag Carl Winter, 1993.

Germania Pontificia, vol. 10/1, *Provincia Treverensis: Archidiocesis Treverensis.* Ed. Egon Boshof. Göttingen: Vandenhoeck and Ruprecht, 1992.

Gesta episcoporum Cameracensium, continuatio. Ed. Ludwig Bethmann in MGH *SS* VII. Hannover: Hahn, 1846: 489-500.

Gesta episcoporum Tullensium. Ed. Georg Waitz in MGH *SS* VIII. Hannover: Hahn, 1848: 631-48.

Les Gestes des évêques d'Auxerre. Ed. Guy Lobrichon and Monique Goullet. Les classiques de l'histoire de France au moyen âge. Paris: Les Belles Lettres, 2002.

Gori, Antonio Francesco, ed. *Thesaurus veterum diptychorum consularium et ecclesiasticorum.* 3 vols. Florence: Caietani Albrazzini, 1759.

Gregory I. *Dialogues. PL* 77: 143-428.

_____. *In librum primum Regum expositionem libri vi.* Ed. Patrick Verbraken. *CCL* 144. Turnhout: Brepols, 1963.

_____. *Registrum Epistularum.* Ed. Dag Norberg. *CCL* 140. Turnhout: Brepols, 1982.

Gregory VII. *Das Register Gregors VII.* 2 vols. Ed. Erich Caspar. MGH *ES* 2. Berlin: Weidmann, 1920.

Hermann of Reichenau. *Chronica.* Ed. G.H. Pertz in MGH *SS* V. Hannover: Hahn, 1844: 67-133.

Hermann von Lerbeck. "Catalogus episcoporum Mindensium." Ed. K. Löffler in *Mindener Geschichtsquellen.* Münster: Aschendorff, 1917.

Hrabanus Maurus. *De clericorum institutione. PL* 107:293-420.

Hucbald of St.-Amand. *Vita Sanctae Rictrudis. PL* 132: 829-48.

Hugh of Langres. *Tractatus de corpore et sanguine Christi. PL* 142: 1325-1334.

(John of Fécamp). *Confessio fidei. PL* 101: 1027-98.

John of St.-Arnoul. *La Vie de Jean, abbé de Gorze.* Ed. and trans. Michel Parisse. Paris: Picard, 1999.

John the Deacon. *S. Gregorii magni vita. PL* 75: 59-242.

Kallfelz, Hatto, ed.. *Lebensbeschreibungen einiger Bischöfe des 10.-12. Jahrhunderts. AQDGM* 22. Darmstadt: Wissenschaftliche Buchgesellschaft, 1973.

Lebeuf, Jean. *Mémoires concernant l'histoire civile et ecclésiastique d'Auxerre et de son ancien diocèse.* New ed. by M. Challe and Maximilien Quantin. Vol. 4, *Recueil de monuments, chartes, titres et autres pièces inédites.* Auxerre: Perriquet, 1855.

Le Liber pontificalis. 3 vols. Ed. Louis Duchesne. Paris: E. Thorin, 1892.

The Lives of the Ninth-Century Popes. Trans. Raymond Davis. Liverpool: Liverpool University Press, 1995.

Necrologium Lundense: Lunds domkyrkas nekrologium. Ed. Lauritz Weibull. Lund: Berlingska, 1923.

Obituaires de la province de Sens, vol. 3. *Diocèses d'Orléans, d'Auxerre, et de Nevers.* Ed. Alexandre Vidier and Léon Mirot. Paris: Imprimerie nationale, 1909.

Opus Caroli regis contra synodum (Libri Carolini). Ed. Ann Freeman. MGH *Conc* II, Suppl. 1. Hannover: Hahn, 1998.

Ordines coronationis Franciae: Texts and Ordines for the Coronation of Frankish and French Kings and Queens in the Middle Ages. 2 vols.. Ed. Richard A. Jackson. Philadelphia: University of Pennsylvania Press, 1995.

Die Ordines für die Weihe und Krönung des Kaisers und der Kaiserin (Ordines coronationis imperialis). Ed. Reinhard Elze. MGH *Fontes* 9. Hannover: Hahn, 1960.

"Ordo ad benedicendum ducem Aquitanie." In *Recueil des Historiens des Gaules et de la France*, new ed., vol. 23, ed. Léopold Delisle. Paris: V. Palmé, 1872: 451-53.

Papsturkunden 896-1046. 2 vols. Ed. Harald Zimmerman. Vienna: Österreichische Akademie der Wissenschaften, 1988-89.

Paschasius Radbertus. *De corpore et sanguine Domini, cum appendice Epistola ad Fredugardum*. Ed. Beda Paulus. CCCM 16. Turnhout: Brepols, 1969.

Paul the Deacon. *S. Gregorii magni vita*. PL 75: 41-59.

Paulinus of Nola. *Epistulae*. Ed. Wilhelm Hartel. CSEL 29. Vienna: Tempsky, 1894.

Peter Lombard. *Sententiae*. PL 192: 521-962.

The Peterborough Chronicle, 1070-1154. 2nd ed. Ed. Cecily Clark. Oxford: Clarendon, 1970.

Prosper of Aquitaine. *Expositio Psalmorum*. Ed. P. Callens. CCL 68A. Turnhout: Brepols, 1972.

Radulfus Glaber. *Opera*. Ed. John France, Neithard Bulst, and Paul Reynolds. Oxford: Oxford University Press, 1989.

Rather of Verona. *The Complete Works of Rather of Verona*. Trans. Peter L.D. Reid. Binghamton, NY: Medieval and Renaissance Texts and Studies, 1991.

Ratramnus of Corbie. *De corpore et sanguine Domini*. PL 121: 125-70.

Recueil des chartes de l'abbaye de Cluny. Ed. Auguste Bernard and Alexander Bruel. 6 vols. Paris: Imprimerie nationale, 1876–1903.

Regino of Prüm. *Chronicon*. Ed. Friedrich Kurze. MGH SSRG 50. Hannover: Hahn, 1890.

"Ribe Bispekrønike." Ed. Ellen Jørgensen in *Kirkehistoriske Samlinger*, ser. 6, vol. 1. Copenhagen: G.E.C. Gad, 1933-1935: 23-33.

Roskildekrøniken. 2nd. ed.. Trans. Michael H. Gelting. Højbjerg: Wormianum, 2002.

Ruotger. *Vita sancti Brunonis*. In *Lebensbeschreibungen einiger Bischöfe des 10.-12. Jahrhunderts*, ed. Kallfelz, 178-261.

Thangmar. *Vita Sancti Bernwardi*. In *Lebensbeschreibungen einiger Bischöfe des 10.-12. Jahrhunderts*, ed. Kallfelz, 272-360.

The Theodosian Code and Novels and the Sirmondian Constitutions. Trans. Clyde Pharr. Princeton: Princeton University Press, 1952.

Theodulph of Orléans. *Capitulare*. PL 105: 207-24.

Thietmar of Merseburg. *Chronicon*. Ed. Werner Trillmich. *AQDGM* 9. Darmstadt: Wissenschaftliche Buchgesellschaft, 1957.

——. *Chronicon*. Ed. Robert Holtzmann. MGH *SSRG*, n.s. 9. Berlin: Weidmann, 1935.

——. *Ottonian Germany: The Chronicon of Thietmar of Merseburg*. Trans. David Warner. Manchester and New York: Manchester University Press, 2001.

Urkundenbuch zur Geschichte der mittelrheinischen Territorien. 3 vols. Ed. Heinrich Beyer. Coblenz: J. Hölscher, 1860-74.

La Vie du Pape Léon IX (Brunon, évêque de Toul). Ed. Michel Parisse. Les Classiques de l'Histoire de France au Moyen Age 38. Paris: Les Belles Lettres, 1997.

Vita Dunstani ("B" version). In *Memorials of Saint Dunstan*, ed. William Stubbs. Rolls Series 63. London: Rolls Commissioners, 1874: 3-52.

Vita Meinwerci episcopi Patherbrunnensis. Ed. Franz Tenckhoff. MGH *SSRG* 59. Hannover: Hahn, 1921.

Vitae sanctorum Danorum. Ed. M. Cl. Gertz. Copenhagen: G. E. C. Gad, 1908-12.

Widukind of Corvey. *Res Gestae Saxonicae*. In *Quellen zur Geschichte der sächsischen Kaiserzeit*, ed. Albert Bauer and Reinhard Rau. *AQDGM* 8. Darmstadt: Wissenschaftliche Buchgesellschaft, 1971.

William of Jumièges *et al. The "Gesta Normannorum Ducum" of William of Jumièges, Orderic Vitalis, and Robert of Torigni*. Ed. Elisabeth M. C. Van Houts. 2 vols. Oxford: Clarendon, 1992-95.

Wulfstan of Winchester. *The Life of St Æthelwold*. Ed. Michael Lapidge and Michael Winterbottom. Oxford: Oxford University Press, 1991.

* * *

Achter, Irmingard. "Die Kölner Petrusreliquien und die Bautätigkeit Erzbischof Brunos am Kölner Dom." In *Das erste Jahrtausend: Kultur und Kunst im werdenden Abendland an Rhein und Ruhr*, 3 vols., ed. Kurt Böhner *et al*. Düsseldorf: L. Schwann, 1962: 2: 948-81

Althoff, Gerd. "Verwandschaft, Freundschaft, Klientel. Der schwierige Weg zum Ohr des Herrschers." In *Spielregeln der Politik im Mittelalter. Kommunikation im Frieden und Fehde*. Darmstadt: Wissenschaftliche Buchgesellschaft, 1997: 185-98.

———, ed. *Form und Funktion öffentlicher Kommunikation im Mittelalter*. Sigmaringen: Thorbecke, 2001.

Anderson, Benedict. *Imagined Communities: Reflections on the Origin and Spread of Nationalism*. 2nd ed. London: Verso, 1991.

Andrieu, Michel. "Le Sacre épiscopal d'après Hincmar de Reims." *Revue d'histoire ecclésiastique* 48 (1953): 22-73.

Appuhn, Horst, Christian Radtke, and Walter Körber, ed.. *850 Jahre St.-Petri-Dom zu Schleswig*. Schleswig: Schleswiger Druck- und Verlagshaus, 1984.

Arup, Erik. "Kong Svend 2.s Biografi." *Scandia* 4 (1931): 55-101.

Atsma, Hartmut and Jean Vezin. "Remarques paléographiques et diplomatiques sur les actes originaux des évêques de France du VIIe siècle à l'an mil." In *Die Diplomatik der Bischofsurkunde vor 1250*, ed. Haidacher and Köfler, 209-221

Babelon, Ernest. *Catalogue des camées antiques et modernes de la Bibliothèque Nationale*. Paris: E. Leroux, 1897.

Bachrach, Bernard S. "Geoffrey Greymantle, Count of the Angevins, 960-987: A Study in French Politics." *Studies in Medieval and Renaissance History* 17 (1985): 1-67.

Bak, Janos M.. "Introduction: Coronation studies—past, present, and future." In *Coronations: Medieval and Early Modern Monarchic Ritual*, ed. Janos M. Bak. Berkeley: University of California Press, 1990: 1-15.

———. "Medieval symbology of the state: Percy E. Schramm's contribution." *Viator* 4 (1973): 33-63

Barlow, Frank. *Thomas Becket*. Berkeley: University of California Press, 1986.

Barraud, P.C.. "Des bagues à toutes les époques et en particulier de l'anneau des évêques et des abbés." *Bulletin monumental* 30 (1864): 5-74, 353-422, 501-28, and 613-70.

Barthélemy, Dominique. *L'an mil et la paix de Dieu. La France chrétienne et féodale, 980-1060*. Paris: Fayard, 1999.

———. *La mutation de l'an mil a-t-elle eu lieu? Servage et chevalerie dans la France des Xe et XIe siècles*. Paris: Fayard, 1997.

Bautier, Robert-Henri. "Apparition, diffusion et évolution typologique du sceau épiscopal au Moyen Age." In *Die Diplomatik der Bischofsurkunde vor 1250*, ed. Haidacher and Köfler, 225-241.

Bedos-Rezak, Brigitte Miriam. "Une image ontologique: sceau et ressemblance en France préscolastique (1000-1200)." In *Etudes d'histoire de l'art offertes a Jacques Thirion, des premiers temps chrétiens au XXe siècle*, ed. Alain Erlande-Brandenburg and Jean-Michel Leniaud. Paris: Ecole des chartes, 2001: 39-50.

———. "Medieval Identity: A Sign and a Concept." *The American Historical Review* 105 (2000): 1489-1533.

———. "Replica: Images of Identity and the Identity of Images in Pre-scholastic France." In *The Mind's Eye: Art and Theological Argument in the Medieval West*, ed. Jeffrey Hamburger and Anne-Marie Bouché (forthcoming).

———. "Ritual in the Royal Chancery: Text, Image, and the Representation of Kingship in Medieval French Diplomas (700-1200)." In *European Monarchy. Its Evolution and Practice from Roman Antiquity to Modern Times*, ed. Heinz Duchhardt, Richard A. Jackson, and David Sturdy. Stuttgart: Franz Steiner, 1992: 27-40.

Benson, Robert L.. *The Bishop-Elect: A Study in Medieval Ecclesiastical Office*. Princeton: Princeton University Press, 1968.

Benz, Karl-Josef. *Untersuchungen zur politischen Bedeutung der Kirchweihe unter Teilnahme der deutschen Herrscher im hohen Mittelalter. Ein Beitrag zum Studium des Verhältnisses zwischen weltlicher Macht und Kirchlicher Wirklichkeit unter Otto III. und Heinrich II.* Kallmünz: M. Lassleben, 1975.

Berglar, Peter and Odilo Engels, ed.. *Der Bischof in seiner Zeit. Bischofstypus und Bischofsideal im Spiegel der Kölner Kirche*. Cologne: J.P. Bachem, 1996.

Berschin, Walter. *Biographie und Epochenstil im lateinischen Mittelalter*, vol. 4, *Ottonische Biographie, erster Halbband, 920-1070*. Stuttgart: Anton Hiersemann, 1999.

Bloch, Peter and Hermann Schnitzler. *Die Ottonischen Kölner Malerschule*. 2 vols. Düsseldorf: Schwann, 1970.

Bolin, Sture. *Om Nordens äldsta historieforskning: Studier över dess metodik och källvärde*. Lunds Universitets årsskrift, n.s. 1/27 no. 3. Lund: H. Olsson, 1931.

Bonnassie, Pierre. *From Slavery to Feudalism in South-Western Europe*. Trans. Jean Birrell. Cambridge and New York: Cambridge University Press, 1991.

Boockmann, Andrea. *Geistliche und weltliche Gerichtsbarkeit im mittelalterlichen Bistum Schleswig*. Neumünster: Karl Wachholtz, 1967.

Boshof, Egon. "Köln, Mainz, Trier—Die Auseinandersetzungen um die Spitzenstellung im deutschen Episkopat in ottonisch-salischer Zeit." *Jahrbuch des Kölnischen Geschichtsvereins* 49 (1978): 19-48.

Botte, Bernard. "Conficere Corpus Christi." *Année théologique* 8 (1947): 309-15.

Bouchard, Constance Brittain. "Merovingian, Carolingian, and Cluniac Monasticism: Reform and Renewal in Burgundy." *Journal of Ecclesiastical History* 41 (1990): 365-388.

_____. *Spirituality and Administration: The Role of the Bishop in Twelfth-Century Auxerre*. Speculum Anniversary Monographs 5. Cambridge, MA: Medieval Academy of America, 1979.

_____. *Sword, Miter, and Cloister: Nobility and the Church in Burgundy, 980-1198*. Ithaca: Cornell University Press, 1987.

_____. *"Those of My Blood": Constructing Noble Families in Medieval Francia*. Philadelphia: University of Pennsylvania Press, 2001.

Bouman, Cornelius. *Sacring and Crowning*. Groningen: J. B. Wolters, 1957.

Boussard, Jacques. "Les évêques en Neustrie avant la Réforme grégorienne (950-1050 environ)." *Journal des Savants* 3 (1970): 161-96.

Brandt, Michael and Arne Eggebrecht, ed. *Bernward von Hildesheim und das Zeitalter der Ottonen. Katalog der Ausstellung, Hildesheim 1993*. 2 vols. Hildesheim: Bernward Verlag, 1993.

Breengaard, Carsten. *Muren om Israels hus: Regnum og sacerdotium i Danmark 1050-1170*. Copenhagen: G. E. C. Gad, 1982.

Brentano, Robert. *A New World in a Small Place: Church and Religion in the Diocese of Rieti, 1188-1378*. Berkeley: University of California Press, 1994.

_____. *Two Churches: England and Italy in the Thirteenth Century*. Berkeley: University of California Press, 1988.

Bresslau, Harry. *Handbuch der Urkundenlehre für Deutschland und Italien*. Leipzig: Veit, 1889.

_____. *Jahrbücher des Deutschen Reichs unter Konrad II*. 2 vols. Berlin: Duncker and Humblot, 1879-84.

Brown, Peter. "Arbiters of the Holy: The Christian Holy Man in Late Antiquity." In *Authority and the Sacred: Aspects of the Christianization of the Roman World*. Cambridge and New York: Cambridge University Press, 1995: 55-78.

_____. *Power and Persuasion in Late Antiquity: Towards A Christian Empire*. Madison, WI: University of Wisconsin Press, 1992.

_____. "The Rise and Function of the Holy Man in Late Antiquity." In *Society and the Holy in Late Antiquity*. Berkeley: University of California Press, 1982: 103-52.

Brunel, Ghislain. "Chartes et chancelleries épiscopales du Nord de la France au XIe siècle." In *A propos des actes d'évêques*, ed. Parisse, 227-44.

Brunner, Herbert, ed. *Schatzkammer der Residenz München, Katalog*. 3rd ed. Munich: Bayerische Verwaltung der staatlichen Schlösser, Gärten und Seen, 1970.

Bührer-Thierry, Geneviève. *Evêques et pouvoir dans le royaume de Germanie. Les Eglises de Bavière et de Souabe, 876-973*. Paris: Picard, 1997.

Büttner, Heinrich. "Die Mainzer Erzbischöfe Friedrich und Wilhelm und das Papsttum des 10. Jahrhunderts." *Geschichtliche Landeskunde* 3/1 (1966): 2-14.

Catalogue d'objets d'art et de curiosité formant la collection de feu M'r le Comte Girolamo Possenti de Fabriano. Rome: 1880.

Chassel, Jean-Luc. "L'apparition du sceau dans les actes de la chancellerie de Langres au XIe siècle." *Cahiers Hauts-Marnais* 167 (1986): 77-95

_____. "L'essor du sceau au XIe siècle." *Bibliothèque de l'Ecole des chartes* 155 (1997): 221-34.

Chauney, Martine. "Deux évêques bourguignons de l'an mil: Brunon de Langres et Hughes Ier d'Auxerre." *Cahiers de civilisation médiévale* 21 (1978): 385-93.

Chazelle, Celia. *The Crucified God in the Carolingian Era: Theology and Art of God's Passion*. Cambridge and New York: Cambridge University Press, 2001.

_____. "Figure, Character, and the Glorified Body in the Carolingian Eucharistic Controversy." *Traditio* 47 (1992): 1-36.

Chédeville, André and Noël-Yves Tonnerre. *La Bretagne féodale, XIe-XIIIe siècle*. Rennes: Ouest-France, 1987.

Choux, Jacques. "Plaque de reliure d'un évangéliaire carolingien de la cathédrale de Toul." *Annales de l'Est* (1958): 65-67. Reprinted in *La Lorraine chrétienne au moyen age. Receuil d'études*. Metz: Editions Serpenoise, 1981: 327-29

Christiansen, Tage E.. "De gyldne Altre, I. Tamdrup-Pladerne." *Aarbøger for Nordisk Oldkyndighed og Historie* (1968): 153-205.

Cinthio, Erik. "Dalby kungsgård: Medeltidsarkeologien som historisk vetenskap." *Kungl. Vitterhets, Historie och Antikvitets Akademiens Årsbok* (1983): 89-100.

———. "Kungapalatset i Dalby." *Ale: Historisk tidskrift för Skåneland* (1966, no. 3): 16-19.

Clanchy, Michael. *From Memory to Written Record: England 1066-1307*. 2nd ed. Oxford: Blackwell, 1993.

Cohen, Adam. *The Uta Codex. Art, Philosophy, and Reform in Eleventh-Century Germany*. University Park, PA: Pennsylvania State University Press, 2000.

Comaroff, John and Simon Roberts. *Rules and Processes: The Cultural Logic of Dispute in an African Context*. Chicago: The University of Chicago Press, 1981.

Constable, Giles. *Letters and Letter-Collections*. Typologie des sources du Moyen Age occidental 17. Turnhout: Brepols, 1976.

Coué, Stephanie. "Acht Bischofsviten aus der Salierzeit—neu interpretiert." In *Die Salier und das Reich*, ed. Weinfurter, 3: 347-413.

———. *Hagiographie im Kontext: Schreibanlass und Funktion von Bischofsviten aus dem 11. und vom Anfang des 12. Jahrhunderts*. Arbeiten zur Frühmittelalterforschung 24. Berlin: Walter de Gruyter, 1997.

Courtois, Michèle. "Remarques sur les chartes originales des évêques antérieures à 1121 et conservées dans les Bibliothèques et Archives de France." In *A propos des actes d'évêques*, ed. Parisse, 45-77.

Cowdrey, H. E. J. *The Cluniacs and the Gregorian Reform*. Oxford: Oxford University Press, 1970.

Cristiani, Marta. "La controversia eucaristica nella cultura del secolo IX." *Studi Medievali* 9 (1968): 167-233.

Cutler, Anthony. "A Byzantine Triptych in Medieval Germany and Its Modern Recovery." *Gesta* 37 (1998): 3-12.

———. "The Date and Significance of the Romanos Ivory." In *Byzantine East, Latin West*, ed. Moss and Kiefer, 605-13.

———. "From Loot to Scholarship: Changing Modes in the Italian Response to Byzantine Artifacts, ca. 1200-1750." *Dumbarton Oaks Papers* 49 (1995): 237-67.

———. *The Hand of the Master: Craftsmanship, Ivory, and Society in Byzantium (9th-11th Centuries)*. Princeton: Princeton University Press, 1994.

———. "Misapprehensions and Misgivings: Byzantine Art and the West in the Twelfth and Thirteenth Centuries." *Medievalia* 7 (1981): 41-77.

———. "La 'questione bizantina' nella pittura italiana: una visione alternativa della 'maniera greca'." In *La Pittura in Italia. L'Altomedioevo*, ed. Carlo Bertelli. Milan: Electa, 1994: 335-54.

———. "Reuse or Use? Theoretical and Practical Attitudes towards Objects in the Early Middle Ages." In *Ideologie e pratiche del reimpiego nell'alto medioevo*. Settimane di studio del Centro italiano di studi sull'alto medioevo 46. Spoleto: Presso le Sede del Centro, 1999: 1057-83.

Dahlhaus, Joachim. "Zu den Gesta Episcoporum Tullensium." In *Papstgeschichte und Landesgeschichte. Festschrift Hermann Jakobs*. Cologne: Böhlau, 1995: 177-94.

Danmarks Kirker, ed. Victor Hermansen *et al*, vol. 19, *Ribe Amt*, vol. 1. Copenhagen, G.E.C. Gad, 1979.

Dehio, Georg. *Geschichte des Erzbistums Hamburg-Bremen bis zum Ausgang der Mission*. 2 vols. Berlin: W. Hertz, 1877.

Delogu, Paolo. "Vescovi, conti et sovrani nella crisi del regno italico." *Annali della scuola speciale per archivisti e bibliotecari dell'Università di Roma* 8 (1968): 3-72.

Deloche, Maximin. *Etude historique et archéologique sur les anneaux sigillaires et autres des premiers siècles du moyen âge*. Paris: Leroux, 1900.

———. "Le port des anneaux dans l'antiquité romaine et dans les premiers siècles du Moyen Age." *Mémoires de l'Académie des Inscriptions et Belles-Lettres* 35/2 (1896): 64-70.

Demay, Germain. *Inventaire des sceaux de Normandie*. Paris: Imprimerie nationale, 1881.

Demidoff, Lene. "The Poppo Legend." *Mediaeval Scandinavia* 6 (1973): 39-67.

Demouy, Patrick. "Les sceaux des archevêques de Reims des origines à la fin du XIIIe siècle." In *Actes du 109e Congrès national des Sociétés savantes, Dijon, 1984: section d'histoire médiévale et de philologie*, vol. 1. Paris: C.T.H.S., 1985: 687-720.

Demus, Otto. *Byzantine Art and the West*. New York: New York University Press, 1970.

Duby, Georges. *La société aux XIe et XIIe siècles dans la région mâconnaise*. 2nd ed. Paris: SEVPEN, 1971.

———. *The Three Orders: Feudal Society Imagined*. Trans. Arthur Goldhammer. Chicago: The University of Chicago Press, 1980.

Duguet, Jacques. "La famille des Isembert, évêques de Poitiers et ses relations (Xe-XIe siècles)." *Bulletin de la Société des antiquaires de l'Ouest*, 4th ser., 11 (1971-72): 163-86.

Dvornik, Francis. *The Idea of Apostolicity in Byzantium and the Legend of the Apostle Andrew*. Cambridge, MA: Harvard University Press, 1958.

Eck, Walter. "Der Einfluß der konstantinischen Wende auf die Auswahl der Bischöfe im 4. und 5. Jahrhundert." *Chiron* 8 (1978): 561-85.

Effenberger, Arne. "Byzantinische Kunstwerke im Besitz deutscher Kaiser, Bischöfe, und Klöster im Zeitalter der Ottonen." In *Bernward von Hildesheim*, ed. Brandt and Eggebrecht, 1: 145-59.

Ehlers, Joachim. "Die Reform der Christenheit. Studium, Bildung und Wissenschaft als bestimmende Kräfte bei der Entstehung des mittelalterlichen Europa." In *Deutschland und der Westen Europas im Mittelalter*, ed. Joachim Ehlers. Vorträge und Forschungen 56. Stuttgart: Thorbecke, 2002: 177-209.

Ellard, Gerald. *Ordination Anointings in the Western Church before 1000 A.D.*. Cambridge, MA: Medieval Academy of America, 1933.

Engels, Odilo. "Der Pontifikatsantritt und seine Zeichen." In *Segni e riti nella chiesa altomedievale occidentale*. Settimane 33. Spoleto: Centro Italiano di studi sull'alto Medioevo, 1987: 707-70.

———. "Theophano, the western empress from the East." In *The Empress Theophano: Byzantium and the West at the turn of the first millennium*, ed. Adelbert Davids. Cambridge and New York: Cambridge University Press, 1995: 28-48.

Erkens, Franz-Reiner. "*In tota cunctis gratissimus aula?* Egbert von Trier als Erzbischof," in *Egbert, Erzbishof von Trier*, ed. Ronig, 2: 37-52.

Evans, Helen C., and William D. Wixom, ed.. *The Glory of Byzantium: Art and Culture of the Middle Byzantine Era, A.D. 843-1261.* New York: Metropolitan Museum of Art, 1997.

Ewald, Paul. "Die Papstbriefe der Brittischen Sammlung." *Neues Archiv der Gesellschaft für ältere deutsche Geschichtskunde* 5 (1880): 275-596.

Favreau, Robert. *Épigraphie médiévale.* L'atelier du médiéviste 5. Turnhout: Brepols, 1997.

Ferguson, Margaret W.. "Saint Augustine's Region of Unlikeness: The Crossing of Exile and Language." *The Georgia Review* 29 (1975): 842-63.

Fichtenau, Heinrich. "Die Ketzer von Orléans (1022)." In *Ex ipsis rerum documentis*, ed. Herbers *et al*, 417-27.

_____. *Lebensordnungen des 10. Jahrhunderts: Studien über Denkart und Existenz im einstigen Karolingerreich.* Monographien zur Geschichte des Mittelalters 30. Stuttgart: Anton Hiersemann, 1984. English translation by Patrick Geary as *Living in the Tenth Century: Mentalities and Social Orders.* Chicago: The University of Chicago Press, 1991.

Finck von Finckenstein, Albrecht Graf. *Bischof und Reich. Untersuchungen zum Integrationsprozess des ottonisch-frühsalischen Reiches (919-1056).* Studien zur Mediävistik 1. Sigmaringen: Thorbecke, 1989.

Fisher, Annika. "Making the Body of Christ: The Crucifix of Archbishop Gero of Cologne." Paper presented at the conference "*Genus Regale et Sacerdotale*: The Image of the Bishop Around the Millennium," Chicago, October 1999.

Fleckenstein, Josef. *Die Hofkapelle der deutschen Könige.* 2 vols. MGH Schriften 16. Stuttgart: Anton Hiersemann, 1959-66.

_____. "Problematik und Gestalt der ottonisch-salischen Reichskirche." In *Reich und Kirche vor dem Investiturstreit. Vorträge beim wissenschaftlichen Kolloquium aus Anlass des 80. Geburtstag Gerd Tellenbach*, ed. Karl Schmid. Sigmaringen: Thorbecke, 1985: 83-98.

_____. "Zum Begriff der ottonisch-salischen Reichskirche." In *Geschichte, Wirtschaft, Gesellschaft. Festschrift für Clemens Bauer zum 75. Geburtstag.* Berlin: Dunker and Humblot, 1974: 61-71.

Fletcher, Richard. *The Conversion of Europe: From Paganism to Christianity, 371-1386 A.D.* London: Fontana Press, 1998.

Folz, Robert. "Adelbéron II, évêque de Metz 984-1005." in *Ex ipsis rerum documentis*, ed. Herbers *et al*, 399-415.

Foreville, Raymonde. *Thomas Becket dans la tradition historique et hagiographique*. London: Variorum, 1981.

Forsyth, Ilene. "Art with History: The Role of Spolia in the Cumulative Work of Art." In *Byzantine East, Latin West*, ed. Moss and Kiefer, 153-62.

Frase, Michael. *Friede und Königsherrschaft. Quellenkritik und Interpretation der* Continuatio Regionis *(Studien zur ottonischen Geschichtsschreibung)*. Studia Irenica 35. Frankfurt am Main: Peter Lang, 1990.

Fuhrmann, Horst. "Die Synoden von Ingelheim." In *Ingelheim am Rhein*, ed. Johanne Autenrieth. Stuttgart: Ernst Klett, 1964: 147-73.

———. "Studien zur Geschichte mittelalterlicher Patriarchate. III. Teil (Schluss)." *ZSfR* 41 (1955): 95-183.

Gallistl, Bernhard. "Byzanz-Rezeption und Renovatio-Symbolik in der Kunst Bernwards von Hildesheim." In *Byzanz und das Abendland im 10. Und 11. Jahrhundert*, ed. Evangelos Konstantinou. Cologne: Böhlau, 1997: 129-60.

Geary, Patrick J. "Monastic Memory and the Mutation of the Year Thousand." In *Monks and Nuns, Saints and Outcasts: Religion in Medieval Society*, ed. Sharon Farmer and Barbara H. Rosenwein. Ithaca: Cornell University Press, 2000: 19-36.

Gechter, Marianne. "Die Grablege des Bischofs Rudolf von Schleswig in St. Kunibert." *Colonia Romanica: Jahrbuch des Fördervereins Romanische Kirchen Köln e.V.* 12 (1997): 17-20.

Gelting, Michael. "Cronica ecclesiæ Ripensis (Chronicle of the Church of Ribe)." In *Medieval Nordic Literature in Latin*, ed. Lars Boje Mortensen *et al* (forthcoming).

———. "Chronicon Roskildense." In *Medieval Nordic Literature in Latin*, ed. Lars Boje Mortensen *et al* (forthcoming).

Giddens, Anthony. *Central Problems in Social Theory: Action, Structure, and Contradiction in Social Analysis*. Berkeley: University of California Press, 1979.

Ginzburg, Carlo. "Clues: Roots of an Evidential Paradigm." In *Clues, Myths, and the Historical Method*, trans. John and Anne Tedeschi. Baltimore: The Johns Hopkins University Press, 1986: 96–125.

Godelier, Maurice. *The Enigma of the Gift*. Trans. Nora Scott. Chicago: The University of Chicago Press, 1999.

Goetz, Hans-Werner. *Geschichtschreibung und Geschichtsbewusstsein im hohen Mittelalter.* Berlin: Akademie Verlag, 1999.

Goldschmidt, Adolph. *Die Elfenbeinskulpturen aus der Zeit der karolingischen und sächsischen Kaiser (VIII.-XI. Jahrhundert).* 2 vols. Berlin: Bruno Cassirer, 1918.

―――― and Kurt Weitzmann, ed. *Die byzantinischen Elfenbeinskulpturen des X. bis XIII. Jahrhunderts.* 2 vols. Berlin: Bruno Cassirer, 1934.

Guenée, Bernard. *Between Church and State: The Lives of Four French Prelates in the Late Middle Ages.* Trans. Arthur Goldhammer. Chicago: The University of Chicago Press, 1996.

Gulliver, Philip. "On Mediators." In *Social Anthropology and Law*, ed. Ian Hamnett. London and New York: Academic Press, 1977: 15-52.

Guyotjeannin, Olivier, Jacques Pycke, and Benoît-Michel Tock. *Diplomatique médiévale.* Turnhout: Brepols, 1993.

Guyotjeannin, Olivier, Laurent Morelle, and Michel Parisse, ed. *Les cartulaires. Actes de la Table Ronde organisée par l'Ecole nationale des chartes et le G.D.R. 121 du C.N.R.S. (Paris, 5-7 décembre 1991).* Paris: Ecole des chartes, 1993.

Haarländer, Stephanie. "Die Vita Burchardi im Rahmen der Bischofsviten seiner Zeit." In *Burchard von Worms*, ed. Hartmann, 129-60.

―――― . *Vitae Episcoporum. Eine Quellengattung zwischen Hagiographie und Historiographie, untersucht an Lebensbeschreibungen von Bischöfen des Regnum Teutonicum im Zeitalter der Ottonen und Salier.* Monographien zur Geschichte des Mittelalters 47. Stuttgart: Anton Hiersemann, 2000.

Haidacher, Christoph and Werner Köfler, ed. *Die Diplomatik der Bischofsurkunde vor 1250 / La diplomatique épiscopale avant 1250. Referate zum VIII. Internationalen Kongress für Diplomatik, Innsbruck, 27. September-3. Oktober 1993.* Innsbruck: Tiroler Landesarchiv, 1995.

Hamilton, Sarah. *The Practice of Penance, 900-1050.* Woodbridge, Suffolk: Boydell Press, 2001.

Handelman, Susan A.. *The Slayers of Moses: The Emergence of Rabbinic Interpretation in Modern Literary Theory.* Albany: State University of New York Press, 1982.

Harries, Jill. *Law and Empire in Late Antiquity.* Cambridge: Cambridge University Press, 1999.

Hartmann, Wilfried, ed.. *Burchard von Worms 1000-1025*. Mainz: Gesellschaft für mittelrheinische Kirchengeschichte, 2000.

Hauck, Albert. *Kirchengeschichte Deutschlands*. 3rd ed. 5 vols. Leipzig: J.C. Hinrich, 1912.

Haussherr, Reiner. *Der tote Christus am Kreuz. Zur Ikonographie des Gerokreuzes*. Ph.D. dissertation, Friedrich-Wilhelms-Universität zu Bonn, 1963.

Head, Thomas. "Art and Artifice in Ottonian Trier." *Gesta* 36/1 (1997): 65-82.

――――――. "The Development of the Peace of God in Aquitaine (970-1005)." *Speculum* 74 (1999): 656-86.

―――――― and Richard Landes, ed. *The Peace of God: Social Violence and Religious Response in France around the Year 1000*. Ithaca: Cornell University Press, 1992.

Heinzelmann, Martin. *Bischofsherrschaft in Gallien: Zur Kontinuität römischer Führungsschichten vom 4. bis zum 7. Jahrhundert. Soziale, prosopographische und bildungsgeschichtliche Aspekte*. Beihefte der Francia 5. Munich: Artemis, 1976.

Hefele, Charles-Joseph. *Histoire de conciles*. Trans. and aug. Henri Leclercq. 10 vols. Paris: Letouzey, 1907-38.

Helveg, Ludvig. *De Danske Domkapitler: deres Oprindelse, Indretning og Virksomhed, før Reformationen*. Copenhagen: C. G. Iversen, 1855.

Herbers, Klaus, Hans-Henning Kortüm, and Carlo Servatius, ed. *Ex ipsis rerum documentis: Beiträge zur Mediävistik. Festschrift für Harald Zimmerman zum 65. Geburtstag*. Sigmaringen: Thorbecke, 1991.

Herkenrath, Rainer Maria. "Das Diplom Kaiser Heinrichs II. für Bischof Berthold von Toul." *DA* 28 (1972): 537-42.

Hertzberg, Ebbe and Alexander Bugge. *Norges historie*, vol. 2/1, *Tidsrummet 1030-1103*. Kristiania: Aschehoug, 1915.

Hlawitschka, Eduard. "Zur Erschliessung der Memorialüberlieferung aus dem Kloster Fulda." *DA* 38 (1982): 166-179.

Hoffmann, Erich. "Beiträge zur Geschichte der Beziehungen zwischen dem deutschen und dem dänischen Reich für die Zeit von 934 bis 1035." In *850 Jahre St.-Petri-Dom zu Schleswig*, ed. Appuhn *et al*, 105-132.

Howe, John. "The Nobility's Reform of the Medieval Church." *American Historical Review* 92 (1988): 317-39.

Hunt, Noreen. *Cluny Under Saint Hugh, 1049-1109.* London: Edward Arnold, 1967.

Hussong, Ulrich. "Studien zur Geschichte der Reichsabtei Fulda bis zur Jahrtausendwende. Erster Teil." *Archiv für Diplomatik* 31 (1985): 1-225.

Innes, Matthew. *State and Society in the Early Middle Ages: The Middle Rhine Valley, 400-1000.* Cambridge and New York: Cambridge University Press, 2000.

Instinsky, Hans Ulrich. *Bischofsstuhl und Kaiserthron.* Munich: Kösel-Verlag, 1955.

Jakobs, Hermann. "Zu den neuen Thesen über die Fuldaer Papsturkunden." *DA* 37 (1981): 792-95.

Jaeger, C. Stephen. *The Envy of Angels: Cathedral Schools and Social Ideals in Medieval Europe, 950-1200.* Philadelphia: University of Pennsylvania Press, 1994.

_____. *The Origins of Courtliness: Civilizing Trends and the Formation of Courtly Ideals, 939-1210.* Philadelphia: The University of Pennsylvania Press, 1985.

James, Edward. "'*Beati Pacifici*: Bishops and the Law in Sixth-Century Gaul." In *Disputes and Settlements: Law and Human Relations in the West*, ed. John Bossy. Cambridge and New York: Cambridge University Press, 1983: 25-46.

Janson, Henrik. *Templum nobilissimum. Adam av Bremen: Uppsalatemplet och konfliktlinjerna i Europa kring år 1075.* Avhandlingar från Historiska institutionen i Göteborg 21. Göteborg: Historiska institutionen, 1998.

Jørgensen, Ellen. *Helgendyrkelse i Danmark: Studier over Kirkekultur og kirkeligt Liv fra det 11te Aarhundredes Midte til Reformationen.* Copenhagen: Hagerup, 1909.

Jungmann, Joseph A.. *The Mass of the Roman Rite: Its Origins and Development.* 2 vols. Trans. Francis A. Brunner. New York: Benziger Brothers, 1951-55.

Kahle, Barbara and Ulrich Kahle. "St. Andreas." In *Köln: Die romanischen Kirchen von den Anfängen bis zum zweiten Weltkrieg*," ed. Hiltrud Kier and Ulrich Krings. Cologne: J.P. Bachem, 1984: 154-82.

Kaiser, Reinhold. *Bischofsherrschaft zwischen Königtum und Fürstenmacht. Studien zur bischöflichen Stadtherrschaft im westfränkisch-*

französischen Reich im frühen und hohen Mittelalter. Bonn: Röhrscheid, 1981.

———. "Les évêques neustriens du Xe siècle dans l'exercice de leur pouvoir temporel d'après l'historiographie médiévale." In *Pays de Loire et Aquitaine de Robert le Fort aux premiers Capétiens*. Poitiers: Société des Antiquaires de l'Ouest, 1997: 117-43.

Källström, Olle. "Ein neuentdecktes Majestätsdiadem ottonischer Zeit." *Münchner Jahrbuch der bildenden Kunst*, ser. 3, 2 (1951): 61-72.

Keller, Hagen. "Herrscherbild und Herrschaftslegitimation. Zur Deutung der ottonischen Denkmäler." *FmS* 19 (1985): 290-311.

Kirmeier, Josef, Bernd Schneidmüller, Stefan Weinfurter, and Evamaria Brockhoff, ed., *Kaiser Heinrich II. 1002-1024*. Bamberg: Konrad Theiss Verlag, 2002.

Klein, Holger. "Aspekte der Byzanz-Rezeption im Abendland." In *Byzanz: Der Macht der Bilder. Katalog der Ausstellung im Dom-Museum Hildesheim*, ed. Michael Brandt and Arne Effenberger. Hildesheim: Staatliche Museen zu Berlin-Preussischer Kulturbesitz, 1998: 122-53.

Kleinheyer, Bruno. "Ordinationen und Beauftragugen." In *Gottesdienst der Kirche: Handbuch der Liturgiewissenschaft*, ed. Hans Bernard Meyer et al, vol. 8, *Sakramentliche Feiern II*. Regensburg: Friedrich Pustet, 1984.

Kluger, Helmuth, ed., *Series episcoporum ecclesiae catholicae occidentalis ab initio usque ad annum MCXCVIII*, vol. VI/2, *Archiepiscopatus Lundensis*. Stuttgart: Anton Hiersemann, 1992.

Knudsen, Gunnar, Marius Kristensen, and Rikard Hornby, ed., *Danmarks gamle Personnavne*, vol. 1/1. Copenhagen: G. E. C. Gad, 1936.

Köhler, Oskar. *Das Bild des geistlichen Fürsten in den Viten des 10., 11. und 12. Jahrhunderts*. Abhandlungen zur mittleren und neueren Geschichte 77. Berlin: Verlag für Staatswissenschaften und Geschichte, 1935.

———. "Die ottonische Reichskirche. Ein Forschungsberichte." In *Adel und Kirche. Festschrift für Gerd Tellenbach dargebracht von Freunden und Schülern*, ed. Josef Fleckenstein and Karl Schmid. Freiburg: Herder, 1968: 141-204.

Kolsrud, Oluf. *Noregs kyrkjesoga*, vol. 1, *Millomalderen*. Oslo: Aschehoug, 1958.

Kopytoff, Igor. "The cultural biography of things: commoditization as process." In *The Social Life of Things: Commodities in cultural perspective*, ed. Arjun Appadurai. Cambridge and New York: Cambridge University Press, 1986: 64-91.

Kottje, Raymund. "Oratio periculosa—Eine frühmittelalterliche Bezeichnung des Kanons?" *Archiv für Liturgiewissenschaft* 10/1 (1967): 165-168.

Koziol, Geoffrey. *Begging Pardon and Favor: Ritual and Political Order in Early Medieval France.* Ithaca: Cornell University Press, 1992.

Krug, Antje. "Die Bekrönung des Egbertschreins." *Trierer Zeitschrift* 63 (2000): 353-63.

Kuder, Ulrich. "Die Ottonen in der ottonischen Buchmalerei: Identifikation und Ikonographie." In *Herrschaftsrepräsentation im ottonischen Sachsen,* ed. Gerd Althoff and Ernst Schubert. Sigmaringen: Thorbecke, 1998: 137-234.

Ladner, Gerhart B.. *Ad Imaginem Dei: The Image of Man in Mediaeval Art.* Latrobe, PA: Archabbey Press, 1965.

Laharie, Muriel. "Evêques et société en Périgord du Xe au milieu du XIIe siècle." *Annales du Midi* 94 (1982): 343-68.

Lambert, Malcolm. *Medieval Heresy: Popular Movements from the Gregorian Reform to the Reformation.* 2nd ed. Cambridge, MA: Blackwell, 1992.

Landes, Richard. *Relics, Apocalypse, and the Deceits of History: Ademar of Chabannes, 989-1034.* Cambridge, MA: Harvard University Press, 1995.

Lasko, Peter. *Ars Sacra, 800-1200.* 2nd ed. New Haven: Yale University Press, 1994.

Laudage, Johannes. *Priesterbild und Reformpapsttum im 11. Jahrhundert.* Beihefte zum Archiv für Kulturgeschichte 22. Cologne: Böhlau, 1984.

Laurent, René. *Sigillographie.* Brussels: Archives Générales du Royaume, 1985.

Laurentin, René. *Marie, l'Eglise et le Sacerdoce.* 2 vols. Paris: Nouvelles Editions Latines, 1952-53.

Lawson, M.K.. *Cnut: The Danes in England in the Early Eleventh Century.* New York: Longman, 1993.

Legendre, Pierre. *Dieu au miroir. Etude sur l'institution des images.* Paris: Fayard, 1994.

Lepin, Marius. *L'idée du sacrifice de la messe, d'après les théologiens depuis les origines jusqu'à nos jours.* Paris: Gabriel Beauchesne, 1926.

Leyser, Karl. "Ottonian Government." In *Medieval Germany and Its Neighbors, 900-1250*. London: Hambledon Press, 1982: 69-101.

———. *Rule and Conflict in an Early Medieval Society: Ottonian Saxony*. Oxford: Blackwell, 1979.

Lobrichon, Guy. "Arras 1025, ou le vrai procès d'une fausse accusation." In *Inventer l'hérésie? Discours polémique et pouvoirs avant l'inquisition*, ed. Monique Zerner. Nice: Centre d'études médiévales, 1998: 67-85.

Lotter, Friedrich. *Die Vita Brunonis des Ruotger*. Bonner Historische Forschungen 9. Bonn: Röhrscheid, 1958.

Lutterbach, Hubertus. "The Mass and Holy Communion in the Medieval Penitentials (600-1200): Liturgical and Religio-Historical Perspectives." In *Bread of Heaven. Customs and Practices Surrounding Holy Communion*, ed. Charles Caspers, Gerard Lukken, and G.A.M. Rouwhorst. Kampen: Kok Pharos, 1995: 61-81.

MacDonald, A.J.. *Berengar and the Reform of Sacramental Doctrine*. London: Longmans, Green, 1930; repr. Merrick, NY: Richwood, 1977.

Macy, Gary. *The Theologies of the Eucharist in the Early Scholastic Age*. New York: Oxford University Press, 1984.

Maguire, Henry. "The Heavenly Court." In *Byzantine Court Culture from 829 to 1204*, ed. Henry Maguire. Washington, DC: Dumbarton Oaks, 1997.

Mango, Cyril and Marlia Mango. "Cameos in Byzantium." In *Cameos in Context: The Benjamin Zucker Lectures, 1990*, ed. Martin Henig and Michael Vickers. Oxford: Ashmolean Museum, 1993: 57-76.

Marcone, Arnaldo. "Late Roman Social Relations." In *The Cambridge Ancient History*, vol. 13, *The Late Empire, A.D. 337-425*, ed. Averil Cameron and Peter Garnsey. Cambridge and New York: Cambridge University Press, 1998: 338-70.

Margue, Michel and Jean Schroeder. "Zur geistigen Ausstrahlung Triers unter Erzbischof Egbert." In *Egbert, Erzbischof von Trier*, ed. Ronig, 2: 111-20.

Mariaux, Pierre-Alain. "La Vierge dans l'atelier de Tuotilo. De l'artiste médiéval considéré comme un 'théodidacte'." *Revue de l'Histoire des religions* 218/2 (2001): 171-93.

Marin, Louis. *Portrait of the King*. Minneapolis: The University of Minnesota Press, 1988.

Markus, R.A.. *Gregory the Great and His World*. Cambridge and New York: Cambridge University Press, 1997.

Martin, Eugène. *Histoire des diocèses de Toul, de Nancy et de Saint-Dié*, vol. 1, *Des origines à la réunion de Toul à la France*. Nancy: A. Crépin-Leblond, 1900.

Mathews, Karen R. "Expressing Political Legitimacy and Cultural Identity through the Use of *Spolia* on the *Ambo* of Henry II." *Medieval Encounters* 5/2 (1999): 156-83.

Mathisen, Ralph. *Roman Aristocrats in Barbarian Gaul: Strategies for Survival in an Age of Transition*. Austin, TX: University of Texas Press, 1993.

May, Otto Heinrich. *Regesten der Erzbsschöfe von Bremen*, vol. 1 (787-1306). Veröffentlichungen der Historischen Kommission für Hannover, Oldenburg, Braunschweig, Schaumburg-Lippe und Bremen 11. Hannover: Historische Kommission, 1937.

Mayr-Harting, Henry. *Ottonian Book Illumination*. Rev. ed. 2 vols. London: Harvey Miller, 1999.

McLaughlin, Megan. *Consorting With Saints: Prayer for the Dead in Early Medieval France*. Ithaca: Cornell University Press, 1994.

McNulty, Patricia M. and Bernard Hamilton. "Orientale lumen et magistra latinitas: Greek influence on Western Monasticism (900-1100)." In *Le Millénaire du Mont Athos 963-1963: Etudes et mélanges*, vol. 1. Venice: Editions de Chevetogne, 1963: 181-216.

Meisterwerke aus Elfenbein der Staatlichen Museen zu Berlin. Berlin: Staatliche Museum zu Berlin-Preussischer Kulturbesitz and Braunschweig: Herzog Anton Ulrich-Museum, 2000.

Miller, Maureen C.. *The Bishop's Palace: Architecture and Authority in Medieval Italy*. Ithaca: Cornell University Press, 2000.

Montclos, Jean de. *Lanfranc et Bérenger: La controverse eucharistique du XIe siècle*. Louvain: Spicilegium sacrum Lovaniense, 1971.

Mor, Carlo Guido and Heinrich Schmidinger, ed.. *I poteri temporali dei vescovi in Italia e Germania nel Medioevo*. Bologna: Il Mulino, 1979.

Morelle, Laurent. "Archives épiscopales et formulaire de chancellerie au XIIe siècle. Remarques sur les privilèges épiscopaux connus par le *Codex* de Lambert de Guînes, évêque d'Arras (1093/94-1115)." In *Die Diplomatik der Bischofsurkunde vor 1250*, ed. Haidacher and Köfler, 255-267.

———. "La pratique épistolaire de Lambert, evêque d'Arras (1093-1115)." In *Regards sur la correspondance (de Cicéron à Armand Barbès)*, ed. Daniel Odon Hurel [= *Les Cahiers du GRHIS* 5 (1996)], 37-57.

Moss, Christopher and Katherine Kiefer, ed.. *Byzantine East, Latin West: Art-Historical Studies in Honor of Kurt Weitzmann*. Princeton: Department of Art History and Archaeology, 1995.

Nelson, Janet L.. "The earliest surviving royal *ordo*: some liturgical and historical aspects." In Nelson, *Politics and Ritual*, 341-60.

———. "Kingship, law and liturgy in the political thought of Hincmar of Rheims." In Nelson, *Politics and Ritual*, 133-71.

———. "National synods, kingship as office, and royal anointing: an early medieval syndrome." In Nelson, *Politics and Ritual*, 239-57.

———. *Politics and Ritual in Early Medieval Europe*. London: Hambledon Press, 1986.

Nelson, Robert S.. "Byzantine Art and the West: An Asymmetrical Relationship." In *Actes du XXe Congrès International des Etudes byzantines* (forthcoming).

Nightingale, John. *Monasteries and Patrons in the Gorze Reform: Lotharingia c. 850-1000*. Cambridge and New York: Cambridge University Press, 2001.

Norden, Walter. *Erzbischof Friedrich von Mainz und Otto der Grosse*. Berlin: E. Ebering, 1912.

Nordenfalk, Carl. "Archbishop Egbert's 'Registrum Gregorii'." In *Studien zur Mittelalterlichen Kunst, 800-1200. Festschrift für Florentine Mütherich zum 70. Geburtstag*, ed. Katharina Bierbrauer, Peter Klein, and Willibald Sauerländer. Munich: Prestel-Verlag, 1985: 87-100.

Nuvolone, Flavio. "Il *Sermo pastoralis* pseudoambrosiano e il *Sermo Girberti philosophi papae urbis Romae qui cognominatus est Silvester de informatione Episcoporum*. Riflessioni." In *Gerberto: scienza, storia e mito*. Piacenza: Editrice degli Archivi Storici Bobiensi, 1985: 379-565.

Nyberg, Tore S. *Die Kirche in Skandinavien: Mitteleuropäischer und englischer Einfluss im 11. und 12. Jahrhundert. Anfänge der Domkapitel Børglum und Odense in Dänemark*. Beiträge zur Geschichte und Quellenkunde des Mittelalters 10. Sigmaringen: Thorbecke, 1986.

———. *Monasticism in North-Western Europe, 800-1200*. Aldershot: Ashgate, 2000.

Nyborg, Ebbe and Niels Jørgen Poulsen. *Tamdrup*. Danmarks Kirker, Århus amt, 52. Heming: Nationalmuseet/Poul Kristensen, 2002.

Ohnsorge, Werner. "Die Legation des Kaisers Basileios II. an Heinrich II.." *Historisches Jahrbuch* 73 (1954): 61-73.

Oursel, Raymond, and A.-M. Oursel. *Les églises romanes de l'Autunois et du Brionnais*. Mâcon: Imprimerie Protat frères, 1956.

Pacaut, Marcel. *Louis VII et les élections épiscopales dans la royaume de France*. Paris: J. Vrin, 1957.

Parisse, Michel. "Les évêques de France et le pape, à la lumière des actes du concile de Saint-Basle (991)." In *Gerbert moine, évêque et pape: d'un millénaire à l'autre*. Aurillac: Association catalienne, 2000: 171-94.

_____. "Importance et richesse des chartes épiscopales. Les exemples de Metz et de Toul, des origines à 1200." In *A propos des actes d'évêques*, ed. Parisse, 19-44.

_____. "Princes laïques et/ou moines: les évêques du Xe siècle." In *Il secolo di ferro: mito e realtà del secolo X*. Settimane 38. Spoleto: Presso le Sede del Centro, 1991: 449-513.

_____. "La recherche française sur les actes des évêques. Les travaux d'un groupe de recherche." In *Die Diplomatik der Bischofsurkunde vor 1250*, ed. Haidacher and Köfler, 203-208.

_____, ed.. *A propos des actes d'évêques. Hommage à Lucie Fossier*. Nancy: Presses universitaires de Nancy, 1991.

Petrucci, Armando. *La scrittura: Ideologia e rappresentazione*. Turin: G. Einaudi, 1986. English translation by Linda Lappin as *Public Lettering: Script, Power, and Culture*. Chicago: The University of Chicago Press, 1993.

Pfister, Christian. *Etudes sur le règne de Robert le Pieux (996-1031)*. Paris: F. Vieweg, 1885.

Plotzek, Joachim. "Zur Initialmalerei des 10. Jahrhunderts in Trier und Köln." *Aachener Kunstblätter* 44 (1973): 101-28.

Poly, Jean-Pierre, and Eric Bournazel. *The Feudal Transformation, 900-1200*. Trans. Caroline Higgitt. New York: Holmes and Meier, 1991.

Radford, C.A. Ralegh. "St. Magnus Cathedral, Kirkwall, and the Development of the Cathedral in Northwest Europe." In *St Magnus Cathedral and Orkney's Twelfth-Century Renaissance*, ed. Barbara E. Crawford. Aberdeen: Aberdeen University Press, 1988: 14-24.

Radtke, Christian. "Anfänge und erste Entwicklung des Bistums Schleswig im 10. und 11. Jahrhundert." In *850 Jahre St.-Petri-Dom zu Schleswig*, ed. Horst Appuhn *et al*, 133-60.

Ramsey, Nigel *et al*, ed.. *St. Dunstan: His Life, Time, and Cult*. Woodbridge: Boydell and Brewer, 1992.

Rathsack, Mogens. *Fuldaforfalskningerne: en retshistorisk analyse af klostret Fuldas pavelige privilegier, 751- ca. 1158*. Copenhagen: Juristforbundet, 1980. Translated by Kortnum Mogensen as *Fuldaer Fälschungen: eine rechtshistorische Analyse der päpstliche Privilegien des Klosters Fulda von 751 bis ca. 1158*. 2 vols. Päpste und Paptsttum 24. Stuttgart: Anton Hiersemann, 1989.

Refskou, Niels. "Det retslige indhold af de ottonske diplomer til de danske bispedømmer." *Scandia* 52 (1986): 167-210.

Reuter, Timothy. "Ein Europa der Bischöfe: das Zeitalter Burchards von Worms." In *Burchard von Worms 1000-1025*, ed. Hartmann, 1-28.

_____. "*Filii matris nostrae pugnant adversum nos*: bonds and tensions between German prelates and their milites in the high middle ages." In *Chiesa e mondo feudale nei secoli X-XII*. Miscellanea del Centro di studi medioevali 14. Milan: Vita e pensiero, 1995: 247-76.

_____. "The 'Imperial Church System' of the Ottonian and Salian rulers: A Reconsideration." *Journal of Ecclesiastical History* 33 (1982): 347-74.

_____. "*Pastorale pedum ante pedes ipsius apostolici posuit*: Dis- and reinvestiture in the era of the Investiture Contest." In *Belief and Culture in the Middle Ages: Studies presented to Henry Mayr-Harting*, ed. Richard Gameson and Henrietta Leyser. Oxford: Oxford University Press, 2001: 197-210.

_____. "Property transactions and social relations between rulers, bishops and nobles in early eleventh-century Saxony: The evidence of the *Vita Meinwerci*." In *Property and Power in the Early Middle Ages*, ed. Wendy Davies and Paul Fouracre. Cambridge and New York: Cambridge University Press, 1995: 165-99.

_____. "*Velle sibi fieri in forma hac*: Symbolisches Handeln im Becketstreit." In *Form und Funktion öffentlicher Kommunikation im Mittelalter*, ed. Althoff, 201-25.

Reynolds, Susan. *Fiefs and Vassals*. Oxford: Oxford University Press, 1994.

Roesdahl, Else. *Viking Age Denmark*. London: British Museum Publications, 1982.

Ronig, Franz, ed. *Egbert, Erzbischof von Trier, 977-993. Gendenkenschrift der Diözese Trier zum 1000. Todestag*. 2 vols. Beiheft zur Trierer Zeitschrift für Geschichte und Kunst 18. Trier: Rheinische Landsmuseum Trier, 1993.

———. "Erzbischof Egbert und die Entstehung seines Evangeliars." In *Codex Egberti: Teilfaksimile des Ms. 24 der Stadtbibliothek Trier*, ed. Gunther Franz and Franz Ronig. Wiesbaden: L. Reichert, 1983: 29-46.

———. "Der Psalter Erzbischof Egberts von Trier in Cividale." In *Egbert, Erzbischof von Trier*, ed. Ronig, 2: 163-68.

———. "Der Trierer Dom und sein Verhältnis zur Antike." *Zeitschrift des Deutschen Vereins für Kunstwissenschaft* 44 (1990): 112-23

Rosenwein, Barbara H.. *Rhinoceros Bound: Cluny in the Tenth Century*. Philadelphia: University of Pennsylvania Press, 1982.

Rubin, Miri. *Corpus Christi: The Eucharist in Late Medieval Culture*. Cambridge and New York: Cambridge University Press, 1991.

Santantoni, Antonio. *L'ordinazione episcopale: storia e teologia dei riti dell'ordinazione nelle antiche liturgie dell'occidente*. Studia Anselmiana 69: Analecta Liturgica 2. Rome: Editrice Anselmiana, 1976.

Santifaller, Leo. *Zur Geschichte des ottonisch- salischen Reichskirchensystems*. 2nd ed.. Sitzungsberichte der österreichischen Akademie der Wissenschaften, phil.-hist. Klasse 229/1. Vienna: R.M. Rohrer, 1964.

Sassier, Yves. *Recherches sur le pouvoir comtal en Auxerrois du Xe au début du XIIIe siècle*. Auxerre: Société des fouilles archéologiques et des monuments historiques de l'Yonne, 1980.

Sauerland, H.V. and Arthur Haseloff. *Der Psalter Erzbischof Egberts von Trier. Codex Gertrudiana in Cividale*. Trier: Gesellschaft für nützliche Forschungen, 1901.

Sawyer, Birgit and Peter Sawyer. *Medieval Scandinavia: >From Conversion to Reformation, circa 800-1500*. Minneapolis: University of Minnesota Press, 1993.

Sawyer, Peter. *Anglo-Saxon Charters: An annotated list and bibliography*. London: Royal Historical Society, 1968.

———. "The process of Scandinavian Christianization in the tenth and eleventh centuries." In *The Christianization of Scandinavia: Report of a Symposium held at Kungälv, Sweden, 4-9 August 1985*, ed. Birgit

Sawyer, Peter Sawyer, and Ian Wood. Alingsås: Viktoria Bokförlag, 1987: 68-87.

Schetter, Rudolf. *Die Intervenienz der weltlichen und geistlichen Fürsten in den deutschen Königsurkunden von 911-1056*. Bottrop: Postberg, 1935.

Schieffer, Rudolf. *Der geschichtliche Ort der ottonisch-salischen Reichskirchenpolitik*. Rheinisch-Westfälische Akademie der Wissenschaften, Geisteswissenschaften, Vorträge G 352. Opladen: Westdeutscher Verlag, 1998.

──────. "Karolingische und ottonische Kirchenpolitik." In *Mönchtum-Kirche-Herrschaft, 750-1000*, ed. Dieter Bauer and Josef Semmler. Sigmaringen: Jan Thorbecke Verlag, 1998: 311-24.

──────. "Der ottonische Reichsepiskopat zwischen Königtum und Adel." *FmS* 23 (1989): 291-301.

Schlesinger, Walter. "Unkonventionelle Gedanken zur Geschichte von Schleswig/Haithabu." In *Aus Reichsgeschichte und Nordischer Geschichte*, ed. Horst Fuhrmann, Hans Eberhard Mayer, and Klaus Wriedt. Stuttgart: Ernst Klett, 1972: 70-91.

Schramm, Percy Ernst. "Grundbegriffe des Bereichs: Herrschaftszeichen und Staatssymbolik." In Schramm, *Kaiser, Könige und Päpste*, 4: 682-705.

──────. "Das Grundproblem dieser Sammlung: Die 'Herrschaftszeichen', die 'Staatssymbolik' und die 'Staatspräsentation' des Mittelalters." In Schramm, *Kaiser, Könige und Päpste*, 1: 30-60.

──────. *Herrschaftszeichen und Staatssymbolik*. 3 vols. MGH Schriften 13. Stuttgart: Anton Hiersemann, 1955.

──────. *Kaiser, Könige und Päpste. Gesammelte Aufsätze zur Geschichte des Mittelalters*. 4 vols. Stuttgart: Anton Hiersemann, 1968-71.

──────. "Sacerdotium und Regnum im Austausch ihrer Vorrechte: imitatio imperii und imitatio sacerdotii. Eine geschichtliche Skizze zur Beleuchtung des Dictatus papae Gregors VII.." In Schramm, *Kaiser, Könige und Päpste*, 4: 57-106.

Schreiner, Klaus. "'Nudis pedibus': Barfüßigkeit als religiöses und politisches Ritual." In *Formen und Funktionen öffentlicher Kommunikation*, ed. Althoff, 53-124.

Schütte, Sven. "Zur frühen Baugeschichte von St. Kunibert in Köln und zur Grablege des Bischofs Rudolf von Schleswig." *Colonia Romanica: Jahrbuch des Fördervereins Romanische Kirchen Köln e.V.* 12 (1997): 9-16.

Seegrün, Wolfgang. *Das Papsttum und Skandinavien bis zur Vollendung der nordischen Kirchenorganisation (1164)*. Neumünster: Karl Wachholtz, 1967.

Seibrich, Wolfgang. "Egbert als Metropolit und Erzbischof von Trier." in *Egbert, Erzbischof von Trier*, ed. Ronig, 2: 187-95.

Seiler, Sven and Marianne Gechter. "Das Grab des Bischofs Rudolf von Schleswig in St. Kunibert zu Köln." In *Ein Land macht Geschichte: Archäologie in Nordrhein-Westfalen*, ed. Heinz Günter Horn, Hansgerd Hellenkemper, Harald Koschik, and Bendix Trier. Cologne: Römisch-Germanisches Museum der Stadt Köln, 1995: 300-03.

Sewell, William H., Jr. "A Theory of Structure: Duality, Agency, and Transformation." *American Journal of Sociology* 98/1 (July 1992): 1-29.

Skyum-Nielsen, Niels. *Kvinde og Slave*. Copenhagen: Munksgaard, 1971.

Sot, Michel. *Gesta episcoporum, gesta abbatum*. Typologie des sources du Moyen Age occidental 37. Turnhout: Brepols, 1981.

_____. "Rhétorique et technique dans les préfaces des *gesta episcoporum* (IXe—XIIe s.)." *Cahiers de civilisation médiévale* 28 (1985): 181-200.

Stock, Brian. *The Implications of Literacy: Written Language and Models of Interpretation in the Eleventh and Twelfth Centuries*. Princeton: Princeton University Press, 1983.

Suckale, Robert. *Rogier van der Weyden, die Johannestafel. Das Bild als stumme Predigt*. Frankfurt am Main: Fischer Taschenbuch Verlag, 1995.

Surmann, Ulrike. "Der Meister der Wiener Gregortafel." In *Egbert, Erzbischof von Trier, 977-993*, ed. Ronig, 1: 207-29.

_____. *Studien zur ottonischen Elfenbeinplastik in Metz und Trier*. Witterschlick and Bonn: M. Wehle, 1990.

Thompson, Michael. *Medieval Bishops' Houses in England and Wales*. Aldershot: Ashgate, 1998.

Toch, Michael. *"Dunkle Jahrhunderte": Gab es ein jüdisches Frühmittelalter? 3. "Arye Maimon-Vortrag" an der Universität Trier, 15. November 2000*. Kleine Schriften des Arye-Maimon-Instituts 4. Trier: Arye-Maimon-Institut für Geschichte der Juden, 2001.

Trommer, Aage. "Komposition und Tendenz in der Hamburgischen Kirchengeschichte Adam von Bremens." *Classica et mediaevalia* 18 (1957): 207-57.

Tschan, Francis. *Saint Bernward of Hildesheim*. 3 vols. Notre Dame: University of Notre Dame Press, 1942, 1951-1952.

Van Engen, John. "Letters, Schools, and Written Culture in the Eleventh and Twelfth Centuries." In *Dialektik und Rhetorik im früheren und hohen Mittelalter*, ed. Johannes Fried. Munich: Oldenbourg, 1997: 97-132.

de Venutis, Phillipus. *De cruce Cortonensi dissertatio*. Livorno: J.P. Fantechi, 1751.

Vescovi e diocesi in italia nel medioevo (secoli IX-XIII). Padua: Antenore, 1964.

Vessey, Mark. "The Origins of the *Collectio Sirmondiana*: A New Look at the Evidence." In *The Theodosian Code: Studies in the Imperial Law of Late Antiquity*, ed. Jill Harries and Ian Wood. London: Duckworth, 1993: 187-99.

Vöge, Wilhelm. "Ein deutscher Schnitzer des 10. Jahrhunderts." *Jahrbuch der Königlich-preussischen Kunstsammlungen* 20 (1899): 118-25.

Wallace-Hadrill, J.M. "The *Via Regia* of the Carolingian age." In *Early Medieval History*. Oxford: Basil Blackwell, 1975: 181-200.

Warner, David A. "Ritual and Memory in the Ottonian *Reich*: The Ceremony of *Adventus*." *Speculum* 76 (2001): 255-83.

Weinfurter, Stefan, ed. *Die Salier und das Reich*. 3 vols.. Sigmaringen: Thorbecke, 1991.

_____ and Odilo Engels, ed. *Series episcoporum ecclesiae catholicae occidentalis ab initio usque ad annum MCXCVIII*, vol. 5/2, *Archiepiscopatus Hammaburgensis sive Bremensis*. Stuttgart: Anton Hiersemann, 1984.

Wentzel, Hans. "Das byzantinische Erbe der ottonischen Kaiser: Hypothesen über den Brautschatz der Theophanu." *Aachener Kunstblätter* 40 (1971): 11-84 and 42 (1972): 11-96.

Werner, Karl-Ferdinand. "Heeresorganisation und Kriegführung im deutschen Königreich des 10. und 11. Jahrhundert." In *Ordinamenti militari in Occidente nell'alto Medioevo*. Settimane 15. Spoleto: Centro Italiano di studi sull'alto Medioevo, 1968: 791-843.

Westermann-Angerhausen, Hiltrud. "Blattmasken, Maskenkapitelle, Säulenhäupter: Variationen über ein vorgegebenes Thema." *Boreas: Münster'sche Studien zur Archäologie* 6 (1983): 202-11.

_____. *Die Goldschmiedearbeiten der Trierer Egbertwerkstatt*. Trier: Spee-Verlag, 1973.

———. "Heinrich der Löwe: ein Mäzen?" In *Heinrich der Löwe: Herrschaft und Repräsentation*, ed. Johannes Fried and Otto-Gerhard Oexle (forthcoming).

———. "Das Nagelreliqiar im Trierer Egbertschrein—Das 'künstlerisch edelste Werk der Egbertwerkstätte'?" In *Festschrift für Peter Bloch zum 11. Juli 1990*, ed. Hartmut Krohm and Christian Theuerkauff. Mainz: P. von Zabern, 1990: 9-23.

———. "Spolie und Umfeld in Egberts Trier." *Zeitschrift für Kunstgeschichte* 50/3 (1987): 305-36.

———. "Spolie—Zitat—Tradition: Die vorgotischen Emails und der Vorgänger des Schreins." In *Schatz aus den Trümmern: Der Silberschrein von Nivelles und die europäische Hochgotik*, ed. Hiltrud Westermann-Angerhausen and Gudrun Sporbeck. Cologne: Schnütgen-Museum, 1994: 117-34.

———. "Die Stiftungen der Gräfin Gertrude: Anspruch und Rang." In *Der Welfenschatz und sein Umkreis*, ed. Johannes Ehlers and Dietrich Kötzsche. Mainz: Philipp von Zabern, 1998: 51-76.

Westwood, John O.. *A Descriptive Catalogue of the Fictile Ivories in the South Kensington Museum*. London: Eyre and Spottiswoode, 1876.

Williams, John R.. "The Cathedral School of Rheims in the Eleventh Century." *Speculum* 29 (1954): 661-677.

———. "The Cathedral School of Rheims in the time of Master Alberic, 1118-1136." *Traditio* 20 (1964): 93-114.

Wirth, Jean. *L'image à l'époque romane*. Paris: Editions du Cerf, 1999.

Wolf, Gunther. "Zur Datierung des Buchdeckels des Codex aureus epernacensis." *Hêmecht* 42 (1990): 147-51.

Yorke, Barbara, ed.. *Bishop Aethelwold: His Career and Influence*. Woodbridge: Boydell and Brewer, 1988.

Zielinski, Hubert. *Der Reichsepiskopat in spätottonischer und salischer Zeit (1002-1125)*. Stuttgart: Franz Steiner, 1984.

Zink, Jochen. "Die Baugeschichte des Trierer Doms von den Anfängen im 4. Jahrhundert bis zur letzten Restaurierung." In *Der Trierer Dom*, ed. Gustav Bereths and Franz Ronig. Neuss: Verlag Gesellschaft für Buchdruckerei, 1980: 17-111.

Index

Acta Synodi Atrebatensis, 145

Adalbero, archbishop of Hamburg-Bremen, 193

Adalbero, archbishop of Reims, 92, 101, 125

Adalbero, bishop of Laon, 19

Adalbero, bishop of Metz, 12, 86, 91, 93, 94, 99, 100, 102, 103

Adalbero, brother-in-law of Henry II, 72

Adalbero Crucifixion, 91, 100

Adalbert, archbishop of Hamburg-Bremen and papal vicar, 183, 187, 188-89, 190, 191, 192, 199, 200

Adalbert of St. Maximin, Trier (later archbishop of Magdeburg), 63, 65, 71

Adalbold of Utrecht, 67, 89

Adaldag, archbishop of Hamburg-Bremen, 70, 173, 174, 175

Adam of Bremen, xvii, 169, 173, 174, 175-78, 179-80, 181, 182-84, 188, 189, 191, 193, 197, 200

Adelaide, countess of Chalon and Anjou, 40, 43

Adelheid, queen of Italy, queen of Germany, empress, wife of Otto I, 59, 114

Ademar, bishop of Chabannes, 31, 158

Adventius, bishop of Metz, 69, 70

adventus ritual, 29

Aethelnoth, archbishop of Canterbury, 176

Aethelwold, bishop of Winchester, 28

Alberic, bishop of Osnabrück, 183

Albric, bishop of Wendila, 198

Aldenburg (Starigard) (diocese), 172, 173, 180, 182

Alduin, bishop of Limoges, 31

Alexander II, pope, 192

Amalarius of Metz, 159

Ambrose, St., 52, 159

Andrew, St., 119-21

Ansgar, archbishop of Hamburg-Bremen, 172, 198

Apostolic Constitutions, 58

apostolic succession, 65, 119, 123

arbitration. *See* mediation

Århus (diocese): discontinuation, 173; foundation, 172; reformation, 188-89

Arnulf, archbishop of Reims, 14, 16

Arnulf, bishop of Halberstadt, 31, 71, 72

Arnulf, bishop of Orléans, 11

Arras, Synod of, 145

artists, 155, 162, 165, 166; signatures of, 155-56

Arup, Erik, 193 n 97

Atto, bishop of Vercelli, 158-59

Augustine, St., 52, 146-47, 159

Auxerre, 3, 4, 37, 43, 45, 46-47. *See also* Hugh, bishop of Auxerre

Avoco, bishop of Sealand, 179, 182-83, 188

Bedos-Rezak, Brigitte, xvi, 82 n 27, 98 n 92

Benedict III, pope, 96

Benedict VII, pope, 71

Benson, Robert, xiv, 33

Berengar of Tours, xvi, 143-44, 145, 146, 163-64

Bernard, titular bishop of Scania, 176-77, 182

Bernard II, duke of Saxony, 180

Berno of Baume, abbot of Cluny, 42

Berno of Reichenau, 157, 158

Bernward, bishop of Hildesheim, 18, 76, 77, 94, 99, 100-101

Berthold, bishop of Toul, xv, 77-78; and Adalbero of Metz, 76, 91, 94; as artistic patron, 77-78, 87-88, 90, 92-95, 99, 102-103; and Berlin *Hodegetria*, 83, 91, 92, 95-99, 102-103; as builder, 86-87; career, 85-90; as courtier, 86, 88, 90; and Henry II, 88-89; identification of, 84-85; sources for, 90-95; and Trier, 92-94; uses of epigraphy, 83, 95-99, 102-103

Bertulf, archbishop of Trier, 69-70

Bescelin Alebrand, archbishop of Hamburg-Bremen, 173, 180, 181-82, 187

bishop: as advisor, 12, 15, 62, 69, 117; as aristocrat, 9, 22, 38-39, 47, 48; as artist, xvi-xvii, 155, 165-66; as builder, 39, 46, 86, 115; burial, 27-30, 31, 184; consecration, 26, 31, 34; as courtier, 15, 18, 20, 70-71, 88-90, 113; as cultural patron, 18, 76-78, 79-80, 86-88, 91-95, 96, 99-103, 113, 114-15, 115-16, 119, 125-26; death, 27, 29-30; education, 13, 18, 117; election, 10, 18, 24, 31, 34, 35, 44, 71-72, 72-73, 113; as fighter, 44-45, 49; images of, xv-xvi, 99-101, 102-3, 117-19, 121-24, 125, 129-31, 136, 142, 148, 149-51, 152, 154; installation, 11, 21, 31-32, 33, 35, 188-91; as intercessor, xv, 51, 54-56, 61, 66-73;

231

as judge, 12, 14-15, 45, 58; as mediator, xiii, xv, 51-52, 56-67, 73, 76, 77, 158, 162, 178; as missionary, 174, 175-76, 197-98; as peacemaker, 16-17, 39, 47, 49, 57-60, 61-66, 67, 178; as preacher, 54, 68-69; qualities, 4-5, 8-10, 18-19; as reformer, 38, 43, 48, 63, 120, 144-45; regalia, 11, 26; as ruler, xiv, 12, 24-26, 32-33, 124, 158-59; sacramental functions, 11-12, 52-53, 155, 157-58, 165-66; staff, 7-8, 15-16, 137, 139; tenure, 19-20

Botte, Bernard, 159

Bouchard, Constance Brittain, xv

Brentano, Robert, xiv, 24

Brown, Peter, 55

Brun, bishop of Augsburg, 67

Brun, archbishop of Cologne, xiii, 27, 113, 119, 121, 122

Brun, bishop of Toul. *See* Leo IX

Brun, bishop of Verden, 70

Bührer-Thierry, Geneviève, xiv

Burchard, archbishop of Lyon, 18

Burchard, bishop of Worms, 18, 21, 29-30

Büttner, Heinrich, 65

Byzantium: artistic production, 78-79, 80-81, 99, 125; relationship to West, 78-80, 84, 90-91, 103, 119, 178

Cambrai, 3, 4, 6, 35, 137, 141, 145

Canterbury, 2, 177, 187, 189

cartularies, 6-7

cathedral, 11, 28, 29, 32, 34, 36; of Auxerre, 44, 46; of Bamberg, 90, 97; of Bremen, 174, 179; of Cologne, 121; of Lund, 175-76; of Magdeburg, 30; of Nancy, 92; of Ribe, 184; of Toul, 87, 93, 94; of Trier, 114, 115, 120, 122; of Winchester, 28; of Worms, 29

chancery, episcopal, 16, 137-39, 143, 145

chancery, royal, 15, 113, 137, 142

chapel, royal, 15, 18, 20, 70, 71

chapter, cathedral, 7, 13, 14, 16, 18, 21, 25, 39, 46, 71, 72, 139, 170, 197

Charlemagne, Frankish emperor, 15, 118

Charles "the Bald", West Frankish king and emperor, 120, 142 n. 14

charters, episcopal, xv, 5-8, 16, 39, 47, 85, 138-40; rise of in France, 140-41; semiotic function of, 140

Chazelle, Celia, 163

Christian, bishop of Ribe, son of Odinkar the Younger, 184, 187, 189

Chronica ecclesiae Ripensis (Chronicle of the Church of Ribe), 184

Chronicon Roskildense (Roskilde Chronicle), 197

Cicero, 116, 126

Clement of Alexandria, St., 121

Cluny, 38, 39, 40, 42-43, 45, 46, 48

Cnut "the Great", king of Denmark, 173, 175, 198; conquest of England, 176; death, 180; installation of bishops, 176-77, 182, 193, 197; relations with Germany, 178-79, 180, 199-200; relations with Hamburg-Bremen, 176, 179-80, 200

Codex Aureus of St. Emmeram, 120-21, 134

Codex Egberti. *See* Egbert Codex

Cohen, Adam, 77 n. 11

Cologne, 5, 119, 121-22, 172, 180-81, 182, 183

confection. *See* consecration, eucharistic

Conrad "the Red", duke of Lotharingia, 58, 59, 62

Conrad II, king of Germany and emperor, 178-79, 180, 199

consecration, eucharistic, 144, 156, 157-58; and confection, 159-60, 162, 163, 164-65

Constantine I, Roman emperor, 118

Couches, 43

councils, royal, 15, 18, 76

counts, xv, 1, 10, 15, 17, 20, 37, 38, 40, 43-44, 47, 49

Cutler, Anthony, xv-xvi

Dalby (episcopal seat), 188, 190-91

Denmark: church in, xvii, 169-200; episcopacy of, xvii, 169-70, 172-77, 180-84, 187, 188-90, 191-93, 197, 198-200; historiography of, xvii, 169-70, 197, 200; relations with England, 175-77, 190, 193, 198, 199; with Germany, 178-80, 187-88, 199-200; with Hamburg-Bremen, 170, 172, 176-77, 179-80, 181-83, 187-89, 191-93, 199-200; royal dynasty of, 171, 176, 180, 181, 187-88, 191, 198-99; saints of, 198-99

Dhuoda, 54

Dietrich, archbishop of Trier, 115

Dietrich, count of Holland, 113

diocesan organization, 1, 12, 23-24, 34, 169, 172-73, 177, 187, 188-90, 191, 199-200

Dortmund, Synod of (1005), 174

Duby, Georges, 38, 48 n. 39, 54

Dunstan, archbishop of Canterbury, 27

Dvornik, Francis, 119

Eberhard, duke of Franconia, 61

Echternach, 115

Egbert, archbishop of Trier, xvi, 17, 76, 101; as artistic patron, xvi, 77, 92-93, 94, 103, 113, 114, 116, 117, 118, 120, 121-22, 126; as builder, 115, 119; episcopacy, 113-14, 116; and Gregory the Great, 118-19; historical appraisal of, 113-14; and Otto II, 117, 118; self-representation, 118-19, 121-24, 125-26, 130, 131; upbringing, 113

Egbert Codex, 114, 119, 124, 131

Egbert Psalter, 114, 118, 123, 130

Egbert Shrine, 114, 119-21, 122, 124, 132, 133, 135

Egino, auxiliary bishop at Dalby, 190-91, 192

Ehlers, Joachim, 21

Eid, bishop of Meissen, 31

Eilbert, bishop of Funen, 188

Ekkihard (Esico), titular bishop of Schleswig, 174, 179, 180

election, episcopal, 3, 4, 10, 13, 17, 18, 24, 31, 34, 39, 71, 73

Emma, queen of Denmark, wife of Cnut the Great, 179

epigraphy: definition of, 96-97; function of, 91, 95-96; as historical evidence, 83, 97-98; as indication of patronage, 77-78, 98, 99-103

episcopacy: autonomy, 11-12, 21, 22, 63-66; centrality, xiii, xiv, 1, 51-55, 73, 158-59; and community, 11-12, 16, 23-25, 29-30, 32, 34-35, 58; cultic role, 1, 11-12, 52-55, 68-69, 121, 125-26, 155, 156-58, 160-61, 165-66; and cultural production, xv-xvi, 14, 18, 76-78, 79-80, 83-84, 86, 88, 91-96, 97-103, 113, 114-26; in Denmark, xvii, 169-200; economic power, 13-14, 18, 21-22, 143-45; in England, 2, 5, 6, 28-29, 176-77, 190, 198, 199; and eucharistic controversy, xvi, 143-47, 164-65; in France, xvi, 2, 5, 6-7, 10, 18-20, 21, 31-32, 35, 37-49, 137-51; in Germany, xv-xvi, 1-2, 4-5, 17-18, 19-21, 29-31, 58-66, 68-73, 76-78, 79-80, 83-103, 13-36, 172-73, 178-79, 180-82, 183, 188, 193, 197, 199-200; government by, 11-12, 15-17, 23-24, 33-34; hereditary succession to, 184, 189; historiography of, xiv, xvii, 1-2, 61, 65-66, 75-76, 170, 193 n. 97; in Italy, 1, 5; and Jews, 30, 36; in Late Antiquity, 55-57, 66-67; and lay rulership, xv, 15, 17-19, 20-21, 37-38, 44-45, 47, 48-49, 55-57, 66-68, 70-73, 88-91, 113-14, 175-77, 178, 181-82, 187-93, 198-200; military role, xv, 20-21, 44-45, 180; and Peace of God, 16-17, 37-38, 39, 47, 48-49; and reform, 38-39, 43-44, 48; representation of, 116-36, 137-42, 147-51; seals and, xvi, 141-54; sources for, 3-8, 36, 39-40, 60-61, 85-88, 169-77, 184, 197; symbolism of, 27-36; and writing, 14-15, 138-41, 147-48

Erkens, Franz-Reiner, 114

Ernest, brother of Margrave Henry of Bavaria, 67

Erp, bishop of Verden, 69

Esico. *See* Ekkihard

eucharist, xvi-xvii, 137, 142-43, 144-45, 146, 147, 148, 155, 156-58, 159-66

Eucharius, St., 122, 123

Eusebius Bruno, bishop of Angers, 144

Everger, archbishop of Cologne, 97 n. 78

excommunication, 12, 139. *See also* interdiction

Fleckenstein, Josef, 63

Florus of Lyon, 159

Frase, Michael, 63

Frederick, archbishop of Mainz, 61-63, 64, 65-66

Fulcran, bishop of Lodève, 19

Funen (diocese), 174, 176, 177, 181, 183, 188; bishops of, 194. *See also* Odense

Gelting, Michael, xvii

Geoffrey Greymantle, count of Anjou, 40, 43

Gerald, bishop of Limoges, 31-32

Gerbert of Aurillac, 9, 15, 92, 93, 125-26

Gerhard of Augsburg, 58-60

Gerard, bishop of Cambrai, xvi, 11, 35, 145

Gerard, bishop of Toul, 90 n. 52

Gerbrand, bishop in Sealand, 176-77, 178, 179

Gero, archbishop of Cologne, 165

gesta episcoporum, 3-4, 25

Gesta episcoporum Cameracensium (Deeds of the Bishops of Cambrai), 4, 35, 140

Gesta episcoporum Tullensium (Deeds of the Bishops of Toul), 85-87, 88, 94

Gesta Hammaburgensis ecclesiae pontificum (Deeds of the Bishops of the Church of Hamburg), 169

Gesta pontificum Autissiodorensium (Deeds of the Bishops of Auxerre), 3-4, 10, 40, 44

Gezo of Tortona, 163

Giddens, Anthony, 60

Gilbert, duke of Lotharingia, 61

Gilsdorf, Sean, xv

Gisela, queen of Hungary and sister of Henry II, 98

Giselher, bishop of Merseburg and archbishop of Magdeburg, 71

Godelier, Maurice, 103

Gofridus, sculptor, 155

Gori, Antonio, 82 n. 26

Gorze, 115, 117-18

Gotebald, missionary bishop in Denmark, 175-76

Gottschalk, bishop of Freising, 68-69

Gregorian Reform, 3, 22, 24, 33, 34, 38, 44, 48, 53, 199

Gregory I, pope, xiii, 51, 54, 155, 160; and Egbert of Trier, 118-19; and images, 125-26; as reform model, 117-18; representations of, 114, 116, 117, 119, 129

Gregory VII, pope, 48, 160, 192, 193

Gregory, bishop of Tours, 67

Guenée, Bernard, xiv

Gunhild, daughter of Cnut the Great, 178, 180

Guy, bishop of Amiens, 145

Guy, archbishop of Reims, 144

Haarländer, Stephanie, xiv

hagiography. *See vitae episcoporum*

Haithabu, 179

Hamburg-Bremen (diocese): foundation and early history, 172; missionary activity, 172-73, 191-92, 199; relations with Danish church, 169, 172, 176, 178, 179-80, 183, 188-90, 192-93, 199-200; relations with papacy, 187, 193, 197; Scandinavian claims, 170, 176, 181-82, 187-88, 193, 197, 199

Harald Bluetooth, king of Denmark, 169, 172, 173, 197

Harald II, king of Denmark, 176

Harries, Jill, 58

Harthacnut, king of Denmark, 180, 181

Hartpert, bishop of Chur, 58-60

Hauck, Albert, 63 n. 39

Head, Thomas, 38 n. 6, 122 n. 28

Heldric, abbot of St.-Germain d'Auxerre, Flavigny, and Moutier-St.-Jean, 42-43

Henry, bishop of Lund, 176, 188, 190, 191

Henry (I), duke of Bavaria and brother of Otto I, 58, 59, 61, 62

Henry (II) "the Quarrelsome", duke of Bavaria, 112-14

Henry, duke of Burgundy, 42, 44

Henry I, king of England, 34

Henry II, king of Germany and emperor, 30-31, 67, 68-69, 70, 71-73, 98; as artistic patron, 90-91, 97; and Berthold of Toul, 88-89, 91

Henry III, king of Germany and emperor, 35, 178, 180, 187

Henry IV, king of Germany and emperor, 193

Henry of Schweinfurt, margrave of Bavaria, 67, 68

Heribert, archbishop of Cologne, 17

Heribert, bishop of Auxerre, 3, 44

Heriger of Lobbes, 143, 163

Hermann, bishop of Toul, 94

Hildebert, archbishop of Mainz, 61

Hildebrand, cardinal. *See* Gregory VII

Hildesheim, 174, 183. *See also* Bernward, bishop of Hildesheim

Hildeward, bishop of Halberstadt, 27

Hodegetria, 80, 90, 99, 101; at Berlin (Museum für Spätantike und Byzantinische Kunst), 80-84, 85, 88, 90, 91-92, 94, 95, 99, 102-103

Hrabanus Maurus, 53, 54

Hugh, bishop of Auxerre and count of Chalon, xiv, 4, 37, 51; ancestry, 40-41; as bishop, 38, 44-47; as builder, 41; character of, 46; and Cluny, 39, 42-43, 45, 48; as count, 40, 43-44, 47; election of, 10, 44; as judge, 45; military activities, 4, 44-45, 49; monastic conversion, 46; as monastic reformer, 40, 42-43, 48; and Peace of God, 47, 48-49; retirement, 47; sources for, 39-40, 47; upbringing, 40

Hugh, abbot of Cluny, 39

Hugh, bishop of Langres, 144

Hugh, bishop of Rouen, 19

Hugh, bishop of Toulouse, 19

Hugh Capet, king of France, 4, 21, 44

Hugh "the Great", West Frankish duke, 3

Humbert of Silva Candida, cardinal, 102

Iburg (near Osnabrück), 183

Indiculus loricatorum (981), 20

Innocent II, pope, 193

intercession: as admonition, 68-69; definition of, 51 n. 2; in diplomata, 69; episcopal, xv, 54, 57, 61, 66-73; ideology of, 51, 56-57, 73; judicial, 66-67; and mediation, 51, 56-57, 73; and patronage, 55-56, 67, 69-71; and peacemaking, 62, 66-67; and prayer, 53, 54-55; process of, 67, 69, 71-72; refusal of, 71, 72-73

interdiction, episcopal, 12. *See also* excommunication

ivories, xvi, 77, 89, 92, 94, 115, 118; carving technique, 81, 97; and Henry II, 90-91, 97; inscription of, 82-83, 91, 95-101, 102; reuse of, 79, 80, 82, 90, 102-103. *See also* Adalbero Crucifixion; Hodegetria; Notker ivory; Romanos ivory

Jaeger, C. Stephen, 151 n. 36

James, Edward, 57, 66, 67

Janson, Henrik, 200 n. 111

Jaromir, duke of Bohemia, 68

John, bishop of Auxerre, 4, 44

John, castellan of Cambrai, 35

John the Baptist, St., 81, 83, 99, 100

John of Fécamp, 160

John, abbot of Gorze, 117

John XVIII, pope, 47

Jordan, bishop of Limoges, 32

Jutland, 173, 177, 181, 183, 198

Kallfelz, Hatto, 59

Königsnähe, 70, 71

Lambert, bishop of Arras, 138 n. 3

Lambert, count of Chalon, 37, 40, 42

Lambert, bishop of Langres, 6

Laurentin, René, 164

Leo IX, pope, 3, 22, 87, 88, 102, 144, 187

letters, episcopal, 92, 93, 117, 125, 138-40, 147

Liafdag, bishop of Ribe, 198

Libentius I, archbishop of Hamburg-Bremen, 174-75

Libentius II, archbishop of Hamburg-Bremen, 175, 177, 179, 180

Liemar, archbishop of Hamburg-Bremen, 193

Lietbert of Cambrai, 35

Liudolf, son of Otto I and Edith, 58-60, 62

Liutbert, archbishop of Mainz, 67

Lothar III, king of Germany and emperor, 197

Lotter, Friedrich, 63

Louis "the Pious", Frankish emperor, 15

Louis "the German", East Frankish king, 67

Louis II, East Frankish king, 67

Lund (diocese), 170, 175, 176, 188, 190-92; bishops of, 195; elevation to metropolitan see, 193

Magnus "the Good", king of Norway and Denmark, 181, 182, 187, 191

Mainz, Council of (1049), 182, 187

Maiolus, abbot of Cluny, 40, 43

Mariaux, Pierre-Alain, xvi-xvii

Maternus, St., bishop of Trier, 122, 123

Maurice, son of Geoffrey Greymantle of Anjou, 40

Mayr-Harting, Henry, 117

mediation: between God and man, 52-54, 158, 162; cultural, 76, 77; definition of, 51, 57; ideology of, 51-52, 57-58, 60, 64-65, 66, 73; and intercession, 51, 56-57, 73; and peacemaking, 59-60, 61, 63, 64-66, 67; as political act, 56-57, 63-64, 66, 73

Meingaud, archbishop of Trier, 72-73

Meinwerk, bishop of Paderborn, 27

Miller, Maureen, xiv

monasticism, xiii, 18, 30, 37, 39, 42-44, 48, 52, 63, 89, 117-18

Moyenmoutier, 87, 89, 102

nepotism, 13

nicolaitism, 18, 22

Norden, Walter, 64, 65

Nordenfalk, Carl, 17

North, William, xv-xvi

Notker, bishop of Liège, 18, 94, 99, 100, 143, 154

Notker ivory, 94 n. 71

Odense (diocese), 172. *See also* Funen

Odilo, abbot of Cluny, 42

Odinkar the Elder, missionary bishop, 173-74, 175

Odinkar the Younger, bishop of Ribe: consecration, 175, 177, 179-80; death, 182; education, 175, 177; memorialization, 198; transmission of episcopal office, 184, 187, 189

Ohtric, *magister scholae* of Magdeburg, 71

Olaf, king of Norway, 198

Ordulf, duke of Saxony, 181

Otto I, king of Germany and emperor, xiii, 58-59, 61-63, 64-66, 70, 113, 173

Otto II, king of Germany and emperor, 21, 71, 113, 117, 118

Otto III, king of Germany and emperor, 20, 71, 86, 88, 91, 113-14, 115, 172

Otto-William, duke of Burgundy, 44

Paray-le-Monial, 39, 40, 42-43, 44

Parisse, Michel, xiv-xv, 85 n. 34, 140 n. 9

Paschasius Radbertus, 142, 145, 157, 161-62, 164

Passeri, G.B., 82 n. 26

Paul the Deacon, 118, 119, 155, 156

Peace of God movement, 16-17, 37, 38, 39, 47, 48-49

peacemaking, 57, 60, 63-66, 67. *See also* Peace of God movement

Peter Damian, 164

Peter the Deacon, 164

Peter Lombard, bishop of Paris, 139 n. 5, 152, 166

Peter, St., staff reliquary of, 113, 114, 121-24, 125, 136

Philip Augustus, king of France, 34

Plotzek, Joachim, 118

Poitiers, 2, 7, 13, 31

Poppo, missionary bishop, 173-74, 197

Prosper of Aquitaine, 52

Ralph, bishop of Ribe, 198

Ralph Glaber, 39, 45

Rather, bishop of Verona, 53 n. 10, 158-59

Rathsack, Mogens, 122 n. 28

Ratolf, bishop of Schleswig, 188-89

Ratramnus of Corbie, 14, 157, 161, 163, 164

reform, monastic, 7, 37, 38, 40, 42-44, 48, 63, 117-18, 120

Reginbert, bishop of Funen, 176, 177

Registrum Gregorii (Trier), 114, 117, 119, 128, 129

Reims, 2, 6, 14, 16, 19, 139 n. 6, 141; council of, 144; school of, 144-45. *See also* Adalbero, archbishop of Reims.

relics, 33, 114, 119-20, 121-22, 141, 145

representation, 116-17, 118-19, 121, 122-25, 147; and eucharist, 143-44, 146-47; and seals, 138-39, 141-42, 147-51

Reuter, Timothy, xiii, xv, 17, 37, 73

Reynald, son of Duke Otto-William of Burgundy, 45

Ribe (diocese): bishops, 173, 174, 180, 182, 185, 187, 198; foundation, 172; partition of, 188-89; sources on, 184

Ricwal, bishop of Lund, 192

Robert II "the Pious", king of France, 4, 10, 12, 44

Rodulf, titular bishop of Schleswig, 180-81

Rome, Council of (1059), 164

Ronig, Franz, 113, 123 n. 29, 125

Roskilde (diocese), 170, 188; bishops of, 192, 196. *See also* Sealand; Chronicon Roskildense

Ruodhard, bishop of Strasbourg, 61

Ruotger of Cologne, xiii, 121

St. Andreas, Trier, 119

St.-Bénigne de Dijon, 39, 42

St. Eucharius, Trier, 115

St.-Èvre, Toul, 102

St.-Germain d'Auxerre, 42

St. Kunibert, Cologne, 180-81

St.-Marcel-lès-Chalon, 39, 43

St. Maximin, Trier, 118

St.-Pierre, Chauvigny, 155, 167

Sawyer, Peter, 169 n. 1, 175 n. 23

Scania, 174, 175-76, 177, 182-83, 190. *See also* Lund

Schetter, Rudolf, 69

Schleswig (diocese), 173, 179, 181-82, 187; bishops, 174, 183, 186, 188, 199; foundation, 172

Schmeidler, Bernhard, 175

schools, episcopal, 21, 39, 137, 139, 144-45

seals: authenticity of, 150 n. 35; episcopal, xvi, 137, 141-42, 143, 144, 145, 147-48, 149-51; and eucharistic theology, 137-38, 147, 150; function of, 101 n. 87, 138, 142, 147, 151; historio-graphy of, 137 n. 1; as image, 141-42, 148-50; as metaphor, 148-49; royal, 142

Sealand (diocese), 174, 177, 181, 182, 188. *See also* Roskilde

Sederic, Slavic prince, 179

Seibrich, Wolfgang, 114

semiosis, xvi, 80, 100-101, 137, 139-40, 147; Augustinian theory of, 146-47, 164; and eucharistic theology, 142-44, 150-51, 161-62, 164; of seals, 142, 147-51

Sermo de informatione episcoporum (likely by Ademar of Chabannes), 9, 158

Sevcenko, Ihor, 82 n. 27

Shuffelton, George, 84 n. 29

Sigibert, bishop of Minden, 79, 103

simony, 18-19, 22, 144

Sirmondian Constitutions, 66

spolia, 78-79, 124-25

subjectivity, 153-54

Surmann, Ulrike, 118

Sven, bishop of Roskilde, 192

Sven Estrithson, king of Denmark, 180, 181; ecclesiastical policy, 187-90, 192-93, 199; as informant to Adam of Bremen, 177, 180, 193; relations with Germany, 187, relations with the papacy, 192-93

Sven Forkbeard, king of Denmark, 172, 173, 175, 176

synods, episcopal, 14-15, 15-17, 33, 47, 57, 144, 164, 182, 187

Tagino, archbishop of Magdeburg, 30, 31, 70, 71-72

Thangmar of Hildesheim, 88 n. 45, 95 n. 72

Thankmar, half-brother of Otto I, 61

Theobold, bishop of Chalon, 44, 45

Theodgar, St., Danish missionary, 198

Theophanu, queen of Germany and empress, 74 n. 32, 113, 115

Thietmar, bishop of Merseburg, 27, 30, 31, 67, 68-69, 70-71, 71-73, 76, 91, 165

Thorolf, bishop of Orkney, 191

Thurgot, bishop of Skara, 180

Toch, Michael, 36

Toul. *See* Berthold

Trier: as artistic center, 92-93, 94, 113, 115, 118, 125; manuscript production in, 114-15, 117-18; primatial claims of, 119, 121-24

Udo, bishop of Toul, 88

Ulrich, bishop of Augsburg, 5, 12, 20, 58, 59-60

Unwan, archbishop of Hamburg-Bremen, 73, 173, 174, 176, 177-79

Uta, abbess of Niedermünster, 97

Uto, Slavic prince, 179

Valerius, St., 122, 123

Van Engen, John, 139 n. 5

Vercelli, Council of, 164

Viborg (diocese), 183

vitae episcoporum, 2, 4-5, 8, 12, 23, 28, 39-40, 122

Vöge, Wilhelm, 115

Wal, titular bishop of Ribe, 182-84, 187, 188-89, 200

Walthard, archbishop of Magdeburg, 30-31

Walther, provost of Magdeburg, 71-72

Wendila (diocese), 188, 198

Widukind of Corvey, 60-62, 63, 64, 65, 76

William, archbishop of Mainz, 63

William, bishop of Sealand, 188, 192

William of Jumièges, 45

Willigis, archbishop of Mainz, 17, 67, 70, 113

Wulfstan of Winchester, 28

237